Forthcoming Titles

A Guide to Psychiatric Services in Schools

Understanding Roles, Treatment, and Collaboration

Shawna S. Brent

Routledge
Taylor & Francis Group
New York   London

Routledge
Taylor & Francis Group
711 Third Avenue
New York, NY 10017

Routledge
Taylor & Francis Group
27 Church Road
Hove, East Sussex BN3 2FA

© 2012 by Taylor & Francis Group, LLC
Routledge is an imprint of Taylor & Francis Group, an Informa business

Printed in the United States of America on acid-free paper
Version Date: 20111206

International Standard Book Number: 978-0-415-87101-3 (Hardback) 978-0-415-87102-0 (Paperback)

Library of Congress Cataloging-in-Publication Data

Brent, Shawna S.
 A guide to psychiatric services in schools : understanding roles, treatment, and collaboration / Shawna S. Brent.
  p. cm.
 Includes bibliographical references and index.
 ISBN 978-0-415-87101-3 (hardcover : alk. paper) -- ISBN 978-0-415-87102-0 (pbk. : alk. paper)
 1. Students--Mental health services. 2. Child psychiatry. I. Title.

LB3430.B74 2012
371.7'13--dc23   2011038062

**Visit the Taylor & Francis Web site at
http://www.taylorandfrancis.com**

**and the Routledge Web site at
http://www.routledgementalhealth.com**

Contents

Series Editors' Foreword

The School-Based Practice in Action series grew out of the coming together of our passion and commitment to the field of education and the needs of children and schools in today's world. We entered the process of developing and editing this series at two different points of our career, though both were in phases of transition: one (RWC) moving from the opening act to the main scene, and the other (RBM) moving from the main scene to the final act. Despite one of us entering the peak of action and the other leaving it, we both continue to be faced with the same challenges in and visions for education and serving children and families.

Significant transformations to the educational system, through legislation such as the No Child Left Behind Act of 2001 and the reauthorization of Individuals with Disabilities Education Act (IDEA 2004), have created broad sweeping changes for practitioners in the educational setting, and these changes will likely continue. It is imperative that as school-based practitioners we maintain a strong knowledge base and adjust our service delivery. To accomplish this, we need to understand theory and research, but it is critical that we have resources to move our empirical knowledge into the process of practice. Thus, it is our goal that the books included in the School-Based Practice in Action series truly offer resources for readers to put directly "into action."

To accomplish this, each book in the series will offer information in a practice-friendly manner and will have a companion CD with reproducible and usable materials. Within the text, readers will find a specific icon that will cue them to documents available on the accompanying CD. These resources are designed to have a direct impact on transitioning research and knowledge into the day-to-day functions of school-based practitioners. We recognize that the implementation of programs and the changing of roles come with challenges and barriers, and as such, these may take on various forms depending on the context of the situation and the voice of the practitioner. To that end, the books of the School-Based Practice in Action series may be used in their entirety and present form for a number of practitioners; however, for others, these books will help them find new ways to move toward effective action and new possibilities. No matter which style fits your practice, we hope that these books will influence your work and professional growth.

Dr. Shawna Brent graciously provided us with a much-needed resource, *A Guide to Psychiatric Services in Schools: Understanding Roles, Treatment and Collaboration.* The close working of psychiatrists and school-based mental health professionals is expected in delivering comprehensive care to students with a variety of social and emotional challenges. Dr. Brent offers not only information on psychiatric disorders but also an opportunity to understand and embrace the role of psychiatry in the schools and how the integration of services benefits students. She addresses different diagnoses in children, treatment options including therapeutic modalities and medication, and how to respond to mental health crises. We are excited to have an opportunity to offer school-based mental health professionals a guide to enhance the delivery of psychiatric services in the schools. We trust this will be a valuable resource for those working in schools and will have a beneficial impact on students.

Finally, we want to extend our gratitude to Mr. Dana Bliss and Routledge for their support and vision to develop a book series focused on enriching the practice and service delivery within school settings. Their openness to meet the needs of school-based practitioners made the School-Based Practice in Action series possible. We hope that you enjoy reading and implementing the materials in this book and the rest of the series as much as we have enjoyed working with the authors on developing these resources.

Rosemary B. Mennuti, EdD, NCSP
Ray W. Christner, PsyD, NCSP
Series Editors, School-Based Practice in Action Series

Preface

Educators are finding it increasingly necessary to address the mental health needs of students within the school setting. Mental health diagnoses and treatment are becoming more common. Both the identification and the prevalence of these disorders are increasing. The effect of mental illness in the educational setting can cause significant distress for the identified student and for peers and staff. As educators look for improved ways to maximize success, these problems must be addressed. Fortunately, as the rate and impact of mental health disorders are rising, treatment options and interventions are also increasing.

Often the two disciplines of education professionals and mental health professionals seem to speak different languages. Additionally, each has differing approaches to attempting to solve problems. Educators can become frustrated by the many gray areas of mental health, and mental health professionals can be frustrated by the direct approach of educators. Allowing both disciplines to understand each other can improve communication and can facilitate improved progress of the student.

Mental health professionals will talk about a given diagnosis and how it is impacting the student's functioning. Educators may struggle to look at this same difficulty in a similar way. One common example is depression. Whereas adults present with a sad mood state, children and adolescents appear more often irritable than sad. When irritability is a symptom of depression, a student may refuse to do tasks asked of him or her. A teacher will be frustrated by this oppositional behavior and may place even more demands on the student. The failure to meet any demands can worsen the course of depression for this student. Therefore, as teachers begin to understand that the negative behaviors are a symptom of an illness, there can be an improved pattern of interaction between the two that is helpful for the student's recovery. When educators are increasingly aware of mental health diagnoses and their educational implications, there can be progressive improvement for the entire school community.

Along with communicating with mental health treatment providers who are treating the student in the community, it is

becoming more common to have mental health services delivered directly to students in school. Some students may have a
mental health aide or support with them in regular education
classes. Students with identified emotional disabilities may
receive their education in an emotional support classroom
that has additional therapeutic supports. Psychiatric services
can occur through consultation or directly with students in
emotional support classrooms.

A child and adolescent psychiatrist wrote this book, the
primary goal of which is to begin to provide a bridge for
educators to mental health professionals. Psychiatrists are
medical physicians with unique training in mental health
diagnoses. Additionally, psychiatrists take a biological, psychological, developmental, and social perspective as they
attempt to provide an understanding of a person's struggles.
Psychiatrists first attempt to provide a diagnostic formulation to a set of symptoms that are interfering with a person's
functioning or developmental progress. From the diagnostic
formulation, a diagnosis that conforms with the American
Psychiatric Association's *Diagnostic and Statistical Manual of
Mental Disorders* (*DSM*) is generated. This diagnosis is used to
guide a variety of treatment interventions.

Over the past decade, I have been fortunate to be able to
provide a broad array of mental health services to students
as a consultant to school districts and direct service within
public school settings. As I have expanded this type of work, it
has become clearer to me that educators are seeking a broader
understanding and a variety of interventions to help these students. Interestingly, educators are looking to be educated in
this area. It is hoped that this book will provide a framework
of understanding.

The structure and content of this book are meant to appeal to
a wide variety of individuals in the education system. School
psychologists, guidance counselors, regular education teachers, special education teachers, and administrators should all
find useful content. While explaining a variety of psychiatric
diagnoses and interventions, the emphasis will be on making the information clinically relevant. Clinical cases will be
presented frequently to help highlight the material and to help
emphasize educational implications to the diagnosis.

The book begins with the presentation of two clinical cases.
The names and details have been altered to protect the confidentiality of the student and family. These cases will be
revisited in different sections of the book. It is hoped that

the blending of these cases throughout the book will further explain mental health treatment implications and interventions. The content of the attached CD-ROM provides a concrete example of what a psychiatric evaluation might look like. The psychiatric evaluation is from one of the presented cases.

The second chapter focuses further on psychiatric evaluations. There can be unclear expectations of this process, and it is hoped that this chapter will provide useful information that will set the framework for improved communication among educators, mental health professionals, and psychiatrists in particular. Educators may suggest a psychiatric evaluation to a student or family, and there is improved cooperation with this process if all individuals are aware of the process and expected outcome.

In addition to treating patients in the community through private practice or community mental health treatment centers, psychiatrists may work directly with school systems. They may provide psychiatric evaluations as consultation to districts. They may provide direct consultation to district classrooms. Finally, psychiatrists are increasingly participating directly in schools where they provide direct service to identified students. Each of these roles will be explained in detail in Chapter 3.

The medical training that a psychiatrist receives allows the dispensing of medication to patients. Before further exploring medication treatment in the book, Chapter 4 will focus on explaining some basic pharmacologic principles to facilitate understanding of medication treatment of students.

Subsequent chapters focus on different psychiatric diagnoses. The diagnostic criteria for the disorder will be explained, and there will be an explanation of subtleties of different diagnoses. For example, there are at least four different types of depression. The difference between major depression and dysthymia will be explained. In addition to depressive disorders, disruptive behavior disorders, mood disorders, anxiety disorders, psychotic disorders, eating disorders, and pervasive developmental disorders (autism spectrum disorders) will be discussed. The epidemiology and course of each illness will be explained. Small clinical examples will be given in each chapter to help emphasize the educational implications.

Treatment options will be reviewed as well. Different therapeutic modalities will be explained in relation to each illness. At times individual therapy is preferred over family therapy. Understanding the difference between these interventions can be useful. In addition, some therapists will utilize a cognitive behavioral approach, whereas others will use a psychodynamically based approach. Although both approaches are helpful, one or the other may be more helpful based on the diagnosis.

When discussing the treatment of each disorder, I will also discuss the different medications that may be used for treatment for each condition. When the medication is discussed, the risks and benefits of the potential treatment will be the focus. However, there will be an explanation of the expected response, time to see the response, side effects, and withdrawal effects. It is hoped that as educators are more knowledgeable about medications, communication among the school, parents, and prescriber can improve. As the communication improves, the student benefits from improved compliance and decreased side effects. Medication in children and adolescents is at times controversial. The risks and benefits of pursuing this intervention will be discussed. As a physician, I have seen tremendous benefit in some cases from appropriate diagnosis and medication treatment. However I have likely seen at least the same number of negative outcomes to medications as well. It is hoped that the medication section provides information that is useful, but it is never to be used as the solo intervention for treatment of children and adolescents.

Chapter 12 focuses on medicating children in a variety of contexts when the diagnosis is not clear. The treatment plan is ideally derived from a clear diagnosis. However, at times it is difficult in a single evaluation to clearly identify one psychiatric diagnosis. In this case, however, there may be significant "target" symptoms that are causing impairment and require prompt treatment even before fully understanding the origin of the problem. It is hoped that this information will allow educators to be more informed when talking to students and families about medication.

The final chapter (Chapter 13) reviews a variety of mental health crises and how these can be addressed. Suicide is a significant source of mortality in youth, and this is often first identified by peers and shared with trusted educators. The response to a crisis such as this can be challenging but critical. There is increasing community pressure to identify students who are at risk to commit horrific acts of violence. This task is often completed with psychiatrists in conjunction with educators and is another area that strongly reinforces the need for the two disciplines to communicate well.

Throughout the book there are noted references to information that is included on the CD-ROM. These are intended to be user-friendly resources. For example, there is a form letter that can be filled in to share information with the prescribing physician that may be important for him or her to understand.

Ultimately, it is hoped that this book is both clinically and educationally relevant to a variety of educators. It is hoped that there will be ongoing improvement in communication between mental health providers and educators in the best interest of students.

One

Introduction to Psychiatry in Schools

CLINICAL CASE: ERIN

Erin was a 7-year-old Caucasian female who was referred for a psychiatric evaluation by her school district over 1 year ago. (The original psychiatric evaluation, which was modified to protect Erin's privacy, is included on the accompanying CD: 2.1.) At the time of the evaluation, she was living with her mother, father, and sister. She was a second-grade student who had moved into the referring school district 2 months before the evaluation. The sources of information for this evaluation included a clinical interview with Erin and her parents. Erin was seen individually. Her parents were seen together. In addition, five school personnel were present, including the director of special education, building principal, guidance counselor, classroom teacher, and learning support teacher. Early education records and a previous psychiatric evaluation were reviewed before the clinical interview.

Erin's strengths were described as her intelligence, her ability to learn things quickly when she hears them, and her supportive family. She enjoyed playing outside and riding her bike.

For much of Erin's life, she has presented with challenging behaviors. At the age of 2, it became clear that Erin had significant difficulty with transitions. Her parents recounted the story that when she was 3 years old, she spent three hours, twice a week, with a babysitter. When her mother would drop her off in the kitchen, Erin would refuse to leave that room until her mother returned to take her home. Erin had always presented as extremely strong willed. Many other examples of her having prolonged tantrums with transitions were also provided. Her parents described that it had always been very difficult to have Erin engage in a task that she did not want to do. When her parents attempted to have her stop doing a pleasurable activity, the resulting tantrum could last as long as 30 minutes. Trying to have her complete a chore or simple task became so challenging because of her refusal that her parents had stopped asking her to do tasks. Tantrums would occur equally between the home and in public places. Her degree of tantrums and refusal had resulted in the family being unable to eat in restaurants or go to stores.

Over the past several years, Erin had also begun to display significant physical aggression. She became very physically aggressive to her sister and her mother. This had resulted in her giving bruises, scratches, and bites to these family members. Erin had been significantly physically assaultive at school, to the point of bruising adults and scratching them as well. These episodes of extreme anger tended to be triggered by very minor and typically unpredicted events. The extent of the anger outburst and aggression was nearly always out of proportion to the trigger. Although the outbursts were often unpredictable, it was identified that any attempt to enforce structure or rules would cause Erin to react aggressively. A second identified trigger was related to Erin's perception of perfection. If something did not meet Erin's perceived standards of symmetry or perfection, Erin would become aggressive. For example, Erin wanted a ponytail placed on her Barbie doll on the morning of the evaluation. She did not perceive that her mother had done it perfectly, which resulted in a 1-hour tantrum and scratches to her mother's forearm. It was also noted that during these times of extreme anger, she would revert to talking in baby talk and "gibberish." She became frustrated if people did not respond to her. She also would talk faster than her normal rate and talk excessively.

Over the past 6 to 8 months, Erin had been frequently making comments about wanting to die. She made numerous statements such as "I want to go to heaven, it is easier" or "I do not want to live." She made several specific statements about what she would do to end her own life, including starving herself, slicing her throat, or hitting her head against a metal post. She also requested that her parents do something to kill her. These statements were, at times, made during episodes of anger, but at other times they seemed to occur more spontaneously, when she was unprovoked.

Despite the above-identified difficulties, Erin's parents and school personnel describe that there were many times when she was very compliant, sweet, and developmentally appropriate. During these times, which could last for as long as a day but never as long as 2 days in a row, Erin would be cooperative, compliant, and appropriately engaged. However at least once a day, Erin would have some type of "rage outburst" as described above.

Past mental health treatment was significant for a one-time evaluation completed 6 months previously, which diagnosed Erin with an adjustment disorder. This evaluation was pursued by her former school district, although the report did not clarify why the evaluation was being pursued. The behaviors described were similar to those described above but were less frequent and severe. There were no significant medical problems. There was no history of head injury or seizures.

There were no reported difficulties with Erin's mother's pregnancy. Erin had a broken collarbone upon delivery. It took a week for this to be recognized and may have contributed to difficulty with early breast-feeding and Erin's being very irritable and tearful during her first week of life. Motor milestones were all reached on time or early. Erin began walking at 9 months of age. At a young age, she began climbing to high places. Language milestones were delayed, and she did not begin speaking in sentences until 3 years of age. The family had moved three times in Erin's life, with the most recent move being 2 months before this evaluation. One additional stressor that was identified for Erin was her sister's birth when she was 2 years of age.

Educationally, Erin was a second-grade student within a local school. A review of records from her previous school suggested that there was some instructional support team (IST) involvement for learning concerns but not a high level of behavioral problems at school. IST is a team of educators who provide informal support for a targeted concern in an effort to avoid more intensive interventions in the future. Academically, there seemed to be appropriate progress being made.

At the start of her present school, Erin was seen as a shy and reluctant child. Within a few weeks, Erin began to present with significant aggression and defiance in that setting. It had reached a point where Erin frequently needed to be taken out of the room because of her aggression. The reason for the removal was primarily for the safety of others. She had engaged in a number of high-level risk-taking behaviors that could potentially harm others within the classroom. It was interesting that when she was removed from the classroom, she directed her physical aggression toward herself. For example, numerous times she had attempted to kick out glass from building windows. She had also kicked at concrete walls while not wearing shoes. She had been very physically aggressive to staff. On one occasion, during a restraint, she urinated in what was thought to be a particularly willful way on a teacher. The frequency and patterns of her escalation were difficult to predict. At times academic demands were thought to be a trigger; at others the episodes of physical aggression seemed unprovoked. On at least two occasions, Erin had to leave school early because of concerns about her safety. In addition, at times when her aggression escalated at school, Erin made statements about wanting to harm herself.

Within the school setting, Erin was described as being somewhat isolated from peers. She did not like to interact in groups and would not work on group assignments. In addition, she seemed more isolated on the playground and preferred solitary activities. However, Erin also seemed to have the social skills to interact and a desire to interact, but her negative, defiant, and disruptive behaviors seemed to impair these interactions.

Academically, it is perceived that Erin was capable of doing the work. She had demonstrated advanced artwork and academic work product at times. When she was compliant and engaged with work, she was noted to be highly perfectionistic and would become frustrated if her work was not perfect. However, at other times during classwork assignments, she would scribble on papers to the point where they ripped. She would refuse to do work.

There was report of an extended family member with an autism spectrum disorder. There was no other mental health history known.

Erin presented willingly to her individual portion of the interview. She was casually and stylishly dressed and demonstrated good grooming and hygiene. Her hair was neatly combed and arranged. She was able to separate from her parents without difficulty. She also was able to stop a fun activity that she had been engaged in with her teacher, and she readily participated in her portion of the evaluation. She maintained good eye contact throughout the interview. There were no tics or abnormal behaviors noted. She was moderately fidgety throughout the interview but remained in the same general area within the room. Erin seemed to engage with me quickly with charming mannerisms.

Her speech was of normal rate, tone, and volume. She described her mood as "OK now." Her affect was slightly superficial but generally full range and appropriate. Her thought form was clear and organized. There were no psychotic symptoms elicited. Erin was able to talk about her wishes to die and seemed to have some understanding about the permanency of death. She denied having current ideas or thoughts about wanting to die. She did admit at times to having a high degree of frustration, but she had a difficult time articulating emotions or events that precipitated these.

Erin was able to talk about worries and her desire to have all things perfect. Despite my asking numerous questions, no specific obsessions were identified. Erin was able to discuss her frustration about her difficulty making friends and interacting with others.

My initial diagnostic impressions included mood disorder, not otherwise specified; anxiety disorder, not otherwise specified; and oppositional defiant disorder. I was particularly concerned about whether her explosive pattern of mood dyscontrol was an early presentation of bipolar disorder. In addition, because of her need for order and symmetry and her high level of perfectionism, at times I was also considering if her specific anxiety symptoms were caused by obsessive-compulsive disorder. Because of the high level of potentially harmful behaviors, the unpredictability of her explosiveness, and the need for better diagnostic clarification, she was referred to a partial hospitalization program.

Erin participated for 2 weeks at the partial hospitalization program and was successfully discharged with a diagnosis of mood disorder, not otherwise specified and impulse control disorder. I was not involved in her treatment during her stay, but by report clonidine was prescribed to reduce her impulsivity. She was reported to have learned better ways of expressing her anger and frustration. Her mood was described as more stable and predictable, although she remained easily frustrated and periodically angered. Educational recommendations that were forthcoming from the partial hospitalization program suggested an educational placement in a full-time emotional support classroom. Her local district did not have a full-time emotional support classroom in its district, so she was referred to this type of classroom in a center program.

I was one of the psychiatric consultants at the school to which Erin was referred, and for the remainder of her second-grade year and the beginning of her third-grade year,

I remained peripherally involved in her care. In my consulta tive role with the center, I did not meet with Erin or her parents, but I was available for staff consultation. Within that setting Erin was placed in a first- through third-grade classroom with six other students. The teacher was a special education teacher. A social worker was assigned part-time to the classroom, which included 30 minutes a week of individual therapy for Erin. A behavioral-level system existed within the classroom where positive behaviors were reinforced. At times of excessive behavioral disruption, students were removed from the classroom to a single room where staff was available to help the students deescalate.

Erin continued to display aggressive and oppositional behaviors in the classroom. Her level of aggression put herself and others at risk, as she would throw heavy items at staff and began to strongly bang her head on objects. By the fall of her third grade year, Erin spent more time in a time-out room isolated from her peers than she was able to spend in a classroom doing work. The behavioral outbursts became increasingly unpredictable again. She was noted to cry easily and excessively. She continued to have times of talking in what was described as "gibberish."

During this time, a psychiatrist affiliated with the partial hospitalization program Erin had previously attended managed her medications. Because of her increased mood shifts, the clonidine was changed to Risperdal. During this time, it was becoming clearer that her mood episodes were consistent with mania. It was hoped that Risperdal would stabilize her moods and reduce her aggression. Also during this time Erin received mental health treatment with a team of wraparound providers. Wraparound support is a mental health service where a child can receive individual supports where ever that child is. For example, a therapeutic support staff can provide prompt behavioral redirection in a classroom, on the playground, in the home, or in the community. A behavioral specialist consultant can provide behavioral planning and support to the parents and teachers. A therapeutic support staff was assigned to work with her during the school day. It was hoped that a person with mental health training would be able to prevent some of Erin's anger and frustrations so she could remain within the classroom setting. A mobile therapist was assigned to work with Erin at home, and this person also began to address the conflict at home between Erin and her sister.

Three months into her third grade academic year, it became clear to Erin's home school district, the treatment team at the center, her wraparound agency, and her parents, that she was not making educational or therapeutic progress. Her moods remained labile and unpredictable. She needed to control her environment, and any change was met with significant aggression and oppositionality. She was also becoming increasingly aggressive to her sister, and her parents were having more concerns about her sister's safety at home. A decision was made to have her transitioned to a school-based partial treatment center where she would receive more intensive educational and therapeutic support.

For continuity of care, Erin was transitioned to a program where I was the treating psychiatrist. In this program, Erin was one of eight students with a special education teacher, educational aide, classroom therapist, and classroom mental health aide. A psychiatrist was involved for classroom consultation and medication management. In addition, the family participated in monthly meetings with the psychiatrist and therapist.

This setting allowed some very important information to be added to her clinical history. Erin's mother likely had unrecognized and untreated postpartum depression for the first 6 months of Erin's life. Erin had pronounced irritability during her infancy. She was likely experiencing significant pain while trying to feed because of the unrecognized broken collarbone. From a temperamental perspective, she was difficult to soothe and cried often and easily. Her mother's depression in combination with Erin's irritability made the attachment and bonding more tenuous. Her attachment to her mother was likely insecure. The described difficulty with transitions began to make more sense in the context of an insecure attachment with her mother. Her father was able to soothe Erin more easily, and she seemed to form a strong connection with him.

Erin also had a very difficult time adjusting to her sister's birth when she was 2 years old. The adjustment was complicated by her mother's identified postpartum depression and her father's decreasing availability due to his increased work demands. She returned to her very irritable disposition, which was more apparent because of her sister's easy temperament.

In addition, it was learned that there was a family history of anxiety disorders in numerous extended family members. Not all of these individuals had received formal diagnoses or treatment, but the core struggles were present in several aunts and uncles. These included separation anxiety disorder, generalized anxiety disorder, and specific phobia. There was also a positive family history for mood disorders, specifically postpartum depression in mothers. In addition, several maternal family members likely experienced major depression. Several extended family members were treated with SSRI (selective serotonin reuptake inhibitor) medications successfully.

Erin's aggression was targeted primarily toward her mother and sister. This had been conceptualized as a disrupted psychological connection. Specifically, she had a less secure attachment with her mother, and anger at her sister for "replacing" her. There was an increased genetic likelihood for mood disorders and anxiety disorders, as learned by the family history.

Differences in her parents' style of parenting had also begun to emerge. Erin viewed her father as her primary playmate. He was easygoing and played often with her. Although this was positive, she struggled to comply with parenting requests that he made. Because of her reluctance to cooperate, his solution was to place fewer demands on her to avoid the anger explosions. Her mother was more emotionally distant and often became the primary disciplinarian. This role acted to further distance Erin from her mother, and her mother became the primary target of her anger.

Within this educational setting, Erin had begun to make educational progress. For the first month, she completed very little academic work and would spend long portions of time each day drawing detailed mazes. This activity seemed to be a way to engage the classroom adults and allowed her to remain in a room with other students. As she began to adjust to the classroom participation, in-group activities were encouraged. She initially resisted interacting with peers, preferring the adults, but with gradual and titrated support from staff, she was able to begin to integrate with a few peers. However, she continued to prefer adult attention.

Erin had been able to successfully make use of the adjoining therapy room. Although it took several weeks, she was now able to ask to leave the classroom when frustrated and go to the therapy room where she could have brief breaks of play or other therapeutic interventions. She would frequently make use of a mini trampoline to help her deescalate from her anger.

Behavioral interventions were not the focus of this program, but there was some use of a token economy and achieving points for positive behavior. Erin had been able to use the positive reinforcement in a way that had helped her begin to feel better about herself.

There had recently been some gradual improvement in Erin's mood regulation and behavioral control at home. She had had more positive interactions with her sister. She had also begun to interact with peers in the neighborhood and had been more successful at sharing toys and managing her internal frustrations.

Although there had been progress in both settings, Erin continued to have some difficult times. She continued to struggle with transition and unexpected events. In addition, if she did not win a game or activity, she reacted excessively. She had had a few instances of physical aggression toward her sister. She would at times continue to target her mother with annoying behaviors, which could cause both her and her mother to become excessively frustrated.

From a diagnostic perspective, it had become clearer that Erin had childhood bipolar disorder. Her rage outbursts were often unprovoked. She had episodes of talking faster than normal, in a gibberish kind of way. She had expressed grandiose beliefs and often perceived that she was "above" the rules that apply to others. Her moods rapidly shifted from happiness to anger to sadness. She had at times required less sleep and had no change in her energy level. While obsessive-compulsive disorder was previously considered over the past year, it had become apparent that Erin did not continue to have a high degree of anxiety. Although she remained perfectionistic, there had been no identified intrusive thoughts or ritualistic behaviors.

From a treatment perspective, Erin's parents received extensive therapeutic support and family interventions from the Capital Area Partial Program (CAPP) treatment team (an educational partial hospitalization program). They had been able to begin to try to shift their patterns of interactions in a positive way. Erin was also benefitting from the individual therapy and group therapy that were offered routinely in this program. She was able to seek out adults appropriately if she needed a break. She remained on a low dose of Risperdal, which had been helpful for stabilizing her moods.

Classroom interventions primarily offered continual therapeutic support. The primary theoretical basis for the program was understanding the emotional developmental level of each child and targeting interventions to help this developmental delay to improve. At times of emotional turmoil, Erin could regress to the developmental age of a toddler. As those who worked with her understood this, there was more consistency in the approach to helping her progress.

Erin's case is continued throughout this book to highlight medication interventions, therapeutic interventions, and delivery of psychiatric services within the educational setting.

IMPORTANCE OF PSYCHIATRY IN SCHOOLS

Erin's case highlights the challenge of providing educational services to a student with significant emotional and behavioral struggles. Increasingly, both acutely and chronically mentally ill children are participating in public education settings. The reasons for this are numerous and include a reduction in length of stay of both inpatient hospitalizations and partial hospitalizations, increased stringency requirements for placement in residential treatment facilities, and increased placement of mentally ill children in community homes. A challenge becomes how to program and provide appropriate mental health services to this group of students.

Mental health services can be integrated into the educational setting. Behavioral and mental health supports are available to qualified students. Mental health supports can be used to improve a student's attention to tasks and redirect aggression. Mobile therapists can meet with students in the school setting. Typically, these services are for students who have been diagnosed with a mental illness by a mental health agency.

School districts are also attempting to solve the problem of how to access mental health services for students in need. Some districts are using outpatient mental health agencies to provide individual therapy, group therapy, or substance abuse treatment to students. This therapeutic intervention is often more intense than what can be provided by a guidance counselor. In addition, school districts are beginning to work with psychiatrists in collaborative ways.

CHILD AND ADOLESCENT PSYCHIATRISTS' CONTRIBUTIONS TO THE EDUCATIONAL TEAM

One important role of a psychiatrist is to provide an evaluation of a specific student. The evaluation will address specific questions such as diagnostic clarification, provide an identification of an emotional disability, or make treatment recommendations. This type of evaluation is similar to an independent psychiatric evaluation that can be pursued by the family. However, when it is requested by a school district, educational team members should participate along with the student and family members. This information allows the psychiatrist to obtain additional information that often improves the quality of the evaluation. Educators can play a critical role in providing information regarding academic strengths and weaknesses. Describing the challenging behaviors, antecedents to the negative behaviors, and successful interventions are also desirable. Social interactions and interactions with adults can also be helpful to the diagnostic process. Finally, school personnel often have important social history information, as they may have worked with the student or student's siblings for a number of years.

The school district can use the results of this evaluation to provide more specific educational supports for a student, or it can be used to guide a change in educational placement. In addition, when the educational team understands the emotional contributors to a given problem, it can learn new ways to interact with the student in a more helpful way.

The family can also use this evaluation to obtain recommendations regarding treatment interventions. Different therapeutic interventions, including individual therapy, family therapy, medications, or behavioral supports, can be discussed. Although the family may decide not to pursue the recommendations, many parents and students find the discussion and recommendations helpful.

There are also cases where a psychiatrist can be a consultant for a school district. This consultation can occur for a specific student, classroom, or program. Because of the medical, psychological, and developmental knowledge a psychiatrist has, he or she can provide a unique perspective for a given problem. Consultations to a classroom often occur through direct observation of the room and by obtaining information from administrators and teachers. This observation can sometimes provide valuable information. For example, one classroom observation revealed that a teacher was continually reinforcing negative behavior in several students by placing them in the back of the room where the students continued as a group with worsening behaviors.

Psychiatric consultations can also take place for a specific student. There have been several examples where a school district was concerned about a student, and the parents were uncomfortable pursuing a psychiatric evaluation. Parents may be willing to allow a psychiatrist to sit in on a given class to observe their child. In this case, observation of the student can occur and feedback can be given to the staff.

Finally, psychiatrists are working with school districts to create therapeutic educational settings for severely impaired emotionally disturbed students. Along with helping to design the program, the psychiatrist can maintain an ongoing collaborative treatment role in this type of setting.

When psychiatrists are connected directly with an educational program, they also have the ability to provide medication management for the student. In an outpatient setting, a psychiatrist will see a youth and family for a 20- to 30-minute session to review the response to and side effects of a prescribed medication. Psychiatrists are also able to provide this service within an educational setting. This can be a helpful intervention, because if this occurs within a school setting, the teacher or other personnel are more readily available to provide direct feedback.

Some of the medications that are prescribed by psychiatrists are designed to be effective for part of the day. At times, this length of medication response may mean that the parent does not have direct observation of the child while the medication is most effective. An increase in communicating this information can have a positive treatment effect.

CLINICAL CASE: KAYLA

I have had the opportunity to be involved in one particular student's care over the course of 7 years. This case highlights many advantages of providing psychiatric care to students within an educational setting. My initial contact with Kayla was one of indirect consultation. Her special education team at the elementary school she was attending wanted to discuss some unique challenges of providing educational services to a student who was blind and had behavioral challenges. The primary concern was that Kayla was going to inadvertently harm herself, as she was having occasional times of striking her head when frustrated. The initial contact was arranged by the special education director to allow the opportunity for her teacher, visual support aide, school-based behavioral specialist consultant, and school psychologist to meet with me. The consultation meeting reviewed the educators' concerns particularly regarding Kayla's potential harm to others. During that meeting, the triggers for her frustration were explored, and a plan was created for the behavioral specialist to intervene before the frustration reached a high level.

This behavioral support plan was effective for approximately 6 months. Upon Kayla's return to school the following year, her frustration and anger were more prominent. Strategies, such as her taking scheduled breaks, educators' positively reinforcing her verbalization of negative feelings, and her using a squeeze ball, that had previously been very effective were no longer useful. Her episodic frustration was more intense and more frequent. In addition, she had begun to call out nonsensical words in the middle of class, which was disruptive to other students. Because of Kayla's visual limitations, her mother was able to observe her behavioral outbursts in the classroom without Kayla being aware that her mother was there. This allowed her parents to pursue a psychiatric evaluation.

Kayla was seen for a psychiatric evaluation at the age of 9 when she was a third-grade student. It was determined during the evaluation that Kayla was experiencing psychotic symptoms. She believed in magical thinking in a way that was not developmentally appropriate. She talked at various points during the interview as if SpongeBob were in the room. Kayla had conversations with this TV character and could not accept that he was not real or present. It was difficult to determine if this was truly a visual hallucination or if it was her imagination "filling in" visual stimulation. She also described auditory hallucinations, and her affect while describing the voices was significantly distressed and anxious. Her thought form became very tangential and at times disorganized when there was no structure to the interview.

At the time of the evaluation, Kayla's parents did not report significant concerning behaviors at home. She would sometimes become oppositional and struggled with transitions, but she did not display significant physical aggression toward herself, and they had no other safety concerns. Her parents endorsed that at times she seemed to have imaginary conversations with herself.

The school was reporting significant problematic behaviors in numerous settings. She was frequently removed from the classroom because of her physical aggression of throwing books, tipping over her desk, waving her cane, and trying to run out of the classroom. Although it did not seem that these behaviors were targeted at people because of her blindness, there were times that other students and staff were at risk, as she could not see where she was throwing things. In addition, her classroom was on the second floor of the building, and there were concerns that she could fall down the steps when she tried to run down the hallway. Her frustration was at times triggered by academic demands but at other times seemed to be unpredictable. However, when the classroom was less structured, her behavioral problems intensified.

The medical component to her presentation was also a critical one. It was learned that the reason for Kayla's visual impairment was unclear. Review of ophthalmology records showed that she had bilateral optic nerve hypoplasia, but there was also a report that she had septo-optic dysplasia. This was critical, as individuals with septo-optic dysplasia may have pituitary hypoplasia and are at risk for hypothyroidism. Individuals with unrecognized hypothyroidism can develop psychotic symptoms.

I provided diagnoses of psychotic disorder, not otherwise specified; ruled out psychotic disorder due to a medical condition; and oppositional defiant disorder. This evaluation determined that her educational placement in regular education with accommodations for her visual impairment and learning support services was effective. However, she was identified with an emotional disability as well because of the presence of psychotic symptoms. After extensive discussion, it was determined to be in her best interest at the present time to remain in her same classroom with additional supports. A personal care assistant was used to sit near her and immediately reinforce positive behaviors and intervene at times of frustration. Behavioral supports with a therapeutic support staff were recommended, and the personal care aide was used only until this service was put into place. This person became critical to help prompt appropriate behaviors and allowed Kayla to be maintained in a regular education setting.

The information was shared with her pediatrician, who was able to check appropriate laboratory work and to obtain more comprehensive early medical records. Once it was determined that she did not have a low thyroid level or septo-optic dysplasia, her family also decided to treat the psychotic symptoms with an atypical antipsychotic medication.

I had the opportunity to follow Kayla for about a year in a community mental health setting to manage her medications. With the extensive supports and medication, she began to make

progress remaining in reality and better managing her frustration. Her psychotic symptoms resolved with a low dose of
Risperdal. The behavioral supports provided by the same agency
were helping her in all settings. Once she had stabilized in many
areas, her pediatrician agreed to continue her medications.

Two years after the transfer of care to her pediatrician,
Kayla began to display behavioral problems at both home and
school. She presented for an updated evaluation at the request
of her school district. When the problems first returned, there
was a high level of concern for safety, so she participated
in a partial hospitalization program. A review of the discharge information showed that she had significant anxiety,
which was thought to be related to her behavioral problems.
There had been no return of psychotic symptoms. The intensity of the partial program had been helpful, but her refusal
to cooperate at home and at school was becoming increasingly problematic.

Kayla was also noted to perseverate on certain topics, as
seen by her repeatedly asking the same question. Although her
aggressive behaviors had not returned to the severity seen in my
first contact with her, there was noted worsening of her behavioral control during the 3 months before the second evaluation.
During that evaluation, Kayla was strikingly more nervous.
She spontaneously talked about being fearful and worried. She
described being unable to stop worrying, although she could
articulate that these negative thoughts were causing her to feel
worse. There was a question of whether her perseverative behaviors were a feature of a pervasive developmental disorder, but I
did not believe that she had the social deficits or unusual perseverations that are necessary for that cluster of diagnoses. At
that time, I provided diagnoses of generalized anxiety disorder
and oppositional defiant disorder. I recommended treatment
for the anxiety with a low dose of an SSRI medication. I also
recommended outpatient cognitive behavioral therapy to teach
Kayla strategies to manage her anxiety. Educationally, her personal care aide had been discontinued successfully, but it was
decided that itinerant emotional support services would be
helpful to supplement her relaxation strategies.

On two occasions during Kayla's middle school years, I provided brief consultations to her educational team. I was not
involved directly in her care, but in my collaborative role with
her school district, I was available for consultations. These
occurred without new evaluations but were useful to her educational team members. These years were difficult for Kayla,

and she would frequently have very aggressive outbursts. She began to cause injury to herself by biting her arms. The explosiveness, directed at others and herself, was associated with times of increased anxiety. Medication, outpatient therapy, and educational supports were not consistently effective. During these 3 years she had several inpatient hospitalizations because of concerns for her safety.

The primary diagnostic consideration remained an anxiety disorder, but there was also a consideration for bipolar disorder. During one of the hospitalizations, she was also diagnosed with a pervasive developmental disorder. Numerous medications were tried and prescribed. A variety of community mental health supports were also put into place.

As Kayla completed eighth grade, her disruptiveness, aggression, anxiety, and resistance to treatment were becoming concerns to all adults. There was discussion about a placement in a residential facility for more intensive treatment. Her family was reluctant to pursue this option. A decision was made by the family to have her return home from her third inpatient hospitalization. A case manager was assigned to coordinate a high level of care.

Educationally, as she was promoted to ninth grade, she was placed in a therapeutic emotional support classroom. This educational placement was in the high school at her home school district. I was the psychiatrist who worked directly with this program. Within this setting, she received weekly individual therapy, daily group therapy, social work services, and medication management. In addition, she received many visual support services.

This level of intervention had continued for 2½ academic years. Although the course of progress was not always smooth, Kayla had made tremendous progress. She had not needed treatment in an inpatient or partial hospitalization program during this time. She rarely engaged in self-injury by scratching her arms. She did not display overt physical aggression at home or at school. Although her anxiety remained intermittently high, she was able to articulate this emotion and was now able to use behavioral interventions such as progressive muscular relaxation and deep breathing.

The psychiatric medication plan had also been successful. During Kayla's middle school years, she was placed on a mood stabilizer, an atypical antipsychotic, a medication for inattention, and an antidepressant for anxiety. These medications were necessary at the time. However, as her anxiety had decreased and her skills handling difficult situations had improved, there had been a reduction in medication. She had been off the antipsychotic medication for 1 year. The mood stabilizer dose had been reduced by 50%. There was a plan over the next 3 months to stop the medication for inattention. In part this reduction was possible because of the collaborative approach used in this setting.

In this setting I had the opportunity to provide a longitudinal psychiatric assessment. Within the first year it became apparent that Kayla did not have a pervasive developmental disorder. She appropriately interacted with peers and staff. She was a group leader and successfully negotiated some challenging peer interactions. She did not display unusual or perseverative behaviors. She was able to transition more smoothly than she did as a child. She had no unusual fixations, and her cognitive style was not rigid or inflexible. It was also my opinion that Kayla did not have bipolar disorder. Her moods were stable and had remained stable on less antipsychotic and mood stabilizing medications. There had been no sustained grandiosity, decreased need for sleep, flight of ideas, or pressured speech. There had also not been a return of psychotic symptoms without the antipsychotic medication.

It was my opinion that Kayla's primary diagnosis was generalized anxiety disorder. She was now able to articulate having a running thought pattern of different worries. When these worries increased, she became more irritable, edgy, and explosive. In addition, when she was anxious, she had more difficulty articulating her frustrations and emotions. In addition, there was a depressive component as well. Kayla became more depressed and irritable the week before her menses. This symptom was moderately ameliorated with oral contraceptives.

Kayla's case will continue to be discussed in other chapters of this book. Her case is interesting because of the changing diagnostic picture and her overall progress with many supports.

Two

Psychiatric Evaluation and Formulation

PSYCHIATRIST: BACKGROUND INFORMATION

A psychiatrist is a physician who specializes in the treatment of emotional disorders. There is also an emphasis on diagnosis and prevention of these disorders. Some examples of disorders that can be treated by psychiatrists include depression, anxiety, developmental disabilities, psychosis, and substance abuse. Psychiatrists are medical physicians who have received specialized training in the field of psychiatry. The training focuses on the medical, psychological, and social components of emotional and behavioral disorders. Psychiatrists can order diagnostic tests, prescribe medication, perform psychotherapy, and help in times of stress and crisis. In addition, they may consult with primary care physicians, psychologists, social workers, child protective service systems, juvenile justice systems, and education systems.

A psychiatric evaluation is a comprehensive assessment completed by a psychiatrist. This clinician may be board certified in general psychiatry, and if the evaluation is being conducted on youth, then the clinician may be a board certified child and adolescent psychiatrist. To be board certified in this specialty, the physician must have completed medical school, 3 years of a general psychiatric residency, and 2 years of a child and adolescent residency. A portion of the residency program includes several months spent training with a medical internist and several months spent with a neurologist. A board certified physician is one who has successfully passed a national board examination that most often involves both written and oral portions. A board eligible physician is one who has successfully completed the training for the specialty but has not yet taken or passed the board examination.

As a result of this background and training, several unique characteristics are present in child and adolescent psychiatrists. The frame of reference for a psychiatrist tends to be biologically and medically based. The medical school background prepares a psychiatrist to assess both mental health and medical problems. The neurology training also allows a psychiatrist to consider structural brain abnormalities in assessment of behavioral and emotional problems. Finally, the psychiatry training provides the ability to consider strengths and weaknesses in three different domains: the biological, psychological, and social. This three-tier approach, commonly referred to as the biopsychosocial model, allows for a comprehensive view of the student's functioning.

PSYCHIATRIC EVALUATION: REASONS

A parent or pediatrician can recommend psychiatric evaluations. In this situation, an evaluation is requested primarily to answer specific questions. This may include an assessment for use of a psychotropic medication. It may include an assessment for more intense mental health interventions such as hospitalization. There may be particular questions about a response to a therapeutic intervention such as therapy. In this type of evaluation, it is most common to see the individual and family members only.

A psychiatric evaluation should provide helpful information to the family. It can provide information about diagnosis and contributors to the diagnosis. It can also help to define the youth's strengths and how these can be used to improve deficiencies. It can determine if the symptoms present are developmentally appropriate or a sign of pathology. Finally, it is an opportunity to have any medical contributors assessed.

A school district can also request psychiatric evaluations. This evaluation tends to be more complex. The expectation is that the evaluation, along with providing diagnoses, provides recommendations to help the student be more successful educationally. Often, more questions are asked, and there is often more information readily available by a large number of sources. A school may request an evaluation for several reasons. However, typically it is requested if a student's emotional difficulty is interfering with his or her educational progress. At times, an evaluation is requested simply to provide diagnostic information. Understanding the emotional reasons that are contributing to the presenting problems may be helpful. In addition, a school district might request a psychiatric evaluation to ensure that all possible educational interventions are being provided. Finally, identifying a student with an emotional disturbance can lead to additional educational supports.

Children and youth agencies or juvenile probation agencies can also request psychiatric evaluations. In this type of evaluation, more complex questions are asked. Some of these questions may include an assessment of the student's safety in the community or the impact of past experiences on current functioning, or they may determine if more intensive mental health services are needed.

Regardless of who is requesting the psychiatric evaluation, the primary purpose of the diagnostic assessment is to determine whether psychopathology is present. If it is determined that the symptoms are a sign of pathology, then it becomes important to establish a differential diagnosis. A differential diagnosis is a listing in order of importance of all of the potential causes for the problems. From the differential diagnosis, treatment recommendations can be generated.

There may be situations in which the focus of the evaluation, besides conducting a comprehensive evaluation, is appropriately narrowed. Some examples of this include a consultation for a medical physician on an individual who has been hospitalized in a pediatric unit or an emergency evaluation to determine the dangerousness to self or others. In this type of assessment, there is often a more rapid assessment to answer the one immediate question. This answer will guide further treatment and assessment extents.

PSYCHIATRIC STANDARDIZATION: *DSM-IV-TR*

The American Psychiatric Association developed the first edition of the *Diagnostic and Statistical Manual: Mental Disorders* (DSM-I) in 1952. It was created to provide standardization of diagnoses. This system has evolved and changed until the creation of the current psychiatric standard, the *Diagnostic and Statistical Manual of Mental Disorders*, fourth edition, text revision (*DSM-IV-TR*), which was accepted in 2000.

This reference provides a mechanism for mental health clinicians to provide consistent and clear diagnoses. In this system a mental disorder "is conceptualized as a clinically significant behavioral or psychological syndrome or pattern that occurs in an individual and that is associated with present distress or disability" (American Psychiatric Association,

2000, p. xxxi). It is also specified that this pattern must be more than a culturally sanctioned response to an event. The approach that is used is a "categorical classification that divides mental disorders into types based on criteria sets with defining features" (p. xxxi).

The *DSM-IV-TR* lists the diagnostic criteria for all currently recognized mental disorders. The criteria include a specific cluster of symptoms that must be present. For some diagnoses there are many criteria listed, and it is specified what number of these criteria must be present to reach the clinical diagnostic threshold. For example, there are nine recognized criteria for major depression, but an individual needs to have only five current symptoms to meet the diagnostic threshold for the disorder. It is also specified how long these symptoms must be present. At times the age of onset is specified. For example, an individual with attention-deficit/hyperactivity disorder must demonstrate symptoms before age 7. Some disorders specify that the symptoms must be present in several settings. It is always required that the symptoms cause functional impairment. This is a critical component that helps to differentiate psychopathology from normal. Once criteria are met for a given diagnosis, there may be further specification required. For example, if criteria are met for major depression, the severity of the disorder—mild, moderate, severe, or profound— is required. Each clinical diagnosis and specifier is given a unique identifying code.

The organizational plan for the diagnosis includes a multi-axial system for diagnostic clarity. Axis I is reserved for "mental disorders and conditions that are a focus of clinical attention" (*DSM-IV-TR*, p. 28). There may be more than one Axis I diagnosis identified, and if this is the case, they should be recorded in order of importance. Axis II is for recording personality disorders and mental retardation. Axis III is where general medical conditions are listed, particularly those that are affecting the mental health of the individual. Axis IV is where psychosocial and environmental problems are recorded. Again, if multiple stressors are present, they should be listed. Typically, these are grouped together into the following categories: problems with primary support group, problems related to the social environment, education problems, occupational problems, housing problems, economic problems, problems with access to health care services, and problems related to interactions with the legal system. Finally, Axis V is for the clinician to report his or her judgment of the individual's overall level of functioning. This is done using a scale called the Global Assessment of Functioning (GAF) scale. This is a scale from 1 to 100 that is divided into 10 ranges of functioning. More severe impairment is in the lower range, which describes a more severe problem. For example, numbers ranging from 91 to 100 reflect superior functioning, whereas numbers from 41 to 50 are for serious symptoms such as suicidal ideation or serious impairment in functioning, and 1 to 10 are for those individuals who are in persistent danger of severely hurting self or others.

PSYCHIATRIC EVALUATION

Features

The American Academy of Child and Adolescent Psychiatry (AACAP) is an organization that can be a helpful resource to child and adolescent psychiatrists and families. This organization devised a set of guidelines that, although not mandatory to follow, can be used by physicians to ensure that a thorough evaluation is completed. The suggestions in the following section are loosely based on these guidelines.

One unique feature of a psychiatric evaluation is its focus on developmental information. Development occurs on a continuum, and there are several different "developmental lines." Some examples of developmental lines include motor development, speech and language development, social development, educational development, and identity development. The psychiatric evaluation should consider where the youth is on those different lines. This context helps to further identify individual strengths and weaknesses. Therefore, it is important for the psychiatrist to understand normal and abnormal development (see accompanying CD: 2.1).

Along with development, a psychiatric assessment must also consider the student in the context of family and educational settings. A child's functioning is dependent on the interactions with others around him or her. A child does not operate independently, and a full understanding can be achieved only when there has been a consideration of the different settings in which the child functions. Therefore, these features must be understood to help clarify strengths and needs.

A final critical feature of the assessment is the mental status examination. This section is a "snapshot" description of the child at the time of evaluation. However, it must be considered that factors can influence this presentation of the child on that given day. For example, if a child is physically ill on the day of the assessment, the evaluation may not fully reflect the child's presentation on a day he or she feels well. Nervousness about meeting a new person may also skew the presentation. In addition, pressure to perform and do well may change this view in an unrealistically positive way.

Sources of Information

A complete psychiatric evaluation includes information from as many sources as possible. At minimum, the parent and child are required informants. However, information should also be sought from the school, a medical physician, or prior treatment providers. In addition, if the child is involved with other public systems, such as child welfare or juvenile probation, information should be sought from these agencies as well.

It is important that there be the opportunity to see the child and the parents separately. This allows the opportunity for the clinician to ask more direct questions and allows each participant to answer more honestly. However, it is often equally useful to spend a portion of the time with the parents and child together. This allows the clinician the opportunity to see the interactions between the family members.

Parent Interview

The parent interview is critical to a full understanding of the child, and it is often framed with the intention of discovering several objectives. The first goal of the parent interview is to understand the reason for the referral. This includes understanding the child's current difficulties and the impact these difficulties are having on both the child and the family. The second goal is to obtain relevant developmental history to have the appropriate framework in which to place these difficulties. The third objective is to gain understanding of the family's level of functioning and the cultural context in which the family operates. Finally, obtaining information about physical or mental illnesses within the family can contribute to an understanding about biological influences on the problem.

The history should focus not only on obtaining information about the child's struggles, but also on strengths, interests, and talents. This approach helps to foster the self-esteem of the child and bolster the self-construct of the family. In addition, it allows the opportunity to make use of these positives to modify the more challenging behaviors. Strengths should be identified throughout the assessment, but initiating the parent interview with this information often puts the family at ease.

When obtaining information to understand the reason for the referral, it is necessary to inquire about frequency, intensity, duration, and circumstances in which problematic behaviors occur. The attitudes of the parents, child, and others toward the problem are also a helpful line on which to inquire. Often, each parent may have a different perspective of the impact of the problem, and understanding the differing views is helpful. This should include a direct account of several specific instances of the problematic behavior. Once there seems to be a thorough understanding of the behavioral problem, it is important to understand the parental view of the child's perceived distress, the degree to which the behaviors interfere with social and academic activities, and the impact on the child's ongoing development. Finally, it is important to understand the impact this behavior has on others (Cox & Rutter, 1985).

Certain behaviors are developmentally normal, whereas other behaviors become abnormal if they persist beyond a certain age. This is the reason child and adolescent psychiatrists attempt to gain as much information about the child's development as possible. For example, a fear of bugs is developmentally appropriate in a preschool child but can be abnormal in a teenager. It is important to understand motor development, social development, and the development of self-regulation.

As described above, it is important to also understand the ways in which the family system functions. Considering the family's flexibility and conflict resolution skills are often important as they can place the family's ability to manage problematic behavior in different ways. Equally important is the cultural context in which the family operates. Some cultures are more reluctant to share personal and family information with strangers. Some cultures readily embrace the idea of mental illness and therefore are able to be more forthcoming about problems. Extended family members' cultural context and view of information can drive the way a nuclear family functions.

Youth Interview

The clinical interview of the youth allows for the opportunity for the clinician to directly explore the individual's own perception of the presenting problem and the assessment of his or her overall developmental and mental status. This direct contact allows the clinician to learn information that may not be available from other sources. For example, the child's perception of his or her personal suffering can be provided only by the child. In addition, thoughts and feelings such as anxiety, suicide, and obsessions can be given only in a direct child interview. It is also important to assess the child's level of emotional awareness.

There are two main objectives that should be considered during this portion of the assessment: obtaining personal history and conducting a mental status examination. When taking the personal history, the clinician should inquire into the child's life and level of functioning both in the past and in the present. The mental status examination is an assessment and description of the child's appearance and functioning as seen during the evaluation. These two objectives are often addressed simultaneously during the individual assessment.

Unlike an interview with an adult, the interview of a child or adolescent often requires creativity and flexibility to obtain information. The interview must match the child's developmental, cognitive, and language abilities. In addition, the approach and tone of the interview may need to be adjusted regarding the difficulty or intensity of the topic being discussed. Finally the degree of rapport that has been established may guide the speed of the interview.

Particularly with younger children, using interactive play can provide more useful information than asking questions. Children may be limited in their ability to give an explicit verbal account of their feelings or social interactions (Glasbourg & Aboud, 1982). This information may be readily revealed as the child plays with puppets or small figures in an imaginative way. The trained interviewer is able to facilitate such play for diagnostic and rapport-building purpose, without distorting the child's views.

In addition, there are several informal projective techniques that can be used to complement the use of unstructured imaginative play. One of the common projective techniques is to ask the child to draw a picture. Projective questions can be asked including asking a child which three wishes she would like to have granted or what she would take with her if she were on a deserted island. Play and projective techniques and questions can often add an element of fun to the individual interview, which places the child at ease and helps to build a positive rapport.

When beginning the interview with the youth, it is often most helpful not to begin with the presenting problem. The initial time should be spent establishing rapport. It next becomes important to obtain information that assesses the areas of functioning. It is helpful to understand the child's interests, strengths, weaknesses, and feelings in the major areas of the child's life. These include both the external world of family, peers, and school and the inner world, including self-concept. When attempting to understand the symptoms of distress, the clinician should inquire into mood states such as depression and anxiety. There should be some discussion to ascertain if the individual is suffering from low self-esteem or suicidal ideation thoughts. When assessing anxiety the clinician should investigate the existence of unusual fears, obsessions, or compulsions. All youth should be asked about hallucinations and delusions to rule out psychotic symptoms. Finally, there should be questions about eating patterns, delinquent behavior, substance abuse, and a history of traumatic experiences.

Other Informants

As described above, there may be other individuals, along with the student and parents, who have critical information about the child's strengths, challenges, and developmental functioning. Depending on the scope of the evaluation, these individuals should be given the opportunity to provide this information. In some families the student may have frequent contact with extended family members such as grandparents, aunts, or uncles. The family may choose to have these individuals provide direct information or written information.

School personnel often have astute observations of the child's functioning in the educational system. In addition, depending on the age of the child, school personnel may have accurate social information that further supports the evaluation. If school personnel are unable to participate directly in the interview, a teacher may provide a written summary or complete a checklist of observations. A probation officer may be able to provide information more honestly about past illegal behaviors. In addition, probation officers may have had the opportunity to see the student in the context of different social environments. This information further provides diagnostic information. A pediatrician may supply medical records. It is particularly important to review laboratory results if available or review prescribed psychotropic medications.

Formulation

Following the clinical interview, the psychiatrist begins to make an opinion. This medical opinion is called the psychiatric

formulation or psychiatric assessment. In this section the clinician reviews the relevant data and organizes them in a way
to highlight the child's difficulties and biological, social, and
psychological contributors to this problem. The consequences
of the problem to the youth and family are also relevant. It is
also important to understand the factors that may cause the
problem to be maintained and what factors might relieve it.
Definitive answers to these questions may not be apparent at
the conclusion of the initial assessment. In this situation it is
appropriate to consider a differential diagnosis of several possible causes. The subsequent steps that are needed to clarify
the diagnosis and treatment options should be included in
this scenario.

The formulation takes into account the different biological, psychological, and social domains that may be contributing to the identified problems. The interaction between these
domains often becomes critical in both the diagnosis of pathology and the subsequent recommendations for treatment.

PSYCHIATRIC EVALUATION REPORT

Background

The written report of the psychiatric evaluation should provide relevant information regarding the student's thoughts,
feelings, and behaviors. Individual and familial strengths
should be highlighted. When a psychiatric evaluation is conducted for a school system, there should also be emphasis on
which domain is causing interference with a student's ability
to make educational progress. There should be diagnoses provided that conform to the *DSM-IV-TR*. Finally, there should be
recommendations provided to help promote success in areas
that have been a struggle. Although the definitive structure of
the report varies depending on the clinician, there is generally
consistency in the overall format. The expected content of the
report is described below.

Identifying Data

The start of the evaluation should identify the reasons for the
evaluation and specific questions or problems that will be
addressed in the report. Demographic details such as address,
age, constellation of family, and educational placement should
be described. The individuals who provided information
should be listed. Finally, any other resources, such as other

reports or the conclusion of testing, that were used in the formulation, diagnoses, or recommendations should be listed.

History of Presenting Illness

Following the introduction is the history of presenting illness. The purpose of this section is to clearly identify both strengths and challenges of the student. The symptoms that cause the most interference in the student's growth and development are important to highlight. The symptoms may be behaviors. In this case the antecedent to the behavior and a clear description of the concerning behavior should be provided. Any patterns related to the behavioral decompensation or recovery should be noted as well. For example, if a 7-year-old cries and throws items when a request is made, the length of the outburst, the intensity of the behavior, and what helps to stop it should be given. In addition to overt behavioral problems, other symptoms can also interfere in a child's functioning. Withdrawal from interactions with others can cause interference in growth and development. Having extensive internal worries or thoughts that are not consistent with reality may also be a cause for concern. This is a comprehensive section that highlights concerns. The section is meant to reflect information conveyed from a number of sources. The parent interview often provides the majority of the content for this section, but it is also appropriate for the clinician to use information provided by the student or other informants in this portion of the report.

Past Psychiatric History

The third section is a review and summary of past mental health interventions. It is referred to as the past psychiatric history. This section provides the framework in which to consider the concerns highlighted in the previous section. Important components of past history include any known assessments, diagnoses, and treatment. It is important that this section be as complete as possible, because success or failure of past treatments can be an important guide to current recommendations. If prior psychological or psychiatric evaluations have been completed, there should be a listing of the date of evaluation and diagnoses given. It is important to include past psychiatric hospitalizations or participation in partial hospitalization treatment programs. If medications have been tried, the name of the medication should be listed with the dosage, length of the trial, side effects, and any positive response. Specific psychotherapeutic interventions should be reviewed, with a brief summary of outcome.

Past Medical History

Medical problems should be summarized in the next section. There should be particular attention given to illnesses that may compound psychiatric symptoms. For example, a child with asthma may also have anxiety, and each problem may worsen the other. There should also be a consideration in this section for any somatic symptoms for which a medical cause cannot be identified. Commonly, adolescents with depression or anxiety may complain repeatedly of gastric distress for which no known physiologic reason can be found, despite repeated medical procedures. There should also be questions posed to ensure that there is no history of significant head trauma, particularly one that resulted in a loss of consciousness.

Social and Developmental History

Social and developmental history is also an important component of the assessment. This section should include any problems that were experienced during pregnancy and any exposure to medications or illicit substances that might have occurred *in utero.* Delivery complications should be listed, as well as Apgar scores if they are known. Acquisition of developmental milestones helps to put the current symptoms in an appropriate context. This section should also include all relevant social information such as the constellation of the family, supports to the family, and stressors that may be occurring. As described above, it is important to review how the child fits with the family and how the family functions in the context of its culture. This information as it is obtained from the parent interview should be summarized.

A history of physical abuse, sexual abuse, or neglect is also important to include in this section of history. The source of information for this should be both the student and the parents. Understanding past abusive experiences is best explored with the student individually and the parents individually. Finally, there should be a brief discussion about the peer group with whom the student associates. Again this information is best obtained from both the parents and the student.

At times students who are undergoing a psychiatric evaluation have had connections with other systems. This should be included in the social and developmental history. For example, any contact a student has had with the juvenile probation office or children and youth services is relevant. The benefit obtained from these supports should be included, as well as any hindrance that may have occurred.

Substance use is sometimes included in the social and developmental history section, or it may encompass its own section of the report. It is important to include the pattern of tobacco, alcohol, and/or prescription medication abuse and the use of illicit substances. Efforts should be made to ascertain if the pattern of use is escalating and to what degree it is consuming the student. Asking these questions in a nonjudgmental way will often allow the student to be honest. Certainly the student is the primary informant of this information, but at times the parent or school personnel suspect abuse. In this case this information should be included as well.

Educational History

The section regarding educational history is important especially when a psychiatric evaluation is being completed with school personnel present. It is important to note the history of school attendance, behavioral problems, academic successes and failures, and social interactions. If there has been psychoeducational testing, the results should be included. It is important to assess any past special education services and the effectiveness of these programs. A review of the current individualized education program also provides additional insight into the challenges the student faces on a regular basis. School personnel are often in a unique position to observe the student over the course of time, and this observation takes place within a natural setting.

Family Psychiatric History

Family psychiatric history is also an important section. This should describe any family members who have a diagnosed mental illness. If a family member has received successful treatment, the specifics of this should be included, as it may help to identify useful interventions for the identified student. In addition, there are often suspicions that a family member has a mental illness but there has not been a formal diagnosis or treatment. This information should also be included.

Mental Status Examination

The mental status examination is a clinical snapshot of the student at the time of presentation. This section is often equated with a medical physician's physical examination. In the report this section includes only information that was obtained in the clinical interview with the student. There should be a detailed description of the student, including physical attributes, appearance, and hygiene. It has been explained that this description should provide enough detail that a person reading the description should be able to identify the student in a group of individuals. Behavioral or motor abnormalities should be included. For example, some students are restless and unable to sit still. Alternatively, a student might present with psychomotor retardation where there is excessive slowness of movement and thought. Motor or vocal tics may also be observed and should be described in detail.

The characteristics of speech should be described. This includes the rate, tone, and volume of speech, as well as any disarticulations. Mood, which is the individual's description of his or her current feelings, is reported, and at times the exact descriptive words can be put in quotations. Affect, which is the evaluator's view of the individual's mood, should be described. It should also be reported if the affect changes quickly (affective lability) or is inconsistent with the reported mood (incongruent with mood). The individual's thought form reflects the flow of thoughts and can be considered one of the hallmarks of the described mental status examination. Ideally, an individual's thought form is termed "clear and organized" when it is logical and goal directed. Alternatively, if the thought form is disorganized, there should be clarification about the way in which it is not organized. A mild type of disorganized thinking is termed "tangential." In this pattern an individual answers the question but provides excessive detail that gradually shifts the conversation in a different direction. A similar type of disorganization is "circumstantial thought processes." In this case the student answers the question initially but quickly provides excessive detail or changes the topic briefly before returning the topic of conversation back to the initial answer. Another pattern of more severely disorganized thinking is called "flight of ideas." In this pattern the thoughts are loosely related but do not flow well together. For example, "Today is Monday. On Monday I drive to school. I drive a red car. That reminds me that red is my favorite color and blue is my mother's favorite color. She likes blue because it reminds her of the beach." Another type of disorganized thinking is called "clanging." In this pattern the individual will provide two or three rhyming words intermixed within a sentence. The most severe type of disorganized thinking is termed "loosening of association." In this pattern there are no logical connections between the words. It can also be referred to as "word salad," which is a good descriptor. It is important to clearly describe the thought form, as certain types of disorganized thinking suggest certain mental illnesses. Flight of ideas is often heard when an individual is manic, whereas clanging and loosening of associations are most common in schizophrenia.

Thought content is a description of the internal thoughts of the student. This includes a description of the student's internal mood states such as sadness, anxiety, or anger. When reporting symptoms of depression, the clinician should describe the degree of hopelessness and guilt that are experienced and the perversity of this emotional state. When reporting symptoms of anxiety, the clinician should describe the thoughts or situations that trigger this emotion. Anxiety can also cause physical symptoms such as restlessness, racing heartbeat, headaches, abdominal distress, or shortness of breath. Obsessions that are irrational fears or compulsions that are behaviors done repetitively to reduce anxiety can also be other symptoms of this emotional state. Understanding the students' description of anger triggers and the way in which this normal emotion is managed should be reported. Any thoughts that demonstrate poor reality testing such as the presence of hallucinations or delusions should be detailed. Assessing suicidal or homicidal ideas is important to include in this section. It is often better to begin to inquire about these symptoms in broad terms, such as asking "Have you ever wished you had not been born?" before asking more specific questions regarding suicidal intention. The final area that should be reported in the mental status examination should reference the individual's cognition, fund of knowledge, and insight into his or her own internal thoughts and emotions.

Diagnostic Formulation

Following the above-described information should be the diagnostic assessment or formulation section. This section should provide a very brief summary of the identified problem. It should provide details of the interactions between biological, psychological, and social aspects. For example, if a student is presenting with depressive symptoms, the biological contributor may be a genetic history of depression in several family members. The psychological contributor could be the student's process of understanding his or her own identity and forming an appropriate view of him- or herself. The social contributors may include an overbearing and protective family and conflict with peers. Each of these contributors has an impact on the student's presentation right now.

Diagnosis

The diagnosis should be recorded in the format as recommended by the *DSM*. This format includes the five-axis diagnostic system that was highlighted above (see also accompanying CD: 2.2). An example of how this section may appear for a given individual is as follows:

> Axis I: Major depression: single episode, moderate severity; attention-deficit/hyperactivity disorder: primarily inattentive
>
> Axis II: Deferred
>
> Axis III: History of seizure disorder; last seizure 18 months ago
>
> Axis IV: Psychosocial stressors moderate: history of physical abuse, peer conflict, lack of educational success
>
> Axis V: GAF currently 60, highest in past year 75

Recommendations

The final section of the written report is the recommendations. These recommendations should be clear and concise. The recommendations reflect suggestions for treatment. At a minimum there should be recommendations for the following types of services: psychotherapy, medication management, social agency supports, and community supports. Depending on the information available, educational recommendations can also be included. At times it might be determined that a higher level of mental health intervention such as inpatient hospitalization or partial hospitalization may be indicated.

The psychotherapy interventions can include individual, group, or family therapy. In addition, the type of therapy, such as psychodynamic therapy, cognitive behavioral therapy, interpersonal therapy, or supportive therapy, should be specified. If there is an identified provider, that should also be specified, and if there is a suggested frequency of visits, that should also be included. The indication for group therapy should be included if there is an appropriate group available. Finally, if family therapy is recommended, there should be a brief review of the goals of this intervention.

Medication suggestions should be clearly described, including the type of medication, reason for this medication, dose, side effects, expected time course of response, and potential benefits. At times the family may decide during the evaluation to begin medication, and if a prescription is provided, this and a notification that informed consent for medication was given should be documented.

Social service supports vary by state. If there is a concern identified about abuse or neglect, the relevant county department of human services should be notified. Some states have mental health case managers who can help connect families with appropriate mental health services. If it is believed that the family may have difficulty finding providers for the other recommendations, it can be helpful to provide a referral for this service. Juvenile probation referrals are rarely made from a psychiatric evaluation, as this service is court ordered. However, if there is active involvement from this agency, there should be coordination of care and recommendations.

Community supports rarely require the recommendation of a psychiatrist, but these may be discussed as other potential supports. This can include participation in the Big Brothers Big Sisters program, YMCA recreation programs, or church activities.

Finally, based on the severity and intensity of symptoms, it may be determined that a higher level of care is needed. Typically, inpatient care is indicated if the student is unable to ensure the clinician of his or her safety, if there is concern about the safety of others, or if psychotic symptoms are present. This level of care is particularly needed if it is determined that the family is unable to provide the level of monitoring that is needed to keep the individual safe. Alternatively, if there is a moderately high degree of symptoms but the clinician perceives that the student will be safe for some of the day, a referral to a partial hospitalization program can be made. The clinician who makes these recommendations should understand what steps to take to ensure that these higher level interventions are followed.

Psychiatric Report: Conclusion

At the conclusion of the psychiatric evaluation, the findings should be shared with the relevant parties. The physician also generates a report that includes all of the above information. Some psychiatrists will automatically provide a copy of the report to the parents. Others prefer to provide the report with consent only to other clinicians.

PSYCHIATRIC EVALUATION: SUMMARY

A psychiatrist who reviews current symptoms, past intervention, and social aspects of the presenting problem completes a
psychiatric evaluation. From this information based on a set
of necessary symptoms, a psychiatric diagnosis can be given.
The evaluation should, however, provide much more information than a simple diagnosis (see accompanying CD: 2.2). There
should be relevant information reviewing biological, psychological, and social contributors. Recommendations should be
the conclusion of the evaluation, and these recommendations
can guide helpful intervention strategies. Ideally, when a psychiatric evaluation is conducted for a school district, it should
include information to help guide the educational team and
should include educational implications.

Three

Psychiatric Roles

THE PSYCHIATRIST AS A CONSULTANT

Conducting a consult implies that a professional in one system has knowledge and expertise that a professional in another system needs. The consultant believes that he or she can offer a new and helpful solution to the problem. In a private practice or clinic setting, a psychiatrist has a direct relationship with an identified patient and the family. When a psychiatrist is a consultant, the primary relationship is with the individual or agency that requested the consult. A psychiatrist may become a consultant to another medical provider. The most common example of this is when a psychiatrist assesses a patient who has been admitted to a medical unit but is believed to also be struggling with a mental illness. Child and adolescent psychiatrists also serve as consultants in different systems such as juvenile probation, children and youth services, foster care agencies, and schools.

When engaged in a consultation for a school system, the psychiatrist may be asked to provide direct information regarding an individual student. This may include an evaluation or other assessment. Alternatively, the psychiatrist may be consulted to identify and offer solutions to problems. The consultation may take place in the classroom with a team of teachers, with building administrators, or with the community.

Psychiatrists can offer a unique knowledge base when they function as consultants. They blend principles of child development with psychiatric disorders and knowledge of the system in which they are acting as the consultant. Their background in the diagnosis and treatment of mental disorders from a biopsychosocial model further complements these principles. Although not necessarily behavioral experts, they have an appreciation for common reasons contributing to negative behaviors and suggestions to help ameliorate negative

behavior. In addition, they add an appreciation of psychodynamic interaction within the group, family, and individual.

In 2004, the American Academy of Child and Adolescent
Psychiatry (AACAP) provided the opinion that child and adolescent psychiatrists should be able to consult and collaborate
with school systems (*Journal of the American Academy of Child
and Adolescent Psychiatry* [*JAACAP*]). This fact is becoming
more critical in today's mental health system. Epidemiological
data suggest that 9 to 13% of children and adolescents in the
United States, a figure that represents 6 to 9 million children and
adolescents, have a mental disorder associated with significant
functional impairment (Friedman, Katz-Leavy, Manderscheid,
& Sondheimer, 1996). Yet, it is estimated that only one fifth of
young people who need mental health services receives them,
and a much smaller proportion receives services from a child
and adolescent psychiatrist (Burns et al., 1995). Because students spend a large portion of their day in school, providing
mental health access in that location should allow students
easier access to treatment. Educators and school employees are
in a unique position to make important observations that can
further contribute to diagnostic clarity or further help describe
treatment effects.

PSYCHIATRIC CONSULTATION: POTENTIAL ROLES

Psychiatrists can be instrumental in identifying students with
an emotional or mental disability. Once a student has been
identified with a disability, a school system has a legal obligation to provide that individual with an education that best
meets the student's needs. Psychiatrists may also become
involved in determining if an identified student is receiving the
specialized programs that meet his or her educational needs.

In addition, psychiatrists can work directly in a classroom
to provide behavioral support or to provide a broader understanding of problematic relationships that exist within the
classroom setting. They can also address problematic relationships that exist between teachers and administrators or teachers and families. The broad perspective of a psychiatrist can
be particularly helpful within this area.

Schools are charged with the task of keeping students safe.
With the events that have occurred across the nation over the
past decade, there is an increased need to identify students
who might be at risk of harming others. Psychiatrists can
participate in the task of helping to assess the risk of a given

student based on comments, writings, or drawings that were received. Often this takes the form of a "risk assessment."

AMERICAN ACADEMY OF CHILD AND ADOLESCENT PSYCHIATRY RECOMMENDATIONS

In 2004, AACAP created practice parameters that described ways in which psychiatrists can and do collaborate with school systems. These guidelines were established after a panel reviewed more than 200 chapters and articles that were published between 1995 and 2003. After this review there was the formation of different standards that child and adolescent psychiatrists are expected to follow. The practice parameters have been given different weights of importance. The "minimal standard" is an expectation that is accepted by overwhelming evidence and is estimated to be true in more than 95% of the cases. The "clinical standard" is based on strong consensus and is expected to apply more than 75% of the time. The "optional recommendations" are acceptable and can be encouraged but are not required for appropriate care.

The first and perhaps most important expectation, a minimal standard, is that psychiatrists understand the educational rights that protect students with disabilities. The foundation for this protection is the 14th Amendment of the Constitution, which prohibits discrimination. The federal laws continued to be clarified during the latter half of the 20th century and are currently well established. State and local districts may have some unique features of protection, and a consultant should understand what these are.

Another minimal standard or basic expectation is that a psychiatrist should be able to provide advice to school personnel and parents about special education services. This information could include either related services or appropriate accommodations for students with psychiatric disorders. If a child is suspected of having a disability, the student should have a special education evaluation performed to determine eligibility for specialized education services. This evaluation is comprehensive and conducted by individuals of several disciplines. A school psychologist can contribute information regarding intelligence, achievement, and working memory. A teacher can contribute information describing barriers to learning within the classroom. A pediatrician can provide information regarding existing medical conditions that affect learning, and a psychiatrist can contribute information regarding emotional challenges. If personnel are following this assessment, a student is identified with a disability and would benefit from special education services, and the school should develop a written individualized education program (IEP).

It is also expected as a minimal standard that a psychiatrist be able to conduct an assessment that addresses a student's barriers to learning. This is most commonly conducted as a psychiatric evaluation. When this assessment is completed as a consultation to a school district, there is more emphasis placed on what features are preventing the student from making educational progress. This information is obtained from a variety of sources, including school personnel, family members, and the student. If there are barriers to learning based on underlying emotional reasons, then the student may qualify to be identified under the Individuals with Disabilities Education Act (IDEA). The IDEA defines a serious emotional disability as "a disability where one or more of the following characteristics are present over a long period of time and to a marked degree that adversely affects educational performance:

- An inability to learn that cannot be explained by intellectual, sensory, or health factors;
- An inability to build or maintain satisfactory interpersonal relationships with peers and teachers;
- Inappropriate types of behavior or feelings under normal circumstances;
- A general pervasive mood of unhappiness or depression;
- A tendency to develop physical symptoms or fears associated with personal or school problems" (Code of Federal Regulations, Title 34, Section 300.7(b)(9)).

If through the process of a psychiatric evaluation it is determined that at least one of the above factors is present and causing impairment, then there can be an identification with an emotional disability. Common psychiatric diagnoses that may cause an emotional disability are major depression, generalized anxiety disorder, obsessive-compulsive disorder, and schizophrenia, as well as a variety of others.

Along with recognizing and describing emotional disabilities, an assessment can identify a number of other barriers to learning. A number of other psychiatric disorders correspond to IDEA disability designations. Psychiatrists commonly diagnose pervasive developmental disorders such as autistic

disorder or Asperger's disorder, which are educationally classified as autism spectrum disorders. Communication disorders
can be diagnosed or supported through a psychiatric evaluation and be further classified during a speech and language
assessment. The student can receive specialized education
through an IEP with the identification of a speech and language impairment. Attention-deficit/hyperactivity disorder is
often identified as an "other health impairment." Learning disabilities and mental retardation are also other difficulties that
can lead to special education; however, these identifications
are best done through a neuropsychological or psychoeducational assessment.

Once a student has been identified as qualifying for special
education services, the recommendations that are a result of
the psychiatric evaluation can guide educational placement
or support services. The educational setting that is provided
must be appropriate to the child's individual educational
needs and be the least restrictive placement. Schools generally
will attempt to provide special education services on site or
within their district. Itinerant emotional support or emotional
support classrooms where a student spends a portion of his or
her day is often the first intervention attempted. If this level of
support is not sufficient to promote progress or if appropriate
services are unavailable, the school must arrange for an alternative placement out of district.

Another clinical standard put forth by AACAP is that a psychiatrist should be able to participate in treatment team planning with schools, home, and the community. As described
above, psychiatric recommendations can be included in
an identified student's IEP. This can include placement recommendations or the use of other educational supports.
Psychiatric recommendations can result in community services and other treatment alternatives. Once the assessment
is completed, there needs to be a format in place to ensure
that these recommendations are clearly shared with all relevant parties. Some states are providing more intensive mental
health supports to students within the school district. This is
an example of why it is critical that results of the evaluation
are communicated not just to the school but to other potential
sources of support as well.

It is a clinical standard that psychiatrists should understand
how to initiate, develop, and maintain consultative relationships with schools. As a psychiatrist works in this capacity,
he or she should understand the consultant role. This work

should be done in an ethical and courteous manner. It is also a clinical standard that the psychiatric consultant be knowledgeable about the school milieu including administrative procedures, school personnel, and the general culture of the students. As described in the previous chapter, understanding the environment in which the student functions is critical to understanding the degree of psychopathology.

Psychiatrists can collaborate with school personnel to provide consultation to the schools in an indirect way, although this is not a clinical standard. In other words, psychiatrists can provide information to the schools about mental illness or programming for students in a way in which there is no direct student contact. One of these interventions could include the ability to conduct a needs assessment for the district. For example, the clinician can consult with a school to help recognize and then refer for treatment students who are suffering from a mental health disorder such as depression. Psychiatrists could collaborate with school personnel to deliver effective school-based universal prevention programs. This could include working with the district to promote the cessation of bullying. This type of consultation often occurs through lectures to staff, students, and parents.

PSYCHIATRIC EVALUATIONS
FOR A SCHOOL SYSTEM

Reasons

Although psychiatrists may work in consultative roles with schools, they most commonly are involved with providing psychiatric evaluations of one identified individual. If the evaluation is initiated and pursued by the family, the clinician can choose to obtain educational information directly from the school. This should be done if a specific school concern, such as absenteeism, is discussed during the first assessment appointment. Prior to this exchange of information, there must be a signed release of information by the parent and student. The information that is exchanged between the school district and the psychiatrist should be considered confidential information and should not be used in a pejorative way. Once a clinician has obtained information directly from a school-based team member, he or she can then provide educational recommendations that can help to ameliorate the given concern (see accompanying CD: 3.1).

Comprehensive psychiatric evaluations can alternatively be requested and initiated by the school district. If the psychiatric evaluation is recommended by the school district, the school team has a very important role as the idea is presented to the student and parents. A school will most often request a psychiatric evaluation if the parents have not pursued this assessment independently. A school can also request a psychiatric evaluation if a second opinion is requested. A student can be in treatment with a community psychiatrist who is operating under one diagnosis. Through the assessment for special education, the school psychologist might suspect a different diagnosis. In this situation an independent psychiatric evaluation can be requested to clarify the diagnosis. In my personal experience, one of the larger diagnostic issues in the situation of pursuing a second opinion through a psychiatric evaluation is to clarify the presence of an autism spectrum disorder (see accompanying CD: 3.2–3.3).

Another valuable reason for a school to use a psychiatric consultant in a direct service model is to provide a "risk assessment." This is typically a brief and focused assessment of a student's risk to him- or herself or to others. Many schools have mental health professionals or psychologists on the school staff. If so these treatment providers are often involved in conducting an immediate assessment of risk and determining if additional assessment is needed. In some situations a psychiatrist might be consulted to provide a risk assessment. The question of risk can be asked and answered during a comprehensive psychiatric evaluation. In addition, this specific question may be the only question asked of the consultant. If this is the request, a risk assessment can become a focused inquiry into a student's statements, drawings, or writings in order to answer a safety question. When a psychiatrist does this assessment, information regarding development, history of violence, and history of impulse control is obtained from the parents. The student provides information regarding his or her thoughts and intention behind the statement. More information on this topic is included in Chapter 13.

Regardless of the reason that the school system is recommending an evaluation, it is critical that this idea be explained appropriately to the family and student. There are a few facts that are very important that the parents need to understand before they can give consent for a psychiatric evaluation. It must be explained that a psychiatrist is a medical doctor who specialized in diagnosing and treating behavioral problems.

The specific questions that are going to be asked by the psychiatrist should be explained. The parents need to know where the evaluation will be conducted and who will be participating. It is particularly important that the parents understand that school personnel will be present to provide information; without this knowledge ahead of the evaluation, there can be significant animosity on the day of the assessment. If the same psychiatrist is used by the school district, the basic format that the physician uses should be explained. Parents should also understand the length of time of the evaluation and that following the evaluation a report will be written. It should be explained that there might be a change in educational placement as a result of the evaluation. The parents will need to sign a release of information to allow the contact between the school and the psychiatrist to occur (see accompanying CD: 3.2).

School systems can sometimes face extreme reluctance from the parents to pursue a psychiatric evaluation. One helpful point to clarify to minimize resistance is to help the parents understand that a psychiatric diagnosis guides treatment and educational interventions, but this diagnosis does not "define" the child. Another source of resistance for some parents is the perception that an evaluation is being pursued to recommend they medicate their child. Although medications may be discussed as a potential recommendation, there will also be a full complement of other recommendations discussed. If the parents have legal guardianship of the student, it will always remain the family's decision to pursue any recommendation including medications. At times a psychiatrist can be particularly useful to review negative responses to past medications. At other times a psychiatrist might be able to provide written or clinical information about medications that will help parents make a better informed decision about medication in the future.

After consent is given, the parents should be asked if they are going to prepare the student or if they would like school personnel to talk to the student about it. If the parents choose to talk to their child, they should explain to the child the known reasons for the evaluation and also describe the process. It is important that the student understand as much about the process as possible in order to improve his or her comfort during the assessment.

If the school personnel are involved in preparing the child, the school representative who does this should be one with whom the student is very comfortable. It should be explained that a psychiatrist is a doctor who talks about and listens to thoughts, feelings, and actions. The student should know that for a portion of the time, he or she will be talking individually to the doctor. Students should be encouraged to answer questions as truthfully as possible and to ask for clarification to any questions that are not understood. There should be an explanation in developmentally appropriate terms about the reasons for the evaluation and the main topics that may be discussed. It should be clearly explained that the evaluation is being done not because the child is "bad" but to determine what may make the student feel better or perform better (see accompanying CD: 3.3).

Initiation

There are numerous reasons why the school may need to facilitate an evaluation or risk assessment. The family may have financial or insurance limitations that prevent an independent psychiatric evaluation. In addition, there may be limited access to child and adolescent psychiatrists or a significant delay if the family attempts to schedule an appointment, but the school may have easier access to a consultant. Finally, the parents may be reluctant to have a psychiatrist involved. It is very important for the school liaison who is facilitating the evaluation to understand what barriers may be preventing the family from scheduling a private evaluation. Attempts should be made to address these barriers. All efforts should be made by school personnel to help the parents and student understand what to expect during the evaluation and as a result of the evaluation. If there is not proper preparation about the evaluation, the family or student may present in a defensive or hostile way that can negatively alter the assessment. In addition, describing the benefit of this assessment is also helpful to ensure that parents and students are participating in a comfortable way.

Process

The first step of a psychiatric evaluation of a student that is done for a school district is obtaining written consent from the appropriate individuals. The parent or guardian must give permission for the school to speak to the psychiatrist and the psychiatrist to speak to school personnel. There needs to be the ability for the school district personnel to collaborate freely with the psychiatrist, and there needs to be the opportunity for the psychiatrist to share his or her findings with the district in both oral and written forms. Without this permission a psychiatric evaluation cannot occur.

The second step of this process involves a meeting with school personnel and the psychiatrist to clarify the nature, extent, and circumstances of the student's problems. The reason for the consultation should be clarified to make certain that the evaluation addresses the needs of the student and answers the school district's specific questions. Some potential consultation questions may include the following: Does the student meet criteria to be identified with an emotional disturbance? Does the student have an underlying mental health concern that would benefit from school-based treatment? Are there additional services that may be helpful to help the student be more successful in the educational setting? Information should be provided by a variety of different educators who know the student well. Some examples of appropriate sources of information include the director of special education, classroom teacher, guidance counselor, principal, or classroom aides. This information should be shared directly with the psychiatrist alone to allow information to be shared without the informers censoring their concerns. If a face-to-face meeting is not feasible, the consultation questions and information can be communicated to the consultant in writing.

The third step of this type of evaluation includes a meeting with the student and family. This portion of the evaluation closely resembles the interview described in the prior chapter. Depending on the age of the child, there can be a joint meeting, but ideally the parents should provide information to the clinician without the child present, and the child should be seen individually as well. If there are other significant adult family members who have frequent contact with the child, they should be included. For example, grandparents are often involved in the student's life, and they may have an alternative perspective. If there is parental discord, all efforts should be made to include both parents in the evaluation, particularly if educational rights are shared. If it becomes clear during the evaluation process that significant animosity exists between the parents, then each parent should be given the opportunity to be seen individually. All attempts should be made to see a school-age child individually. Depending on the student's temperament, it can be beneficial to start the student portion of the evaluation with a family member with whom the child is comfortable, but ideally when the student is comfortable, the adult should be excused.

If time or locale permit, a fourth step could include observation of the student in several school settings. This step provides very helpful information, but the practicality of arranging this portion is often challenging.

Recommendations

The final portion of the psychiatric evaluation involves the preparation of the written report. This report should be shared with both the parents and the school personnel. The report should include the various sections of the evaluation, including history of presenting illness, past psychiatric history, past medical history, social and developmental history, substance abuse history, educational history, family psychiatric history, mental status examination, formulation, and diagnoses. The recommendation section is critical and should include an explanation of the barriers to learning and should end with helpful educational and therapeutic recommendations. Educational recommendations should include whether the student meets criteria to be identified with an emotional or other disability. If there is more than one disability identified, it is helpful to state which disability is thought to be the primary disability and which is secondary. Placement recommendations can follow and can include what level of support services is used. This could range from the student's receiving itinerant services to placement in a particular type of classroom. If it becomes clear through the evaluation that other supports would help the student make educational progress, these should be listed. If there are classroom management strategies that can be more effective, these should be clarified.

Noneducational recommendations should be viewed as suggestions to further assist the child in other settings. These recommendations are meant to be further supportive to the mental health of the child. The family can choose to follow these recommendations immediately or at some point in the future. However, the family is under no obligation to make use of these recommendations. Some types of recommendations can include medication management, mental health case management, individual or family therapy, or other mental health supports such as behavioral health rehabilitation services. In addition, if it becomes clear that the student requires a higher level of mental health care such as inpatient or partial hospitalization, this should be indicated, and the plan to ensure this happens should be included. If an out-of-home placement is recommended, the medical reasons for this should be clearly identified. Some state mental health programs provide individual support to children using mobile therapists, behavior specialists, or family-based therapy, and often these services are available following a psychiatric evaluation.

DIRECT SERVICE TO IDENTIFIED STUDENTS

There is increased pressure to provide education to acutely mentally ill students. It is my opinion that this is in large part due to societal pressures to treat mentally ill children and adolescents in the community. The length of stay in inpatient and partial hospitalization programs has been decreasing. In central Pennsylvania there are fewer inpatient beds available to children and adolescents than there were a decade ago. There is a new treatment model termed "community residential residence (CRR) host home" where a youth lives in the home of specially trained parents, similar to a foster home. In contrast to a foster home, these are placements for mentally ill children where parents retain custodial rights. These youth receive education within the public school district in which the CRR is located. A longer term treatment option for mentally ill youth has included placement in a residential treatment facility (RTF). Placement in an RTF is significantly difficult to initiate, and the length of stay in these programs is also being shortened. Some individuals who are placed in an RTF are educated within the public school district in the location of the RTF. All of these reasons, in addition to increased recognition of mental health problems, have led to more emotionally disturbed children being educated in public school settings.

Emotional Support Services: Public School

Public schools have emotional support services that can be provided to an identified student at an "itinerant level." Depending on the school district and the need, this can include a teacher or aide working with a student in a regular education classroom to provide individualized instruction as it is needed. There may also be the availability for the student to take "breaks" when needed to help minimize frustration. A special education teacher acts as the case manager, but other individuals such as a school-based therapist or guidance counselor can provide other needed supports.

Emotional Support Classrooms: Public School Based

For students who need more support than an itinerant level, a school district often has emotional support classrooms located within its district. These classrooms are smaller than a traditional classroom and are taught by a certified special education teacher. The teacher provides instruction and case management to the identified students. Typically, a behavioral-level system is created, and rewards are associated with positive behavioral choices. Students within this type of classroom can participate in this classroom for all or part of the day depending on the individual need. An advantage of this type of classroom is the student has the opportunity to interact with regular education peers when it is appropriate.

Therapeutic Emotional Support Classroom: Public School Districts

In part because of the increased number of mentally ill students, there are also other models that are being explored in public districts to meet the needs of severely emotionally disturbed students. One such model that is being used locally is called a "therapeutic emotional support classroom." This emotional support educational setting is within a public school district, and there is intensive therapeutic intervention.

A therapist, who is contracted through a mental health agency for this position, meets with students weekly for individual therapy. Goals that are addressed in this setting are individualized but include improving frustration tolerance, improving self-concept, learning skills of anger management, or learning relaxation skills. In addition, group therapy conducted by the same therapist occurs on a daily basis. This provides an opportunity for students to work on social skills and to learn anger management strategies. In addition, the therapist is available in times of escalated behavior to help the student deescalate and then process triggers to the event to prevent these types of events from recurring. When it is believed that family difficulties are interfering with the student's educational progress, family therapy is also provided.

A child and adolescent psychiatrist may also be directly involved with the students. The psychiatrist conducts family treatment team review meetings at a frequency of every 6 weeks. During these meetings a district social worker, therapist, and psychiatrist review with the family the therapeutic progress that has occurred. Family concerns can be addressed.

The psychiatrist sees students for individual assessment every 6 weeks as well, which allows the psychiatrist to have a better understanding of the therapeutic needs. If the family and student prefer, the psychiatrist will also prescribe and monitor psychotropic medications. If this option is chosen, the psychiatrist has the benefit of obtaining information directly from numerous sources before changing a student's medications. At times a family can choose to maintain a therapeutic relationship with a different psychiatrist. If this is the family's request, the school-based psychiatrist continues to meet with the family and student and subsequently provides feedback to the community psychiatrist. This helps to ensure that the psychiatrist is receiving all necessary information to make treatment decisions.

The therapeutic emotional support program also uses an extensive individualized behavioral support system. The students identify personal goals on which they want to work. They obtain points that support their positive decisions. The points are tallied weekly to reveal on what level the student is placed. Privileges within the classroom are contingent on the given level. There is a therapeutic support staff available within the classroom. This person's job is to ensure that positive behavior is rewarded and that negative behavior is quickly addressed. In addition, this person is instrumental in helping to deescalate a student at times of heightened emotional response.

The students placed within this classroom present with significant psychiatric pathology such as schizophrenia, obsessive-compulsive disorder, various personality disorders, and major depression. Typically, these students have a learning disability as well. This format allows for more intensive educational services and close observation of mental health symptoms and behavioral changes. The additional therapeutic support has enabled some students with severe mental illness to continue to be educated within a public school setting.

Emotional Support Classroom: Center Based

Depending on the severity of the underlying emotional difficulty, the intensity of support available within a public school emotional support classroom may be insufficient to promote educational success. The state of Pennsylvania provides specialized education services to identified students through a series of "intermediate units" (IUs). Public school districts can contract to receive a variety of educational supports through their catchment IU. The IUs typically provide a variety of services out of the home school district at what is referred to as a center-based program.

The least restrictive of the center-based classrooms is an IU emotional support classroom. In this setting, students are provided education in a very small, highly structured classroom. The teacher is certified in special education, and often an educational or behavioral aide is present to provide additional support. This type of classroom relies heavily on a behavioral intervention plan, and intensive behavioral support services are available. The classrooms also use an extensively developed level system. There are significant social work services that provide supportive therapy and case management services. At times adventure-based services are used to promote team building and improvement of self-competency. Adventure-based services are a new type of educational intervention which incorporates activities and team building into group interventions.

A center-based school is smaller than a public school, and many more supportive services are available. This allows the teacher to provide more direct individualized instruction and behavioral support at the time it is most needed.

Educational Partial Program: Center Based

A higher level of support and more restrictive placement is available through an IU. This type of classroom is modeled after a mental health partial hospitalization program but is called a school-based partial program. Within this classroom a certified special education teacher gives the instruction. However, there is a much stronger therapeutic component. Each classroom is assigned both a mental health specialist and a behavioral support specialist to provide therapeutic services. A child and adolescent psychiatrist is involved in evaluating and treating each student and is an integral member of the treatment team. There is a review with the family every 20 days. Individual, group, and family therapy are provided at intervals that are determined to be necessary to meet the student's emotional needs. This classroom allows for students and their family to receive intensive therapeutic support to help them make educational progress. The students participate in this classroom until it is determined by the psychiatrist that it is not medically necessary.

Diagnostic Classroom: Center Based

The third type of classroom that is available in a local IU is called the diagnostic classroom. A public school district with parental approval can request placement in this classroom, which has a 45-day length of stay. During this time the student receives psychoeducational testing, a psychiatric evaluation, social work services, a speech therapy assessment, an occupational therapy assessment, and any other specially identified assessments. The classroom is staffed by a special education teacher or school psychologist who continues to provide longitudinal educational assessments. The classroom is currently for students from kindergarten through 12th grade. Educational demands are shifted. It is expected that the student's current academic level is maintained, but new material is presented in a number of different ways to help determine what teaching style may best match the student's needs. Because there is more direct individual instruction and less intensive group instruction, it becomes easier to understand how much academic frustration is contributing to the former behavioral problems. Following this long-term assessment, the diagnostic classroom treatment team meets with the home school district and family to help determine what type of educational placement might best meet the student's needs.

Students are most commonly placed in this type of classroom when the underlying primary diagnosis is in question. There is increased pressure to differentiate students who have an autism spectrum disorder from those who have an emotional disability. Quite often, an incorrect identification and incorrect placement results in significant behavioral problems. As autism spectrum disorders are increasingly recognized, it has become evident that the structure of traditional emotional support services is counterproductive. Particularly when more mild symptoms of a pervasive developmental disorder (PDD) are present, the child may first be identified with oppositional defiant disorder. Behavioral strategies that are believed to reduce oppositional behaviors can cause a worsening of behavioral problems if the core difficulty is PDD.

The second most common reason a student is placed in this classroom is when numerous educational placements have not been successful. The treatment team may be able to offer an objective opinion, after having had an in-depth assessment of the student, about why prior placements were unsuccessful.

The third common reason for placement in the diagnostic classroom is to use the time to obtain additional information to make appropriate recommendations. For example, if a student has lived in a residential treatment facility for over one year, it might not be immediately clear to educators in which type of educational setting the student should be placed. In addition, if a student lived in a different state and was receiving educational services that are not available in the new state, then time spent in the diagnostic classroom can guide what local educational supports would be most effective.

Behavioral or Emotional Consultation: Public Schools

The training that a child and adolescent psychiatrist completes creates the mind-set of viewing problems with the biopsychosocial model. This can provide a unique mind-set when assessing the difficulties a student is having within the classroom. At times a psychiatrist might consult with school staff to review a student's difficulties or even directly observe the student within the classroom.

For a number of years, I have been consulting with a variety of public schools. Some of this work has involved providing independent psychiatric evaluations. In addition, I provide psychiatric services to a Pennsylvania IU, and I provide direct psychiatric care through the above-described therapeutic emotional support classroom. I have also had the opportunity to provide consultation to the schools without providing direct service to a student. This type of consultation is rewarding, and it has been helpful to a number of students as well. The following text provides a few examples of personal experience in this type of consultation.

I was consulted by one school district to provide information and support to a team of teachers who were struggling to have a 15-year-old female successfully complete oral schoolwork. This girl had a genetic disorder that caused some mild cognitive limitations and was associated with significant anxiety. She was fearful of meeting new people. Her parents were aware that she was having difficulty with the transition to high school and wanted to support her progress. However, they were concerned that speaking to a psychiatrist would increase her anxiety. They perceived that she realized she was not fitting in with peers and believed that her perception would be validated if she spoke to a mental health professional. As the teachers were becoming increasingly frustrated, the parents agreed to allow me to provide support to the teachers in a consultative role. First, I met with the parents and obtained a history. Next, I heard the staff's observations and frustrations. I was then able to help the teachers understand that the behaviors they were seeing were a result of her fear of making a mistake or appearing different from her peers. They began to understand this in the context of anxiety rather than defiance. As the staff began to see that the student's lack of response to their questions was not direct defiance but a result of her fear of speaking in public, they were able to work with her more effectively. We were also able to strategize together to help her show her knowledge through writing rather than verbal means. Throughout the year we met to review progress. In addition, as the parents saw increased flexibility from the teachers, they were better able to support the teachers' decisions, and this promoted better educational progress.

A psychiatrist can also provide direct observation within a classroom to make suggestions to improve the setting. One such observation led to the discovery that a teacher and aide were routinely discussing a student's behavior in front of other students. The student whom they were discussing was not in the room at the time, but a number of classmates were doing independent work. This discussion was occurring because of time constraints of the teacher and aide, and it was well intentioned to ensure that both adults were working together. However, having this conversation in front of other students promoted those students to behave negatively to regain the adults' attention and broke the confidentiality of the discussed student. When this fact was pointed out, steps were put into place within the classroom day to allow the staff to communicate when no students were in the room.

Another observation revealed that a student with significant distractibility was placed immediately inside the door of the classroom. This desk was somewhat isolated from peers, which was helpful, but the location was more distracting to this student, as he would look into the hallway every time someone was passing. Within a 10-minute time, he was visibly off task 35 times. Simply repositioning his seat to the front middle of the classroom reduced his off-task behavior to 10 times in 10 minutes.

In addition, providing information about mental health to school personnel can be important within a school district. In my experience this often takes the form of lectures or case consultation with various personnel. I have provided additional education to school personnel about some specific areas that are in the domain of safety. Specifically within some schools, there is a recent increase in adolescents engaging in self-harm behaviors. Nurses and guidance counselors are often seeking advice to help manage this behavior in an emotionally appropriate way. In addition, school personnel are often looking for additional information to ensure that the risk assessments that they complete on an emergent basis are comprehensive and guide the family in the right direction for further assessment and treatment.

Another use of psychiatric consultation is to provide information about mental health to parents and the community. I have had the opportunity to speak to parent groups individually and in a panel discussion. This format is an excellent way to help provide direct information about mental illness. It is also important to provide tools to families to assist in early identification. When parents are able to attend a panel or a lecture on depression, they can begin to recognize these symptoms in a child early during the illness. Early identification of the problem can lead to more rapid treatment, and many mental health difficulties improve more rapidly with early treatment. In addition, hearing of other people's struggles with a mental illness can help to lessen the stigmatization. If the struggle is perceived to be more "normal," parents might be more willing to pursue treatment.

PSYCHIATRIC ROLES: SUMMARY

A psychiatrist can and should work in a cooperative way with school districts. Children's mental health is improved when schools have an understanding of a student's difficulties. Child and adolescent psychiatrists can be valuable consultants to a school district and can collaborate about mental health topics, assess students for safety, provide identification for the need for special education services, and be supportive to staff. Providing this type of collaborative care is rewarding to the patient, family, psychiatrist, and school team.

Four

Psychopharmacology

GENERAL PRINCIPLES OF PSYCHOPHARMACOLOGY

Over the past three decades, there has been a rapid trans-
formation in the field of psychiatric medicine. Psychiatrists
had previously been very involved in psychological theory,
and understanding a person's unconscious was the preferred
method of intervention. The 1990s were termed the decade of
the brain, and extensive research about how the brain works
occurred. This allowed for the design of additional interventions. Biological theories now exist in more detail to explain
many psychological problems. There has been significant
advancement in the understanding of the brain, which has
resulted in improved identification of mental illness and in
different treatment options.

One of the advancements in biological understanding
of mental illness has been the arrival of new medications.
Numerous medications have been developed over the past
15 years. There have been new classes of medications designed
that are more beneficial in part because of increased tolerability and increased ease of administration. Medications
have been identified to treat mood disorders, anxiety disorders, behavioral disorders, psychotic disorders, autistic disorders, and eating disorders. Medications are also useful in
treating target symptoms such as agitation, aggression, irritability, and sleep disturbance. Each of these medications can
have a role in improving a youth's functioning. It is important to remember that these medications may not change the
underlying disease process and clearly will not change the
stressor that may have initiated the problem. However, benefit
can occur when the intensity of the distress begins to lessen.
Many physicians are of the view that medication can reduce
some symptom intensity, which allows psychotherapeutic
interventions to work more successfully.

Despite the advances in medication and understanding of the brain, the studies supporting the use of psychotropic medication in children and adolescents lag behind the knowledge for use in adults. Many of the treatment interventions are derived from adult studies, but as seen with antidepressants, medications can work differently or be associated with different side effects in children compared to adults. Recently there have been a few large studies that have compared treatment with medication alone, to psychotherapeutic interventions, to a combination of both. This type of study is advancing the knowledge base in child and adolescent psychiatry, but additional information is clearly needed.

Medications should not be used as the only treatment intervention, particularly for children and adolescents. Full resolution of a mental disorder results from a multidiscipline approach that can include psychotherapy, educational supports, social services, and community supports. When medications are indicated and prescribed, the physician should be able to explain the rationale for treatment and must be closely involved in monitoring the response to medication.

Because of the volume of children who present with a need for psychotropic medications, the follow-up care can be significantly improved when there is good communication from individuals to the provider. Educators and school personnel often have the advantage of seeing an identified child in a setting over time. This allows a good setting for the assessment of a response to medication. When school personnel are well informed about the medications and mechanism of action, they can become better informants.

Although this book is not intended to be a comprehensive book on neuroanatomy and psychopharmacology, understanding some basics will improve understanding about medications. Each subsequent chapter of this book includes some discussion about medication used to treat the described diagnosis. The chapter will focus on basic understanding of the brain and basic mechanism of action for each class of medication. Specifics regarding indication for medication and side effects are included throughout the book.

NEUROANATOMY

The study of neuroanatomy is the study of the structure of the brain and nervous system. The human nervous system consists of the central and peripheral systems. The central system includes the brain and spinal cord and is likely of the most importance in the biological understanding of the mind. The brain consists of the cerebral cortex, the cerebellum, medulla, and the brain stem. The cerebral cortex consists of two cerebral hemispheres and is most intimately involved with cognition and emotion, as well as numerous other functions. The cortex is also divided into four lobes called the frontal lobe, the parietal lobe, the occipital lobe, and the temporal lobe. Each lobe serves a different function. The frontal lobe is involved in functions such as the response to the environment, our emotional response, expressive language, and memory. Problems in this area of the brain can affect mood changes, the ability to focus, the ability to complete multistep tasks, and the persistence of single thoughts. The parietal lobe is involved with visual attention, manipulation of objects, and integration of sensory input. Deficits in this area of the brain can cause problems with reading, mathematics, writing, naming objects, and eye–hand coordination. The occipital lobe functions primarily with vision, and deficits can cause a variety of sight problems. The temporal lobe works with memory and categorizing objects. Difficulty in recognizing faces and understanding spoken words can occur with damage to this area of the brain (Lehr, n.d.).

The brain is constructed from individual cells called neurons. These are very specialized cells with the primary function of taking information, processing it, and responding. A neuron has four important parts: cell body, dendrites, axons, and the axon terminals. The dendrites stretch out and act as the receivers of information from other neurons. Once the message is received, it travels through the cell body to the axon, which is covered with a special coating called myelin to allow the electrical message to skip and travel very fast. When the message reaches the axon terminal, a chemical reaction occurs within the cell to release a neurotransmitter so the message can continue to the next neuron. Therefore, the communication between nerves takes place through two different patterns. The first is the electrical transmission down the nerve, and the second is the chemical transmission of neurotransmitters.

NEUROTRANSMITTERS

Synaptic transmission is how neurons communicate with each other. Neurotransmitters cluster in groups and are packaged in a synaptic vesicle. The neurotransmitter is released into the space between the neurons called the synaptic junction. Neurotransmitters range in type and complexity. They can be amino acids such as γ-aminobutyric acid (GABA), peptides such as vasopressin, or messengers called monamines such as serotonin or dopamine. They cross the space, or synaptic junction, to any part of the next nerve (postsynaptic nerve), where they attach to a specific type of receptor. Most receptors are proteins that cross the cell membrane. The binding of the neurotransmitter to the receptor is specific and has been compared to a lock and key. The binding of the neurotransmitter to a receptor induces an intracellular change in the neuron that is considered activation.

Many psychiatric disorders are believed to be related to problems with the communication of neurons that occur at the neurotransmitter level. Some critical neurotransmitters that are believed to be involved in the regulation of mood, thoughts, and feelings include norepinephrine, serotonin, and dopamine. The understanding of these three neurotransmitters is important to the understanding of depression. The neurotransmitters GABA and glutamate are likely important in bipolar disorders. Dopamine and serotonin are important in schizophrenia.

Clearly, there is much more information about how the brain works that is yet to be understood. The development of a psychiatric disorder is more complex than having too little or too much of a specific neurotransmitter. The illness presents based on a combination of genetic influences, environmental experiences, and social interactions.

PRINCIPLES RELATED TO MECHANISMS OF ACTION

To further understand how medications work, it is important to have a broad understanding about the way medications are used and metabolized in the body. This knowledge requires two terms be understood. *Pharmacokinetics* is the understanding of what the body does to medications. This leads to an understanding of drug metabolism and drug interactions. *Pharmacodynamics* is what the medication does to the body. In other words, it is the mechanism of action. Pharmacodynamics is the principle on which new medications are developed. However, sometimes medications are created with the purpose of treating one set of problems, and studies reveal that there is no effectiveness toward the identified problem, but it becomes recognized that the medication has a different benefit. One classic example is that one of the first recognized antidepressants was initially designed to treat tuberculosis. It was found to not be effective at treating this illness, but it was recognized that the individuals who were taking this treatment were less depressed, which is a common problem with tuberculosis. Further study found it treated depression in people who did not have tuberculosis.

Another important consideration is the effectiveness and efficacy of a medication. Efficacy refers to how well the drug treats the condition it is designed to treat. A medication is efficacious if it treats in a majority of people the symptoms it is supposed to treat. Effectiveness is a broader and perhaps more important term that refers to the medication's efficacy and to its tolerability and ease of use. A medication may be efficacious but not effective. The medication may work well, but if it is not tolerated well or if its dosing schedule is complicated, it is less effective when compared to another treatment option.

Medications vary in how long they take to be cleared from the body. Most psychiatric medications are metabolized in the liver and then eliminated from the body in feces or urine. The time it takes for the body to remove half of the amount of medication is called *half-life*. A medication with a short half-life will more quickly leave the body. This can be important, as half-life is a feature on the withdrawal of medications. "Steady state" is reached when the same amount of medication is entering the body as is leaving the body. Typically, it takes between four and six half-lives of the medication for the body to reach steady state. Medication with a short half-life will reach steady state sooner than a medication with a longer half-life.

Many medications become effective when they achieve steady state. However, most psychotropic medications take longer to show efficacy than it takes them to reach steady state. For example, an antidepressant such as sertraline reaches steady state within 6 days, but the antidepressant benefit may not be noted for 3 weeks. However, many side effects will begin to lessen when steady state has been reached.

Interestingly, some medications work before steady state is achieved. The stimulants can have their benefit as the medication is entering the system. This is the reason that for many years the effective medications were short acting and had to be taken three times a day. The new long-acting preparations work by releasing bursts of medication spaced throughout the day to prevent a steady state from being reached.

LEGAL AND ETHICAL ISSUES OF MEDICATION

Medication treatment is not without risks. The first step toward the decision to use medication involves a psychiatric evaluation. If a medication trial is deemed appropriate, informed consent must be given. Each medication has the potential to cause more harm than good. In addition, medications are associated with potential side effects, some of which can become life threatening. Side effects must be understood for people to provide informed consent. The time course of expected response and the recommended length of treatment should all be discussed. The physician who initiates the medication is responsible for it until another provider becomes involved.

The physician has an obligation to make certain that the recommended treatment is prescribed in a way to improve the child's or adolescent's functioning. This can include using more than one medication, or it can include prescribing medications in a way that is not approved by the U.S. Food and Drug Administration (FDA). As long as the rationale is clearly outlined and agreed on, this is the physician's right.

ANTIDEPRESSANTS

It is estimated that 1% of children and 5% of adolescents are suffering from depression (Brent & Birmaher, 2002). It is also believed that approximately 6% of youth have significantly impairing anxiety disorders (Costello, Egger, & Angold, 2004). Both depressive and anxiety disorders respond to the same types of medications, because similar brain pathways and neurotransmitters are involved. The use of antidepressants in children and adolescents has been controversial. Some studies have shown only modest improvement when these medications are used, and there has been concern that the use of the medications increases suicidal thoughts. Recently, there has been accumulating proof that medications when appropriately monitored are safe and beneficial.

Regarding the safety of antidepressants, in October 2004 the FDA announced precautions to safeguard children and adolescents treated with this class of medication. The warning states that antidepressants can increase the risk of suicidal thinking and behavior. It recommends that children who are started on medication should be observed closely for clinical worsening, suicidal thinking, and unusual changes in behavior (U.S. FDA, 2007).

Antidepressants can be helpful to treat major depression, obsessive-compulsive disorder (OCD), panic disorder, and perhaps more mild variants of other depressive and anxiety disorders. The FDA has approved fluoxetine (Prozac) for use in pediatric patients with major depression and OCD. Fluvoxamine (Luvox) and clomipramine (Anafranil) are approved for treatment of pediatric OCD. Escitalopram (Lexapro) has been recently approved to treat depression in adolescents aged 12 to 17 years. In addition, fluoxetine (Prozac) is approved for adults with bulimia nervosa.

As a simplistic explanation, antidepressants reduce symptoms of depression and anxiety by increasing the amount of norepinephrine and/or serotonin available. These two neurotransmitters are needed for neuron communication regarding affective states. Some antidepressants work on both neurotransmitter systems, while others work on only serotonin. Antidepressants increase the amount of neurotransmitters available by either increasing the release from the presynaptic neuron or slowing the breakdown or reabsorption in the post-synaptic cleft.

The classical antidepressants were used from the late 1950s until the 1980s when the class of medications called the SSRIs (selective serotonin reuptake inhibitors) were introduced. The classical antidepressants include the tricyclic antidepressants and monoamine oxidase inhibitors. The tricyclic mechanism of action is to block the reuptake of norepinephrine and serotonin. The monoamine oxidase inhibitors work by preventing the breakdown of neurotransmitters. The SSRIs are effective by preventing the reuptake of serotonin. There are newer classes of antidepressants available, but for children and adolescents, there is the most support for the use of SSRIs.

These medications reach steady state levels within several days. With very few exceptions, the medications do not begin to reduce symptoms of depression for 3 to 4 weeks. The effects are typically gradual, and it is not uncommon that family members report benefit before the child or adolescent notices the change. These medications are taken one time a day. They can be taken in the evening if sedation is a possibility, or they can be taken in the morning if activation can occur. The medications are started at a low dose, which can be increased every 3 to 4 weeks if needed. The medications must be tapered, with the exception of fluoxetine (Prozac) to prevent somatic withdraw symptoms. Fluoxetine has a metabolite that also is effective as an antidepressant, so the combined half-life of medication is several weeks. Because of this extended half-life, fluoxetine self-tapers without causing a significant withdraw.

MOOD STABILIZERS

Mood stabilizers are a group of medications that are helpful to treat mania and stabilize the mood of youth with bipolar disorder. Some mood stabilizers also have antidepressant properties. This class of medication includes lithium, anticonvulsants, and atypical antipsychotic medications. This section will focus on the mood stabilizers other than the atypical antipsychotics, which will be reviewed below.

Lithium was the first medication that was recognized to be helpful in reducing the symptoms of mania. It is approved by the FDA both for the treatment of acute mania and as a prevention of further episodes in children and adolescents. Lithium has a complex mechanism of action and can affect different parts of the brain differently. It affects the serotonergic system by enhancing its release. It also affects the rate at which norepinephrine is made. It can reduce the excretion of norepinephrine when a person is manic but increases the excretion of norepinephrine when a person is depressed (Schatzberg, Cole, & DeBattista, 1997).

Although not approved by the FDA for these uses, lithium can also be useful at low dosages to increase the effect of antidepressants if an individual is not responding to a therapeutic dose of an antidepressant. It can also be used to prevent rapid mood swings in individuals who do not meet criteria for bipolar disorder. Finally, it can be tried to treat rage episodes or severe impulsivity if other interventions have failed.

Lithium has a known range of effectiveness, and blood levels can be checked to ensure the person is on a therapeutic dose. It typically takes 7 to 14 days at a therapeutic dose for benefit to be seen. Lithium should not be used in pregnancy, as it is associated with a specific birth defect, Ebstein's anomaly, which is a serious cardiac abnormality.

Lithium is also started at a low dose that can be increased every several days to weeks depending on the person's response and blood level. Lithium is usually prescribed two or three times a day. Steady state is reached within the first week. Response of gradual initiation takes 2 to 4 weeks. In an inpatient setting, the dose can be escalated more rapidly, and response could occur a little sooner.

The anticonvulsants were first recognized as useful when some similarities were noted between temporal lobe seizures and bipolar disorder. The three most commonly used anticonvulsants are valproic acid, carbamazepine, and lamotrigine. Valproic acid can be more beneficial in the treatment of mixed states. It is not approved for treatment of bipolar disorder in children and adolescents, but it is approved for use in this age group to treat certain types of seizures. Valproic acid's mechanism of action is also complex, but one of its beneficial effects can come from the target of GABA. GABA is an inhibitory neurotransmitter.

Carbamazepine is less commonly used recently because it interacts negatively with other medications. Its mechanism of action is less clear and can have its effect by altering sodium channels in the nerves. Lamotrigine (Lamictal) is useful for treating the depressive phase of bipolar disorder but is not approved by the FDA for individuals who are younger than 18 years of age. Lamotrigine works as a glutamate antagonist. Glutamate is an excitatory neurotransmitter.

The anticonvulsants are also taken two or three times a day, with the exception of Depakote ER, which is an extended release form of valproic acid. The dose is started low and increased every few weeks as indicated. Valproic acid and carbamazepine both have established therapeutic blood levels for treatment of seizures, and these same levels are also believed to be most effective toward stabilizing mood.

ANTIPSYCHOTICS

The class of antipsychotic medications has been in use since the 1950s. These medications have been known to be effective in the treatment of acute psychosis and schizophrenia. Traditional antipsychotic medications work by blocking dopamine receptors. Because of this blockade, predictable neurological side effects are likely, and some of these effects can be lifelong. These medications are less commonly used in children and adolescents because of these side effects.

In the 1990s, a new class of medications was developed that work a little differently. These medications, called the atypical antipsychotics, work by blocking specific dopamine and serotonin receptors. When both dopamine and serotonin receptors are blocked, there is improvement in symptoms with fewer potential neurological side effects. Over the past decade, these medications have also been found to be helpful in treating other mental disorders. They can act as mood stabilizers for individuals with bipolar disorder. They are used to reduce aggression and irritability in children with autistic disorder.

They are also helpful at improving impulse control and rage reactions in some children. Finally, they can be beneficial toward reducing tics in individuals with Tourette's disorder.

The following atypical antipsychotics are approved by the FDA for use in children. Risperdal is approved to treat schizophrenia in adolescents from ages 13 to 17 years. It is approved for the treatment of irritability associated with autistic disorder in children and adolescents between the ages of 5 and 16 years. It is approved alone or in combination with other mood stabilizers for adults with bipolar mania and alone in adults and youth ages 10 to 17 years for the short-term treatment of bipolar mania. Aripiprazole (Abilify) is approved for the treatment of mixed and manic episodes in children ages 10 to 17 years and for the treatment of schizophrenia in adolescents ages 13 to 17 years. The other atypical antipsychotics, olanzapine, quetiapine, and ziprasidone, are not approved for use in children or adolescents but are sometimes chosen to target aggression, irritability, anxiety, and mood swings. Some of these medications could receive approval for children soon.

There has been increased media concern over the past year about the increased number of children who have been prescribed atypical antipsychotics. According to the *New York Times* in November 2008, at panel review 389,000 children and teens were prescribed Risperdal during the past year, and 240,000 of these prescriptions were for children ages 12 or younger (Harris, 2009). It is encouraged that all physicians review the potential long-term risks of these medications with the severity of symptoms that they are attempting to treat.

When being used to treat irritability, aggression, or anxiety in children, very low dosages are initiated. Sedation and a calming effect can be noted within a week, but there can be ongoing benefit several months later. When more moderated dosages are being used to treat psychosis or mania, the dose is started low and can be increased every few weeks. The reduction of acute psychotic symptoms can occur within one month, but there can be increased benefit after several months of treatment.

STIMULANTS

The stimulants are the best-studied class of medications that are used in children. The first reported use was of racemic amphetamine sulfate (Benzedrine) in 1937 to treat behaviorally disordered children (W. H. Green, 1995). Despite this long history of study and knowledge of efficacy, the exact mechanism of action of the stimulants remains unknown. It is known that they stimulate the release of neurotransmitters.

The actual pathophysiology of attention-deficit/hyperactivity disorder (ADHD) remains unclear. Current thinking supports the idea that the prefrontal cortex in the brain that controls executive functions such as planning and impulse control is impaired. It is known that stimulants have effects on nor-epinephrine and dopamine pathways. These medications can increase the brain's ability to promote appropriate executive control (Barkley, 1997).

The profile of the absorption of stimulants is rapid. These medications work before a steady state blood level has been achieved. It is believed that these medications work due to a rapid rise in quantity in the brain. For many years these medications needed to be taken several times a day to stimulate this rise. However, over the past 5 years, a number of extended release preparations have been developed that work by generating small pulses of medication released throughout the day.

Stimulants are approved to treat ADHD in children. The FDA approves all stimulants for the use in children ages 6 years or older, and dextroamphetamine is approved for use in children at age 3 years. Stimulants can be used when ADHD is the only disorder present, or they can be used if ADHD coexists with other disorders. They are also approved to treat narco-lepsy, which is a sleep disorder associated with daytime sleep-iness and uncontrollable sleep attacks during the day.

Stimulants can also be used to treat impulsivity that does not occur in the context of ADHD. This class of medication can also have a role in reducing agitation and negative behavior in children with oppositional defiant disorder or conduct disor-der, but this should never be considered unless other intensive interventions have been tried. Finally, stimulants can have a role in improving psychomotor retardation associated with severe episodes of depression.

Stimulants should be used cautiously if a tic disorder or anxiety disorder is present, as these medications can poten-tially exacerbate the other illness. In addition, stimulants should be used carefully in individuals with substance abuse or with an eating disorder.

It has long been questioned if stimulant exposure in child-hood increases the likelihood of drug-seeking behavior in adolescence. Recent thinking denies this fear. It is now com-monly accepted that individuals with untreated ADHD are more likely to seek illicit substances than those who have been treated.

At the end of June 2009, a study was published in the *American Journal of Psychiatry* that highlighted potential risks of stimulant medications (Gould et al., 2009). This study, which was funded by the FDA and National Institute of Mental Health, compared the use of stimulants in a large number of children who died suddenly while on the medication to the same number of children who died in motor vehicle accidents while on the medication. It concluded that children prescribed stimulants were more likely to die from a sudden death than from a motor vehicle accident. The study had some limitations that might have influenced the findings, and closer inspection of the data is occurring.

As a result of this study, the FDA as of July 2009 has recommended that these medications should not be discontinued without discussing the information with the prescriber. For the present time, the FDA recommends that physicians take a careful medication history of individual and family cardiovascular disease, perform a physical examination with focus on the cardiovascular system, and consider obtaining screening tests such as an EKG if the history or physical examination suggests a risk of heart disease.

Short-acting stimulants such as methylphenidate or dextroamphetamine are taken every 3 or 4 hours. Benefit is noted within 10 to 20 minutes of administration once the correct dose has been reached. Longer acting stimulants such as Concerta, Adderall XR, and Focalin XR last 8 to 10 hours, and benefit is noted within 15 to 30 minutes. There is also a dermal patch preparation of methylphenidate that can be applied to the skin daily. The medication in the patch reaches efficacy within about 15 minutes. Medication continues to be absorbed into the bloodstream while the patch remains adhered to the skin. Active medication remains in the bloodstream for 2 to 3 hours after the patch is removed.

ALTERNATIVE CLASSES OF MEDICATION

Atomoxetine (Strattera) is a nonstimulant alternative to treat ADHD. Its mechanism of action is to promote the release of norepinephrine. It works for 24 hours because of its dependence on achieving a steady state. It takes several days to reach steady state, so therefore benefit is not seen immediately. It is taken one time a day, although if significant sedation occurs, the dose can be divided and taken twice a day to reduce this side effect.

Clonidine and guanfacine are two medications that are sometimes used to treat ADHD, sleep disturbance, or tics. These medications work by stimulating presynaptic alpha-2 receptors. This stimulation reduces the release of norepinephrine. Although not approved by the FDA to treat ADHD, they are sometimes used as an additional treatment if ADHD symptoms are not well controlled with a stimulant alone or if tics are present along with ADHD. These medications can also be useful to reduce tics in a child with Tourette's disorder. However, the original purpose of these medications was to reduce blood pressure. If a dose is missed, there is a possibility that the child can develop rebound hypertension, which can result in serious medical problems.

Although not commonly used in children and adolescents, there is another class of medications used to treat anxiety. The anxiolytics that are effective for this class of disorders include the benzodiazepines such as lorazepam (Ativan), clonazepam (Klonopin), and alprazolam (Xanax), to name a few. These medications work by stimulating GABA, and they work quickly. Benzodiazepines promote sedation and muscle relaxation. They are associated with possible dependence, so their use should be monitored closely.

The nonbenzodiazepines, such as buspirone (Buspar), are also used to treat anxiety, and their mechanism of action is based on serotonin and dopamine. They can be used to treat anxiety but are not approved by the FDA for use in children or adolescents.

PREPARING TO TAKE MEDICATION

There is often anxiety related to a trial of medication. It is clearly recommended that a comprehensive psychiatric evaluation be completed before initiating treatment with a medication. As discussed previously, informed consent is needed, and the risks and benefits of treatment must be reviewed.

School personnel can be involved in the recommendation to pursue a psychiatric evaluation. This recommendation can in part be related to a belief that an underlying mental disorder exists that can benefit from medications. School personnel cannot force the family to medicate a child, and even if a family chooses not to medicate a child, educational interventions might be needed to promote success. However, school personnel can be instrumental in preparing parents to make a decision regarding medication. School staff can be helpful to parents by having some knowledge about medications.

It is important that staff help to make it clear to everyone that medications are not effective to change behavior unless the behavior problem is related to a psychiatric disorder. It is also important that staff understand and communicate that medication is only a piece of the total intervention needed to promote success. When school personnel and families expect the medication to be the only intervention, there is often frustration that some degree of problems persists.

Parents and students can be encouraged to learn the name of the medication and the dose of medication being prescribed. School personnel can be helpful in supporting this knowledge. Parents should also be encouraged to understand the reason for the medication and should be helped to understand the importance of compliance. The school nurse can be an additional resource to help provide information regarding medication interactions and over-the-counter medications to avoid.

Teachers, administrators, guidance counselors, and nurses can assist families by having an understanding of the time it can take to see a response from medication and the timing of the emergence of side effects (see accompanying CD: 4.3). Stimulants can show a beneficial response within the first few days of treatment. Side effects to these medications such as nausea, appetite suppression, and sleeplessness can occur in the first few days of treatment and sometimes decrease after a few weeks of consistent medication. Antidepressants, mood stabilizers, and antipsychotic medications can take several weeks to cause improvement, and the improvement is usually gradual. The side effects such as irritability, sedation, and even cognitive slowing typically occur early in the treatment course and should be monitored closely to ensure they are disappearing with continued treatment.

PSYCHOTROPIC MEDICATIONS
IN THE SCHOOL SETTING

To help ensure safety, most schools have a policy that medications should be brought to school in an original container with prescribing information on the label. There must also be permission from the parent for the student to take the medication at the recommended time. A note must be written or a form must be completed by the prescribing provider that outlines the dose, strength of medication, time of delivery, and potential side effects. When a dosage of medication is changed at school, there will need to be a change in medical order.

Medications are to be kept in a secure setting and perhaps in a locked cabinet. These steps help to ensure that other students do not have access to medication that is not intended for them (see accompanying CD: 4.1).

There may be a format developed to ensure that each student has received the prescribed medication and had the correct time. However, steps must be taken to ensure the student's privacy. It is particularly important to think about how to help a student remember to take the medication at the correct time. Reminders might be needed, but privacy should be considered when deciding who is responsible for this task.

The nurse can become instrumental in communicating concerns regarding side effects. There should be a signed release of information for this communication to occur. A physician might prefer to receive this information via fax. A sample letter is included on the accompanying CD (4.2).

It is also helpful when the parent reports to school personnel that a medication is being started or changed. Even if the nurse is not dispensing the medication, school personnel can be helpful in monitoring response or side effects. This is particularly true if a student is going to begin treatment with an antidepressant that can increase irritability, agitation, or suicidal thoughts early in treatment.

Stimulant medications are less commonly dispensed in schools in recent years because of an increased availability of long-acting stimulant preparations. However, if a stimulant is to be given in school, the timing is important but not necessarily critical. Delaying the dose by an hour or more could result in a drop of amount of medication, and rebound symptoms could occur. This is where there is a brief period of worsening hyperactivity and inattention. However, missing a dose of a stimulant will not cause any significant harm to the child and is not critical, as these medications are not dependent on a blood level to be effective.

Antidepressant medications are usually taken one time a day, so there might not be any medication dispensed at school. Again it is important for the school to be aware if this class of medications is prescribed so side effects can be monitored throughout the day. Occasionally to help ensure compliance and decrease a potential battle at home, these medications can be taken at school. Fluoxetine (Prozac) has a long half-life and has an active metabolite with an even longer half-life. This allows its dosage schedule to be a bit more forgiving, and withdraw effects do not occur if a dose is delayed or even missed for 1 or 2 days. However, the other SSRI and non-SSRI medications have shorter half-lives, so there should be more caution to ensure that the medication is taken close to the same time each day. Withdraw symptoms even with a missed dose can be uncomfortable. Typically, a variety of body complaints such as headache, nausea, muscle aches, and nerve pains can occur.

Atypical antipsychotic medications and mood stabilizers are often dispensed several times a day. These medications can be efficacious if given one or two times a day, but commonly smaller, more frequent dosage strategies are recommended to minimize side effects such as sedation. Efforts should be made to take these medications as close to the same time each day to help ensure consistent blood levels. However, missing one or two dosages will not result in significant withdraw symptoms. Extreme care must be taken with the dispensing of clonidine or guanfacine, as rebound hypertension can occur with a missed dose.

It is also helpful for school personnel to understand what an overdose of medication looks like. If excessive stimulant medications are taken, the response is typically one of agitation and possible psychotic symptoms such as hallucinations and confusion. The pulse and blood pressure can be elevated. An overdose of antidepressants, antipsychotics, or mood stabilizers can present with lethargy or confusion.

If one has any concerns about an overdose, the individual should be referred to an emergency room for physical assessment and management. In addition, following medical treatment, a crisis assessment that can include a psychiatric evaluation is indicated following a known overdose.

PSYCHOPHARMACOLOGY: SUMMARY

Psychotropic medications can have a role in promoting a reduction of psychiatric symptoms. They can improve focus and attention or improve symptoms of sadness and anxiety. They can reduce tics, psychotic symptoms, and binge episodes. However, all medications are associated with potential side effects. The potential benefit of medication must be compared to potential side effects. A psychiatrist should work closely with the family, student, and associate systems to make well-informed recommendations.

Medications should not be used as the only treatment intervention for any disorder. In addition, the prescribing physician must periodically review medications to ensure that the maximum benefit with minimal side effect balance is occurring.

Five

Disruptive Behavior Disorders

DISRUPTIVE BEHAVIOR DISORDERS: INTRODUCTION

The disruptive behavior disorders are a common reason for referral to a psychiatrist. There are three distinct disorders recognized in the *DSM-IV-TR* (American Psychiatric Association [APA], 2000). The first is attention-deficit/hyperactivity disorder (ADHD). Individuals with ADHD can present with symptoms of inattention, hyperactivity, or both, but regardless of type the term ADHD continues to apply. The *DSM-IV-TR* indicates that ADHD primarily inattentive is one subtype, and ADHD primarily hyperactive, or ADHD combined type should be specified. The common name ADD is meant to imply ADHD, primarily inattentive, but the term ADD is not consistent with the *DSM-IV-TR*. The second disorder is oppositional defiant disorder (ODD), which is characterized by a persistent pattern of negative and hostile behaviors. The third is conduct disorder (CD), which is also a pattern of negative behaviors, but these behaviors involve harm to others. For children who display a mix of disruptive behavior with no clear single diagnosis, the term "disruptive behavior disorder, not otherwise specified" can be used (APA, 2000).

Despite being considered in the same class, these disorders have some unique differences. ADHD can be diagnosed with either ODD or CD. However, ODD and CD cannot be diagnosed in the same person at the same time. If the criteria for CD are met, that is the diagnosis. By definition ADHD symptoms have to be present in two or more settings, but the symptoms of ODD can be present in only one setting.

ATTENTION-DEFICIT/HYPERACTIVITY DISORDER

Characteristics

The essential features of ADHD are a persistent pattern of inattention and/or hyperactivity-impulsivity that is more frequent and more severe than is typically seen in individuals at the same developmental level. Some symptoms must be present in the individual before age 7 years, and the impairment must be seen in at least two settings. The symptoms must create significant interference with developmentally appropriate functioning.

Inattention can be present in academic, occupational, or social situations. Six of the following symptoms must be present for an individual to qualify for a diagnosis of significant inattention: failing to give close attention to detail or making careless mistakes, having difficulty sustaining attention in tasks or play, not seeming to listen when spoken to, lacking follow-through on instructions and having difficulty organizing tasks, avoiding or disliking tasks that require a sustained mental effort, losing items necessary for tasks or activities, being distracted by external stimuli, and being forgetful in daily activities (APA, 2000).

For a pattern of hyperactivity and impulsivity to be recognized, an individual must demonstrate six of the following symptoms: fidgets or squirms, leaves seat in classroom, runs about or climbs excessively in situations in which it is inappropriate, has difficulty playing quietly, is often "on the go," talks excessively, blurts out answers before questions have been completed, has difficulty awaiting turn, and often interrupts or intrudes on others (APA, 2000).

A person can have either inattention or hyperactivity-impulsivity symptoms, or he or she can have both clusters. Typically, children who present with more symptoms of hyperactivity are identified first. When there is prominent hyperactivity, parents often report that these symptoms have been present since the child first was able to walk. However, there should be caution in diagnosing this disorder in toddlers, as many toddlers are motorically overactive, and not all of these children develop ADHD. Children with predominantly inattentive symptoms are often identified later in childhood, because this characteristic is harder for adults to identify than hyperactivity.

ADHD is currently recognized as genetically transmitted. In addition, it is recognized as a neurobiological illness. Several different chromosomal abnormalities and genes have been identified as being important in its development. There is a high rate of symptoms in twins, which further supports the genetic component. Neuropsychological testing supports that many individuals with ADHD have executive dysfunction as evidenced by increased deficits in response inhibition, vigilance, working memory, and planning (Willcutt, Doyle, Nigg, Faraone, & Pennington, 2005). Neuroimaging is used in research although it does not have clinical significance at the present time. A variety of brain-imaging studies have shown that children with ADHD have reduced white and gray cortical volume. Some studies (Durston et al., 2004) have also noted specific deficits in the frontal lobe volume. These findings are general and primarily support the neurobiological pathology in this disorder.

Epidemiology and Comorbidity

A number of different studies have been conducted to provide updated epidemiological data regarding ADHD. These studies seem to support that 3% to 7% of school-age children have clinically recognized ADHD (APA, 2000, p. 90).

ADHD is associated with a high degree of comorbidity. About half of children with ADHD also have clinically recognizable ODD. A "significant" percentage of children with ADHD and ODD will develop CD (Pliszka et al., 2007, p. 896.). Adolescents with ADHD are at an increased risk of developing substance abuse disorders.

ADHD is not only associated with other disruptive behavior disorders. There is an estimate that over 25% of children with ADHD have a depressive disorder. Some studies support high rates of mania in children with ADHD as well (APA, 2000, p. 88).

There is a high degree of comorbidity between ADHD and specific learning disabilities. Psychoeducation testing is often important to help distinguish if both disorders are present. An individual with a specific learning disability can appear inattentive if the material is not comprehended, but when the material is presented in an appropriate way, the inattention resolves. Alternatively, individuals with ADHD that is recognized in later school years can be behind academically from missing direct instruction, but when the ADHD is treated, there can be a period of rapid academic advancement. However, there is overlap, with 10% of learning disabilities having ADHD or another disruptive behavior disorder (APA, 2000, p. 50).

Course

It appears that over half of the children identified with ADHD continue to have clinically diagnosable symptoms in their teen years (Biederman et al., 1996). It is believed that some individuals with ADHD continue to have lifelong symptomatology. Like most people, individuals with ADHD are able to sustain focus better when engaged in higher interest tasks. Therefore, with age the symptoms can cause less impairment, as adults have more flexibility to choose high-interest subjects or careers.

It is important to remember that students with ADHD have symptoms and struggles in areas other than in school. There are more peer difficulties noted in individuals with ADHD. Their hyperactivity and impulsivity can cause peers to reject them. In addition, there can be increased family discord when a child has ADHD. This discord can negatively influence relationships with adults and further lead to academic failure. With age, children with ADHD begin to recognize their difficulties and differences, and this can lead to a low self-concept and more rejection. In other words, ADHD can cause significant distress and impairment in all areas of functioning throughout much of a person's childhood and adolescence.

Evaluation

A psychiatric evaluation should include screening for symptoms of ADHD. If it is determined that there is some degree of impairment from inattention, hyperactivity, or impulsivity, then a more thorough diagnostic process should proceed. The most accurate way to determine if ADHD is present is to ask about the above-described 17 symptoms. Specific details regarding the symptoms and the impairment that each symptom causes must be determined. It is important to obtain information from a number of sources. For preschool children, day care providers, in addition to the parents, should provide information. For school-age children, teachers are critical for providing information regarding present symptoms and impairment. Rating scales can be used to help provide more consistent data from a number of sources. The Conners' Teacher Rating Scales and Conners' Parent Rating Scales are commonly used. The Child Behavior Checklist (CBCL) also can be used to identify ADHD symptoms.

If there is no significant medical history present, it is not necessary to obtain blood work or neuroimaging studies to make the diagnosis of ADHD. In addition, unless there is some concern about a learning disability or low cognitive functioning, neuropsychological testing is not necessary to diagnosis ADHD. In other words, there is no single "test for ADHD."

In addition to determining the symptomatology of ADHD, the clinician should also determine if other psychiatric illnesses are present. ADHD must be differentiated from the other behavioral disorders. The hyperactive symptoms must be clearly seen as not being related to stereotypic movements such as rocking and biting that are seen in individuals with pervasive developmental disorders. One of the features of major depression is poor concentration. This must be distinguished from the inattentiveness associated with ADHD. The length of time of symptoms can help to provide this distinction. If the inattention is a recent symptom in a teenager, it is unlikely to be ADHD but more likely to be a feature of a mood disorder.

Treatment Interventions

ADHD is best conceptualized as a chronic disorder, and the treatment plan should be developed with this thought in mind. There needs to be ongoing assessment of the individual's response to treatment throughout development. A strategy that is effective at one age might not be effective in the future.

As with most psychiatric illnesses, psychoeducation is a critical component of treatment. Early support should be provided to both the student and the family so they understand that this is a neurobiological illness that has treatment options. Psychoeducation is also important to help parents understand pending developmental challenges. Advice can also be given to help improve social and academic functioning.

Studies throughout the 1980s and 1990s did not support benefit from psychodynamic therapy, cognitive therapy, or family therapy. Behavioral therapy was believed to be the therapeutic intervention that was most helpful. There has been recognition over this decade that biofeedback can be effective, but no clinical studies have strenuously supported this intervention. In addition, despite various resurgence in the importance of dietary modification, no randomized controlled studies have shown any change in core symptoms when dietary changes are implemented.

The National Institute of Mental Health sponsored a large well-controlled trial, the Multimodal Treatment Study of Attention Deficit Hyperactivity Disorder (MTA), in the late 1990s to establish the most effective treatment interventions for ADHD. This study randomized patients with ADHD into four treatment groups. The first group received medication that was monitored and adjusted monthly based on parent and teacher feedback. The second group received psychosocial intervention that primarily was based on behavioral therapy principles. The third group received both closely monitored medication and psychosocial intervention. The final group received community treatment that included no specific mandated interventions. All four groups showed a reduction in symptoms over the 14 months of the initial study. Both groups that received medication showed a greater improvement compared to those that received the behavioral interventions. There was no significant difference between the psychosocial intervention and the community treatment. This study heavily emphasized the importance of medication in the treatment of ADHD. However, behavioral therapy remains the treatment of choice if mild symptoms are present, if the diagnosis is in question, or if the parents are opposed to medication (MTA Cooperative Group, 1999).

Behavioral therapy interventions that are thought to be helpful include providing education about the symptoms of ADHD, teaching parents to use a token economy system, providing training on the appropriate use of time-out, anticipating future misconduct, and promoting positive behavioral choices. Both short- and long-term behavioral therapy have been shown to be effective.

Medication

If there is moderate to severe impairment in functioning related to inattention, hyperactivity, or impulsivity, then there should be a consideration to try a medication. There are a number of rigorous studies that support the effectiveness of pharmacologic intervention for the treatment of ADHD. The different classes of medications that are generally useful include stimulants, noradrenergic reuptake inhibitors, certain antidepressants, and certain antihypertensive agents. There are a large number of medications that have been approved by the FDA for the treatment of ADHD. The first line of treatment should include one of these approved agents.

The main class of medications that are useful for the treatment of ADHD is the stimulants. This class of medication was discovered to be helpful for "hyperkinetic" children in 1937. By 1996, there were 151 randomized controlled studies of these medications. Clinical studies support an improvement in symptomatology in 65% to 75% of children treated with stimulants compared to 4% to 5% of children treated with placebo (Greenhill, 2002). If a stimulant is chosen for medication, there must be a responsible adult who can monitor and dispense the medication. This class of medications is contraindicated for use by individuals who have previously abused stimulants and should be prescribed cautiously if a member of the household is currently abusing stimulants.

There are two different types of stimulants, and both have equal efficacy and potential side effects. The first type contains methylphenidate, and the second type contains amphetamine. There are short-acting (immediate release) preparations and long-acting (extended release) preparations of both types. Stimulants become effective shortly after consumption, and the effect lasts a defined period of time. Typically, immediate release preparations last 4 hours, and extended release preparations last 8 to 12 hours. Immediate release preparations might need to be taken numerous times throughout the day for sustained efficacy. Studies have been conducted to determine if there is a difference between methylphenidate and dextroamphetamine, but there is no clinically significant difference between the two (Arnold, 2000). Both groups have similar side effects and similar response rates. If a person does not tolerate or respond to one class, then the alternate class should be tried.

The common names for the short-acting stimulants that contain methylphenidate are Ritalin, Metadate, and Focalin. Some long-acting methylphenidate medications include Concerta, Ritalin LA, Focalin XR, and Metadate CD. Short-acting medications that contain amphetamine are Dexedrine and Adderall. Long-acting medications that include amphetamine are Adderall XR and Dextrostat. A "prodrug" is Vyvanse, and a dermal patch that contains methylphenidate is Daytrana (see accompanying CD: 5.1).

Stimulants are not dependent on blood levels to be effective. The effective dose is related to weight, so dosages may need to be increased with growth. There is no known therapeutic window, meaning that each person's dose must be individualized. Dosages that are in excess of what is needed can be associated with increased side effects, and dosages that are too low can be ineffective. A starting dose of medication should be initiated and tried for 1 to 3 weeks. After this time period, the dose can be increase based on response. Stimulants work by targeting dopamine and norepinephrine in the striatum and frontal lobe of the brain.

Stimulants have many potential side effects. When one is assessing the response of medication, the degree of impairment from side effects must be compared with the benefit that it is bringing. If the balance is toward the negative, then an alternative stimulant preparation may be indicated. Currently, this is an easy principle to follow, as there are a large number of stimulant medications.

The most common side effects of stimulants include decreased appetite, weight loss, headaches, and insomnia. Appetite is commonly decreased at lunch when the highest concentration of medication is in the person's body. By evening, the appetite can return. Weight loss can sometimes be prevented by the individual eating evening snacks. There has been concern over the past decades about the effects of stimulants on growth. The MTA study did show that children treated with stimulants gained weight more slowly than those children not on medication, but there was no statistically significant difference in height (MTA Cooperative Group, 1999). If insomnia occurs, changing the timing of the medication can reduce this side effect (see accompanying CD: 5.2).

Less common but more concerning side effects of stimulants are emotional changes. This can include emotional lability, irritability, anxiety, or sadness. These effects can be dose dependent and more likely to occur at higher dosages. Sustained release preparations tend to have less effect on emotionality in part because blood levels are more steady. Somewhat related to emotional changes is the possible side effect of behavioral rebound. This side effect occurs as the medication is leaving the person's body and is observed by a more dramatic return of hyperactivity. If mild, behavioral rebound will often subside with ongoing treatment. However, at times the symptoms can be severe and cause significant impairment. If this occurs, rebound can be ameliorated by a low-dose, short-acting medication given prior to its emergence.

Concerning side effects include the potential lowering of the seizure threshold and the potential increased effect on tics. If ADHD symptoms exist in children with epilepsy, it is reasonable to treat these symptoms with a stimulant if their seizure disorder is well controlled.

When a child or adolescent presents with both anxiety and ADHD, treatment can be complicated. Differentiating these disorders can be challenging, because when someone is anxious, it is difficult to concentrate. Alternatively, when a child becomes aware that he or she is not attending well, this can generate anxiety. Treatment is also complicated because stimulants can increase anxiety that can make the inattention appear worse. However, at times treating the ADHD with a stimulant can have an indirect effect of reducing anxiety. Caution and close monitoring are in order when these two problems coexist.

Another treatment challenge is the treatment of ADHD in a child who also has a tic disorder such as Tourette's disorder. As described above, stimulants can cause tics, and if a tic disorder is present, they can also exacerbate tics. Stimulants are no longer absolutely contraindicated with tics, but there should be close monitoring of tics when a stimulant is chosen.

There has long been concern about the risk of abuse of this class of medication. Stimulants are considered substances of abuse, as seen in lab experiments by self-administration and preference over food. There was previously a belief that exposing a child's developing brain to stimulants may sensitize the brain to desire more of this substance. Recently, there has been a shift in opinion to the belief that adolescents with untreated ADHD actually have an increased risk of substance-seeking behavior in an effort to self-medicate (Wilins & Spencer, 1999). The medications themselves can become agents of abuse. At times these medications can be crushed and inhaled to promote a more rapid onset of "high." Longer acting preparations tend to be less desirable for abuse because of their pharmacokinetic properties. In addition, the construction of one medication in particular, Concerta, makes it nearly impossible to crush. The dermal form of methylphenidate, Daytrana, was also designed to make it difficult to misuse. If the patch is removed from the skin it will not adhere for a second time. This prevents the patch from being used by more than one person. It is also difficult to separate the membranes to obtain intact medication.

All children should have a physical exam before starting stimulants. It is important to have a documented baseline of blood pressure, pulse, height, and weight. Stimulants can have cardiovascular side effects and should be used cautiously when there are known underlying cardiac problems. This concern was highlighted in the previous chapter.

The timing of dosage can be important in effective symptom control. The extended release stimulants often lose efficacy by late afternoon. Depending on the youth's schedule, there may be a need for improved focus and attention in the evening. In this situation a short-acting stimulant can be used in the early afternoon. If this option is chosen, there should be close monitoring of sleep. If sleep disturbance becomes severe, the short-acting stimulant should be discontinued.

Because of stimulants' rapid onset and efficacy without a constant blood level, some families elect to provide "medication holidays" by not dispensing a stimulant on weekends or holidays. This can be helpful particularly if the child is having appetite suppression, as the time off medications can prevent weight loss. However, if a child or teen is distractible and inattentive, there can be benefit from continuing these medications daily, just as someone who needs glasses to see typically needs them on weekends as well. This decision is best made by the physician in conjunction with the family.

Stimulants can be used in preschool children, but this age group tends to experience more side effects than older children. These medications are metabolized more slowly in preschool children. Dexedrine is approved by the FDA for use in children younger than 6 years, but a clinician can prescribe methylphenidate preparations. There is some belief that treating symptoms of ADHD early in the development of a child's brain, such as during the preschool years, can promote improved outcomes later in life.

The second class of medications that is approved for treating ADHD is called the noradrenergic reuptake inhibitors. Currently the only medication in this class is atomoxetine (Strattera). This medication has been approved for the treatment of ADHD in children, adolescents, and adults. Unlike the stimulants this medication is dependent on a steady blood level to be most effective. Improvement can be seen in 1 week, but the most improvement is seen beginning after 6 weeks of treatment. The benefit of this medication is that it is effective for 24 hours. This is important particularly for adolescents and adults who have reasons to be attentive throughout the day. Because of this mechanism of action, this medication is recommended to be taken daily for best results. Depending on the prescribed dose, there can be withdraw side effects from missing a dose. In addition, missing weekend dosages lowers the amount of medication in the bloodstream, therefore decreasing its effectiveness.

Common and generally mild side effects of atomoxetine include upset stomach, decreased appetite, tiredness, and mood swings. Some of these side effects can be minimized by changing the dosage time or schedule. For example, if tiredness occurs the individual can take the medication in the evening to promote sleep, and because of the medication's 24-hour efficacy, it is still working the following day. A more concerning side effect includes suicidal thoughts. According to Lilly, the manufacturer of Strattera, 4 out of 1,000 children or adolescents developed suicidal thoughts while treated with this medication. Less common but still concerning side effects include priapism (a sustained erection) and trouble urinating. Stroke and heart attacks have also occurred, and it is suggested that this medication be used cautiously if there are cardiac abnormalities or a family history of heart problems (see accompanying CD: 5.3).

When ADHD is present in an individual with a tic disorder or anxiety, there can be a role for atomoxetine. Because of atomoxetine's mechanism of action, the symptoms of ADHD can be improved without exacerbating either underlying problem. Atomoxetine can be the preferred first-line treatment in both situations.

If there is not significant improvement in symptoms after adequate trial length and adequate dosages of two of the approved medications (either two different stimulants or one stimulant plus atomoxetine), the next step is to review the diagnosis. Failure to show response can be a sign that there is another comorbid or different diagnosis that might have been overlooked. If the diagnosis is reconfirmed, there can be consideration that a different medication strategy must be implemented. Some individuals do not respond adequately to a single approved treatment. Clinically, it can be beneficial to combine two different approved medications. Atomoxetine and a stimulant can be combined and result in more improved symptom resolution for an individual than either medication alone.

There are other medications that can be used in the treatment of ADHD if the diagnosis is certain and there has not been response to approved medications. These medications were more commonly used in the past before there was such an extensive list of other approved treatment options. The FDA has not approved these medications for the treatment of ADHD. Tricyclic antidepressants, bupropion (another antidepressant), and alpha-2 adrenergic agents can be used. Currently, these medications are more frequently prescribed with a stimulant to increase efficacy.

The alpha-2 adrenergic agents (clonidine and guanfacine) can be helpful in reducing impulsivity and aggression that can be present in individuals with ADHD. In addition, these medications are sedating, so taking them at bedtime can improve the individual's sleep and indirectly reduce inattention when the child is more rested. Bupropion or a tricyclic antidepressant can be used in combination with a stimulant if the juvenile is irritable or edgy from the stimulant but it becomes clear that the stimulant is helpful and needed.

Clinical Case

Angie was a 10-year-old Caucasian female who was seen for a psychiatric evaluation at the request of her school district. She was a fourth-grade student who was not completing class work or homework. She was described as sitting in class, staring out the window as she pulled sections of her hair out of her head. Her family stated that as a preschool child, Angie was anxious and fearful. She would not separate easily, and family members had to act as her babysitter. With the transition to grade school, she remained fearful. As early as first grade, teachers began commenting on her failure to pay attention to detail and her disorganization. She was often forgetful, and when called on she was often "in a daze." Her parents reported that when she was playing soccer, a game at which she excelled, the coach often had to call to her numerous times before she would respond.

There was no prior psychiatric treatment. There were no medical problems. She was an only child in a well-to-do family. Apart from her reluctance to separate from her family, there were no developmental difficulties. Family history was positive for panic disorder in her mother and a single episode of major depression in her father in the remote past. There were two cousins with ADHD.

On Angie's mental status examination, a 2-inch-circumference bald spot on the top of her head was observed. Her appearance was otherwise consistent with an attractive girl. There was no hyperactivity or restlessness; however, she spent much time during the interview twirling her hair. Her speech was of normal rate, tone, and volume. She described her mood as "worried." Her affect was anxious, full ranged, and mood congruent. Her thought form was clear and organized. There were no psychotic symptoms. There was no consistent sadness. Angie was able to articulate that she spent much of her day "daydreaming." Many of the daydreams consisted of planning what she would do after school or imagining herself a "soccer star." She denied that she spent time worrying about negative things.

Her hair twirling, hair pulling, history of separation difficulties, and fearfulness at a younger age suggested that some of her inattention could be related to anxiety. However, her description of her internal thought processes was more consistent with inattention. After lengthy discussion with her and her family, it was decided to treat her inattention with atomoxetine. She was started on a low dose that was increased over time to her dose based on weight. The medication was more slowly increased to prevent worsening any underlying anxiety. After 6 weeks she reached her expected atomoxetine dose. A reassessment at that time supported a significant improvement in focus. Her grades had improved. Her soccer coach had frequently complimented her playing and response to direction. Interestingly, she had stopped playing with her hair, and the bald spot had begun to regrow hair.

This example highlights the overlap between ADHD and anxiety, and the first treatment option that was cautiously begun allowed significant symptom reduction.

OPPOSITIONAL DEFIANT DISORDER

Characteristics

Oppositional defiant disorder (ODD) is one of the most common clinical concerns. It is characterized by a recurrent pattern of negative, oppositional, hostile, and aggressive behaviors. This disorder was first recognized in the *DSM-III* in 1966, but the criteria for diagnosis have become more stringent with time. This change has made it somewhat difficult to define the longitudinal outcome of this disorder, but it is quite clear that this disruptive behavioral disorder can cause significant impairment in functioning and significant distress.

ODD is described by a pattern of negativistic, defiant, disobedient, and hostile behavior directed toward authority figures (APA, 2000, p. 100). The pattern must be present for at least 6 months. At least four of the following behaviors must be present: losing temper, arguing with adults, actively defying or refusing to comply with rules and requests, deliberately doing things that will annoy other people, blaming others for mistakes or misbehavior, being touchy or easily annoyed by others, being angry and resentful, or being spiteful or vindictive. Importantly, these behaviors must occur more frequently than is normal for age and developmental level. In contrast to individuals with CD, individuals with ODD do not have major episodes of violating the rights of others.

As with other psychiatric disorders, this illness is believed to have biological, psychological, and social contributors. Although there have been no gene or definitive brain abnormalities found, it is seen that there is a familial risk for the development of ODD. Psychological factors could include insecure attachment, and the behavior can be a signal to the parent to be more responsive. Social factors including inconsistent parenting, poor family unity, and inconsistent discipline can also contribute. Often a pattern can emerge where the parent and child "bring out the worst in each other" (APA, 2000, p. 100).

Epidemiology and Comorbidity

In community samples the rate of ODD is quite variable, ranging from 2% to 16% of the population (APA, 2000, p. 101). This again speaks to the stringency of the diagnostic threshold. It is currently accepted that the pattern is typically present before age 8 years.

Children with ODD have a high likelihood of having other psychiatric problems. ADHD and ODD commonly co-occur. Individuals with both entities are at a high risk for more severe behavioral problems. Interestingly, children with ODD are also at a higher risk than would be expected for developing anxiety disorders and mood disorders.

Course

Brief oppositional behavior is common in preschool children and adolescents, so this must be differentiated from ODD. The onset of ODD is typically gradual and usually becomes evident before the age of 8 years and not later than early adolescence (APA, 2000, p. 101). By description ODD behaviors need to be present in only one setting, but over the course of time, there can be symptoms in numerous settings.

It is estimated that nearly two thirds of individuals with ODD will have a reduction in symptoms in the future. However, the other one third tend to progress into more severe pathological states such as CD or antisocial personality disorder (Connor, 2002). There is a higher likelihood for this progression if the symptoms present at an earlier age. ODD can cause significant impairment in social relations, which can cause distress and dysfunction with age. Often these children recognize their difficulty interacting with adults, and this can lead to negative self-concept.

Evaluation

When assessing a juvenile who is suspected of having ODD, the clinician will find it important to establish a therapeutic alliance with the family and child. Parents who have children with ODD often are aware that their parenting style contributed to the difficulty. They may present very defensively or minimize the behavioral difficulties. Youth also may minimize their symptoms or justify their behavior. Therefore, it is important to obtain information from numerous sources in order to have a comprehensive view of the child. It is also important to keep the behaviors being described in the appropriate cultural context.

Most times the child will not be oppositional toward the psychiatrist in the evaluation. The individual portion of the evaluation should seek to understand the child's thinking behind the negative behaviors and, importantly, should be a time to explore other thought processes that could suggest comorbid illnesses. It is important to quickly work to understand the difference between developmentally normal refusal and ODD. The length of time the symptoms have been present and any potential triggers should be explored.

Rating scales such as the Conners' Parent Rating Scales can also be helpful in discriminating between normal and pathological opposition.

Treatment Interventions

Prevention is believed to be the most effective intervention. Prevention strategies have targeted changing parents' approaches to managing negative behaviors. In addition, providing education to school-age children and adolescents on anger management, conflict resolution skills, and improving social skills have also been helpful.

Once the behavioral pattern has become fixed, parent management training strategies have been shown to be the most effective treatment interventions in two studies (Burke, Loeber, & Birmaher, 2002). The strategies included in this approach are to reduce positive reinforcement of negative behavior, increase positive reinforcement of appropriate behavior, apply consequences for disruptive behavior, and make parental responses predictable. Consistency with applying these strategies is critical and often difficult. In addition, it is important that both parents apply these principles equally. When possible, negative behaviors can be ignored or should have an appropriate consequence. When the parent provides attention or changes the expectation because of the child's negative behavior, the behavior is inadvertently reinforced. Although simplistic in appearance, these strategies are difficult to apply. It is important that parents learn to pick the appropriate battle with the oppositional child. Attempts need to be made to avoid power struggles. Simple and consistent rules and expectations are also helpful. Family therapy is one effective way to ensure that these approaches are consistently used. There are also some parenting training programs that are manualized in their approach. This approach uses workbooks and a definitive structure to the sessions that some families find helpful.

It is clear that prevention is the best "treatment" approach and that parent interventions are most successful at reducing ODD when it occurs. Children with severe ODD require prolonged and extensive treatment. Although the least restrictive placement should always be utilized, there might need to be placement outside of the home if the safety of self or others is involved.

There is no quick solution to ODD. In fact it has been shown in a number of studies (Burke et al., 2002) that dramatic and one-time interventions are not helpful. Showing a person frightening scenarios without providing other behavioral support could worsen the oppositional or aggressive symptoms (Rutter, Giller, & Hagell, 1999).

Medication

There is no medication that is useful to treat ODD. Medication should never be the primary treatment intervention for children with ODD. The first medication strategy is to treat any comorbid conditions with medication. At times reducing the impulsivity associated with ADHD with medication will have an indirect effect of improving compliance. Reducing the irritability by treating associated depressive symptoms can also have the benefit of improving compliance.

If ODD is the only diagnosis present, medications can have a small role in treatment. However, there should be agreement with both the parents and the child about taking a medication. In addition, it should clearly be stated that the medication can reduce some of the symptoms but should not be thought of as "curative." Some classes of medications that have shown some preliminary benefit are the mood stabilizers or atypical antipsychotics. These medications can be particularly helpful in reducing aggression.

CONDUCT DISORDER

Characteristics

Conduct disorder (CD) is a repetitive and persistent pattern of behavior in which the basic rights of others are violated. Alternatively, major age-appropriate societal norms or rules are violated. The potential behaviors fall into four main groups, including aggressive conduct that causes or threatens physical harm to people or animals, nonaggressive conduct that causes property loss or damage, deceitfulness or theft, and serious violation of rules. At least three different behaviors must have been present during the past year, and one behavior must have been present during the past 6 months to qualify for CD (APA, 2000, p. 94).

The aggressive behavior can include bullying and intimidating others or initiating frequent physical fights. The fights or arguments can include use of weapon, including a brick, bat, or gun. Stealing while confronting a victim or forcing someone into sexual activity are other examples of aggressive behavior. Destruction of property can include deliberate fire setting with the intention to cause damage or destroying property in other ways such as breaking windows. Acts of deceitfulness or theft can include breaking into a home, building, or car; frequently lying; breaking promises; or stealing without confronting a victim. The serious violation of rules can include violating school or parental rules. This can include staying out late despite parental prohibition, running away from home overnight, or having significant absence from school (APA, 2000, p. 94).

In addition to having the behaviors described above, individuals with CD could have little empathy for others. They can have common misperceptions about other people's intentions, and they can respond aggressively. Individuals with CD might engage in early onset of sexual behavior, drinking, smoking, and risk-taking behaviors (APA, 2000, p. 96).

Although it is unlikely that a single gene will be identified as associated with CD, there is support for a genetic component because of clustering of the diagnosis that occurs in families. Understanding the role between genetic and environmental influences on the development of CD is difficult. There is likely a temperamental factor, and the interplay between a child's temperament and parenting style can generate additional risk. Children with a difficult temperament can induce more anger in the parent, which can lead to mistreatment. Additional social stressors that can contribute to the development of CD include frequent changes in caregivers, large family size, peer rejection, association with a delinquent peer group, and neighborhood exposure to violence. Poor family functioning, familial substance abuse and psychiatric illness, marital discord, child abuse and neglect, and poor parenting are significant risk factors (Lahey, Piacentini, McBurnett, & Stone, 1988).

Epidemiology and Comorbidity

Population studies provide report rates ranging from less than 1% to 3%. CD is significantly more common in males. In fact, boys outnumber girls by a factor of five to one in childhood. Interestingly, the gender gap narrows with age (Bird et al., 1988), and boys are only three times more likely to meet diagnostic criteria. CD is more common in urban settings.

There is comorbidity between ADHD and CD, and this comorbidity can predict a more ominous outcome. CD can also occur when mood disorders or anxiety disorders are present, and both can be diagnosed if present. Finally, CD in adolescence is associated with an increased risk of developing a substance abuse disorder.

Interestingly, suicide attempts and completed suicides occur at a higher rate than normal in individuals with CD (APA, 2000, p. 97), which could speak to the underlying mood disorders or be a reflection of aggression and misperception of environment.

Course

ODD is often a precursor to CD. The precursor symptoms can begin as early as the preschool years. Typically, the first significant conduct disordered behaviors begin during mid-childhood and continue through mid-adolescence. CD is termed "early onset" if at least one symptom was present before age 10 years. It is rare for the diagnosis to be given after age 16 years (APA, 2000, p. 97).

Although there are no clear longitudinal studies, it is believed that the majority of individuals with CD have remission of symptoms by adulthood. However, many individuals with CD in childhood or adolescence are diagnosed with antisocial personality disorder or substance abuse disorders as adults. Early onset of these behaviors predicts a worse course and a worse outcome. It is often the aggressive behaviors that first come to the attention of adults. A pattern of more severe aggression also predicts a worse outcome.

Evaluation

As with the evaluation of other disruptive behavior disorders, obtaining information from numerous sources is important. Typically, the juvenile will minimize negative behaviors or look to shift the blame for these behaviors to others. Parents might initially minimize the intensity or longevity of the symptoms or be unaware as to the extent of the negative behaviors. Individuals with CD can first come to the attention of a psychiatrist through the school or juvenile probation system. This can help to provide a more accurate representation of the behaviors.

Throughout the evaluation there should be a review of the pattern of negative behaviors. An adolescent who engages in the described behaviors over a short period of time might not meet the criteria for length of symptoms.

An evaluation should screen for other psychiatric disorders. For adolescents there should be a screening for substance use. Mood and anxiety disorders should be reviewed, as irritability can contribute to a pattern of negative behavior.

Treatment Interventions

CD is best considered a chronic difficulty that can be refractory to treatment. Longer term treatment interventions are more helpful than short-term solutions. The best treatments are multimodal in approach. This includes the involvement of numerous systems, including mental health, juvenile probation, and education. In many instances by the time a teen with CD is identified, the parents have lost their power to enforce rules. In this situation juvenile probation can be a very effective agency to help ensure significant consequences for negative behavior. Aggressive community treatment can include close collaboration between a number of different systems.

Providing parent training and focusing on the child's anger management, coping skills, and social interactions can be effective in the treatment of younger children. As the child ages, more emphasis should be placed on teaching the adolescent ways to improve self-regulation. Parent management is less useful for adolescent treatment.

At times the pattern of behavior is so severe that an out-of-home placement is indicated. Depending on the state, these placements can be facilitated by the juvenile probation department or mental health services.

Medication

As with the treatment of ODD, medication is never effective as a solo treatment intervention. There is no medication that can change this behavioral pattern. The first conceptualization for medication use should be to treat any comorbid symptoms. Treating ADHD if present can improve behaviors, as impulsivity is lessened. Treating depression can reduce irritability, which can result in less disruptive behaviors.

If comorbid symptoms have been effectively treated and problems persist, medication treatment can be considered. The atypical antipsychotic medications, particularly Risperdal, have been shown to reduce physical aggression associated with CD (Findling et al., 2000).

Oppositional Defiant Disorder and Conduct Disorder: Clinical Case

Paul was initially referred for a psychiatric evaluation by his parents at the age of 9 years. At that time, 6 years ago, he was refusing to follow requests in the home. Most requests would result in his yelling, screaming, and crying. Any time he was told he could not do something he wanted to do, he would fall to the floor and kick his feet. He demonstrated the most noncompliance with his mother, although at times he would refuse to follow his father's direction. He was doing well academically and behaviorally in school. In addition, he was very social and participated in community recreation programs without difficulty. His parents were becoming increasingly frustrated at how many positive comments they would receive about him from others when they were having such problems at home. There were no medical problems, no significant social or developmental concerns, and no family history of mental illness.

After close review the only diagnosis recognized at the time was ODD. The diagnosis was reviewed with Paul's parents. When they learned that he did not meet the criteria for bipolar disorder, they were relieved and explained that they could "live with the behaviors" and were not interested in pursuing any treatment.

Six years later Paul returned for a psychiatric evaluation at the request of his juvenile probation officer. He was on probation after having made a specific threat to shoot a teacher. Information provided suggested that the past 6 years were consistent with a pattern of escalating behavior. Paul first became noncompliant with completing homework and schoolwork. When confronted first by his parents and later by his teachers, he began doing less work. He also began to have increased conflict with peers and was engaged in a number of physical fights. At the age of 10 years, he was in a fight that resulted in a boy sustaining a mild concussion. When questioned about this incident, Paul reported simply, "He started it." At the age of 12 years, Paul and two boys began doing research on bombs on the Internet. Paul alone printed out the material and made a "bomb," which he lit in the woods behind his house. No damage occurred, but Paul said, "It was the coolest thing ever."

Paul began to smoke marijuana on a daily basis at age 13 years. Within 2 years he had progressed to using cocaine, followed by Klonopin, a benzodiazepine, to "lessen the let down." He admitted to stealing his mother's jewelry and selling it to have money to purchase his drugs.

His parents realized that Paul was "out of control" after he did not return home for 5 days in a row. He had missed school during this time, and when confronted about his whereabouts, he physically assaulted his mother, leaving her with bruises on her arms and face. At this point his parents pressed charges, and he became an adjudicated delinquent.

There were definitive expectations set by his probation officer, and within 2 months it became clear that Paul was not complying with any of the requests. He continued to cut classes at school, was rarely home by curfew, engaged in two other physical fights, and had two random drug screens test positive for cocaine.

After a close review, there were no consistent mood, anxiety, or psychotic symptoms elicited. His pattern of substance use met criteria for cocaine abuse. His behaviors had escalated to meeting criteria for CD. What was concerning was that Paul placed the blame for all of his actions on others and demonstrated no sadness or remorse.

Ultimately, the court had him placed in a facility for juvenile delinquents. A strict behavioral-level system was implemented, and group therapy was utilized. Unfortunately, there was no consistent improvement, and now one year later, Paul remains in the same facility.

Six

Mood Disorders

DEPRESSIVE DISORDERS

Types and Characteristics

Mood disorders can most accurately be thought of as existing on a spectrum. On one end of the spectrum are a variety of depressive disorders, and on the other end are a variety of bipolar disorders. This chapter will focus on both types of mood disorders and diagnosis and treatment options.

There are various types of depression, ranging from mild to severe, which exist along a continuum. Within this spectrum there are a number of recognized distinct clinical disorders, and there can be fluctuations between the presentations at various times in the person's life.

At the most severe end of the spectrum is major depressive disorder (MDD). The hallmark of this depressive disorder is a distinct change in mood or a loss of interest and pleasure in life. For children and adolescents, the mood change most often presents as either sadness or irritability. Typically, this type of depression has an abrupt onset. Along with loss of pleasure or change in mood, there must be five of the following symptoms: increase or decrease in amount of sleep, increased or decreased appetite, psychomotor agitation or retardation, decrease in energy or fatigue, increased preoccupation with worthlessness or guilt, decrease in concentration, and preoccupation with death and suicidal ideas. The symptoms must be present every day for 2 weeks and must cause functional impairment to be considered MDD. In addition, the mood changes must not be directly related to substance use, bereavement, or use of medication (American Psychiatric Association [APA], 2000, p. 356).

Although the same diagnostic criteria are used in children that are used in adults, youth often present with additional associated symptoms. Irritability, decreased frustration tolerance, and temper tantrums are common. If these are present and related to the depression, the behavioral changes represent a change from the child's baseline level of functioning. Somatic complaints and social withdraw can also be associated with MDD (APA, 2000).

A second type of depression on the spectrum is dysthymia. This is noted by persistent and long-term changes in mood. Because of its chronicity, this type of depression is more gradual in its presentation. Symptoms of sadness or irritability in children and adolescents must be present most days for 1 year, which is 1 year less than the time an adult must have a change in mood. In addition, there must be two of the following: poor appetite or overeating, insomnia or hypersomnia, low energy or fatigue, low self-esteem, poor concentration or difficulty making decisions, or feelings of hopelessness. As with all other disorders, there must be functional impairment, and it must not be related to substance abuse, a medical condition, or medication (APA, 2000, p. 380). The severity of sadness is not typically as intense when compared to major depression, but its chronicity causes distress.

The third common type of depression is called an adjustment disorder with depressed mood. In this type of depression, there is an identified stressor that causes excessive sadness. The sadness must begin within 3 months of the stressor. There must be marked distress that is more than a normal response, or there must be significant impairment in social or academic functioning. In addition, the symptoms persist for fewer than 6 months after the stressor has resolved (APA, 2000, pp. 679–680).

Fourth of the distinct depressive disorders is depressive disorder, not otherwise specified (NOS). This classification is for individuals who struggle with depressive symptoms, but these symptoms do not reach threshold criteria for any of the above-described categories of depression (APA, 2000, pp. 381–382). For example, dysthymia must be present for 1 year to meet the time threshold for that disorder. If an adolescent has these symptoms for 6 months, the classification would be depressive disorder, NOS. Another example of a depressive disorder, NOS is a youth who has more than two symptoms of dysthymia but fewer than the five required for major depression. This mild end of the depressive spectrum is where many children with depressive disorders are placed diagnostically.

Epidemiology and Comorbidity

Depressive disorders are common in children and adolescents. It has been estimated that 2% of children and 4% to 8%

of adolescents have clinically significant MDD. Before puberty boys and girls have an equal likelihood of experiencing MDD, but with puberty the risk factor for girls increases by two to four times (Birmaher et al., 1996). It is also estimated that 5% to 10% of community samples have subsyndromal mood disorders (Fergusson, Horwood, Ridder, & Beautrais, 2005) that are best categorized as depressive disorder, NOS.

Individuals with depressive disorders tend to have a higher likelihood of having more than one diagnosis. MDD and depressive disorders commonly co-occur, and this can be termed a "double depression." In addition, it is believed that 40% to 90% of youth who have depression have a second disorder (Birmaher et al., 1996). Anxiety disorders are the most common comorbid conditions, followed by external behavior disorders such as attention-deficit/hyperactivity disorder (ADHD). In teenagers another common co-occurrence is substance abuse disorders.

Course

Most studies support that youth fully recover from a single episode of depression. However, there is increased recognition about the risk of recurrence. It is estimated that up to 70% of youth will have a second episode of depression within 5 years (Birmaher, Arbelaez, & Brent, 2002). These recurrences can persist into adulthood. In addition, there is approximately a 20% to 40% chance that a youth with one episode of MDD will develop bipolar disorder (Geller, Fox, & Clark, 1994).

Evaluation

Standards set forth by the American Academy of Child and Adolescent Psychiatry (AACAP, 2007c) provide guidelines for psychiatrists that outline standards of care when considering if a youth is suffering from a depressive disorder. It is expected that all psychiatric evaluations of youth should include screening for depression. There should be questioning during both the student and the parent portions of the evaluation to elicit potential symptoms of sadness and associated symptoms of depression. This includes an assessment of mood and associated changes in sleep, appetite, energy, interest, and concentration.

A second expectation of all psychiatric evaluations is an assessment of any potential suicidal ideas. It is commonly known that asking a depressed person about suicidal thoughts does not increase the likelihood of suicide. Questions should be asked to identify any current or past thoughts of suicide. If there are recent suicidal thoughts, then more thorough questions regarding suicidal ideas or plans should be explored. There should also be some questions asked to identify thoughts or actions of self-injury.

It is also generally expected that if depressive symptoms are identified, there should be questions asked to help understand what social stressors may be present and contributing to the mood disorder. Understanding the additional social or family pressures with which the youth is struggling helps to place the sadness in context. In addition, understanding social details can also identify supports that the patient can use in a helpful way. For example, a teacher can be recognized as listening to the student's struggles in a way that is helpful for the student.

A psychiatric evaluation should also include a careful assessment of other comorbid conditions. Any teen presenting with depressive symptoms should be carefully assessed for past episodes of grandiosity or mania. It is important to differentiate unipolar depression from bipolar disorder. Anxiety disorders are often comorbid with depression. In addition, ADHD is highly associated with depressive illnesses. Recognizing alternative diagnoses or comorbid illnesses will likely affect treatment interventions and outcomes.

Screening tools (see accompanying CD: 6.1) can sometimes be useful in eliciting symptoms of depression. The Children's Depression Inventory is used both clinically and for research purposes for children ages 7 to 17 years. Each question has three statements from which the youth can pick to the best answer. Individuals with more significant depression have a higher score. Another commonly used instrument is the Children's Depression Rating Scale. This is used for children ages 6 to 12 years and is completed by the evaluator in conjunction with information obtained from the parent, child, and school.

Therapeutic Principles

The treatment approach should be chosen based on the type of depression, the severity of the symptoms, and the degree of functional impairment that is present. Regardless of what treatment approach is chosen, it is helpful to think about treatment as occurring in three phases. The first phase is the acute treatment phase. In this phase the goal is to provide relief from the severity of symptoms and return the youth to the baseline level of functioning. The second phase of treatment is the continuation phase. During this period the effective therapy is continued to promote consolidation of the progress that was made initially. The final phase is the maintenance phase and is very important for youth who have had recurrent depressive episodes, chronic depressions, or very severe symptoms. The treatment goals and length of each phase vary greatly among individuals.

It is recommended that each phase should include supportive management, psychoeducation, and family support (AACAP, 2007c). Although not a formalized therapeutic intervention, supportive management is when the clinician uses active listening and reflects the pieces of relevant information back to the youth and family. Providing a sense of hope for recovery and teaching problem-solving strategies are also helpful supportive interventions. In the acute phase of treatment, psychoeducation is when the treatment provider actively provides education about depression. This information should include a clear description of depression as an illness. The various treatment options and what can happen without any treatment should be explained. It is helpful for both the juvenile and the parents to understand that depression is not a weakness. In addition, it should be explained that depression is not caused by one factor but a result of genetic, temperamental, and environmental influences.

As the course of treatment shifts to the continuation phase, the education offered often includes a review of the individual's depressive symptoms. This is helpful, as it enables a return of illness to be recognized and treated more quickly. The supportive treatment can include a review of problem-solving skills that were particularly helpful and ongoing support of positive management of stressors.

Family involvement in all phases of treatment is important. Even if the distinct treatment approach of family therapy is not selected, the parents are instrumental in a child's recovery from an episode of depression. The parents will need to understand how to support and encourage positive coping strategies. In addition, the parents can have insight into the youth's illness that might not be readily recognized. The parents are often the monitors of safety and help to provide the daily safety net. At times parents must delicately balance parenting strategies. Becoming excessively involved in every decision the youth makes and making excuses for negative choices due to the depression can inadvertently reinforce the depression. On the other hand having too high expectations can cause the youth to feel more stuck and hopeless, which can further entrench the depressive symptoms.

There can also need to be school involvement during
a depressive episode. If an episode is not severe enough to
cause educational difficulties, it can still be crucial to inform
the school team about the depression. If the teacher is aware
that the student is struggling with depression, there can be
some slight informal allowances made that would be helpful
to the student's recovery. In addition, a school psychologist
or guidance counselor can also be instrumental in supportive management.

For juveniles with mild or brief types of depression, offering supportive interventions can effectively resolve the symptoms. For mild depression where there are no suicidal ideas, it
can be appropriate to provide this level of intervention for 4 to
6 weeks before considering other treatment options. However,
if there is severe impairment, particularly with psychotic or
suicidal thoughts, more intensive treatment options should be
discussed upon initial presentation.

When more impairment is present, there must be consideration about whether to begin treatment with psychotherapy or
medication or both. The psychiatrist has the task of presenting to the family and youth the different treatment options
available. It is also important that the psychiatrist be able to
recommend one of the approaches over the other if there is
research-based proof for the use of one treatment over the
other for the individual. It is equally important that the clinician allow the parents and juvenile to ask questions and
provide input into which treatment approach is chosen. The
time course of expected improvement should be explained,
and flexibility in the treatment plan is imperative. If there is
little response to the first treatment intervention, there should
be a change in the plan. During all phases of treatment, it is
important that there be regular follow-up with the clinician.

Psychotherapy Treatment

Psychotherapy is considered an important component of treatment for depression. There are different psychotherapy interventions. Individual therapy is when the patient meets with a
therapist at an agreed-on frequency. For younger children play
therapy is a useful individual approach to improving mood
and coping skills. Older children and adolescents can choose
to participate in talking therapy.

Group therapy is another common treatment approach particularly for adolescents with depression. Many teens report
comfort in learning that other teens suffer from depression.

At times an adolescent can accept confrontation on negative choices from a peer more easily than from an adult.

Family therapy is a third psychotherapeutic intervention. Within the systems model of family therapy, there is investigation into the family's interactions and an exploration why the individual with depression has developed the illness. The family system is supported to change, and less emphasis is placed on the identified child. Although this approach is clinically useful, a study in 1997 found that cognitive behavioral therapy (CBT) was superior to systemic behavioral therapy in the short term (Brent et al., 1997).

If individual therapy is chosen, there should be a clear review with the youth and parents about confidentiality. The parent must understand that the process and much of the content of therapy are confidential. However, the youth must understand that in some instances, this confidentiality may be broken. The instances where confidentiality may be broken include a disclosure of harm to self or others. For example, suicidal intention, homicidal intention, or current abuse must be shared with a parent or appropriate authority.

An agreed-on approach to use in individual therapy is CBT. The premise of CBT is that a person's thoughts and perceptions are related to feelings. A number of randomized controlled studies support that CBT is a very effective therapeutic intervention for depression. The therapist works to identify negative cognition and then to modify these cognitions with behavioral principles. As a general construct CBT is a useful psychotherapeutic treatment of depression. It is a specific and time-limited treatment intervention. The person is assigned "homework" to begin to practice the therapeutic strategies between office visits. The theory from which this treatment evolved was Aaron Beck's belief that negative interpretations of events (schema) can contribute to depression.

When using this treatment model to treat depressed youth, the therapist first helps the person to identify negative or distorted thoughts. Once these negative patterns are identified, they can be challenged and changed. Individuals who are depressed can have "thinking errors" such as overgeneralization. When these thinking errors are recognized and replaced with more realistic thoughts, the depressed feelings begin to resolve. The behavioral portion of CBT for depression can include a list of positive activities that the individual must complete between sessions.

Interpersonal therapy (IPT) is another short-term individual therapy that focuses on the interactions between people and how relationships influence depression. This treatment focuses on the individual's emotions while exploring relationships. IPT studies the way that the individual's current relationships can cause or maintain the symptoms. For example, the following negative patterns of relationships can be causative of depression: unresolved grief, role disputes, role transitions, and interpersonal deficits. Strategies for handling difficult situations with the symptoms are explored as the quality of a person's relationships are improved.

Medication

For many decades the primary class of medications used to treat depression was called "tricyclic antidepressants." This class of medication targeted the release of numerous neurotransmitters in the brain. These medications were found to be effective in adults, but there were a number of significant side effects that made these medications undesirable to many adults. Tricyclic antidepressants were used for a short time in children. When these medications were studied in children for treatment of depression, they were found to not be significantly more beneficial than placebo. However, there were significant side effects in children, and one medication in particular, desipramine, was associated with sudden death in several children likely related to cardiovasular problems.

Subsequent classes of antidepressants have been found, and the first of these classes targets the specific neurotransmitter serotonin. This class of medication specifically targets serotonin by preventing it from being as quickly reabsorbed by the postsynaptic neurons. These medications are called selective serotonin reuptake inhibitors (SSRIs) and are still considered the first line of treatment in adults with depression. SSRIs are effective in adults and are associated with few side effects.

Because of the increased tolerability of these medications, there was an interest in using them in children and adolescents. The research support for SSRI pharmacotherapy of depression is complicated by the conclusion that youth have a very high response to placebo. In the randomized controlled trials of SSRIs, these medications showed a definite improvement in mood symptoms. However, the individuals who received placebo showed almost the same degree of improvement (Wagner et al., 2003). This may speak to the fact that supportive management and recognition of illness are the most important features in recovery.

The FDA has approved fluoxetine for the treatment of child and adolescent depression. Three different randomized controlled studies were completed with this medication, and all were shown that individuals treated with this medication had improvement in mood compared to those on placebo. The first of these studies, conducted by Emslie et al. (1997), showed a particularly robust benefit of fluoxetine over placebo. It is still not clear if the benefit of fluoxetine over placebo is related to a unique feature of this medication or the way in which the studies were designed. Fluoxetine has a long half-life, which can be an important feature related to its positive response. Other SSRIs have been examined in adolescents, including paroxetine, sertraline, citalopram, and escitalopram, and the results were less conclusive. At times any of the above-described antidepressants can be chosen for treatment. Even when there is not FDA approval for a medication, if the psychiatrist sees a therapeutic reason to try an antidepressant, this can be done after gaining informed consent (see accompanying CD: 6.2).

One very important study compared fluoxetine, CBT, fluoxetine and CBT in combination, and placebo. This study occurred in several different areas of the country and was called the Treatment for Adolescents With Depression Study (TADS). A total of 439 adolescents participated, and 351 completed it 12 weeks later. The findings showed that the combination of fluoxetine and CBT showed the greatest improvement, followed by fluoxetine alone. CBT was more effective than placebo, but CBT was less effective than expected (TADS Team, 2004).

There have been a few studies that have assessed youth response to other classes of medications. There can be some improvement with the use of venlafaxine, nefazodone, and bupropion in adolescents with depression. However, there have not been any randomized controlled studies to date.

There are some mild side effects of antidepressants that can be experienced by children and adolescents. These common side effects tend to subside with time. These side effects include gastrointestinal distress, sleep changes (insomnia, somnolence, nightmares, or interrupted sleep), restlessness, headaches, or sexual dysfunction (see accompanying CD: 6.3).

More concerning side effects can emerge in about 5% of youth treated with antidepressants. These include impulsivity, agitation, irritability, and general "behavioral activation." If these side effects occur, they must be differentiated from mania. This cluster of side effects rarely disappears and is an indication to discontinue the medication.

The most significant potential side effect to antidepressants is suicidality. It has long been established that suicidal thinking occurs in the context of depression. It is also well-known that one of the greater time periods in which suicide completion can occur is early in treatment. As an episode of MDD resolves, energy and concentration typically improve faster than the hopelessness and sadness. This allows a window of risk where the individual remains hopeless but now has improved energy and concentration to be able to carry out a suicide plan. Initially, there was thought that the reports of suicidal thinking related to antidepressants were a product of the illness and not a result of the treatment. Concern continued to grow, and it became critical to try to differentiate the cause of reported suicidal thinking in youth.

The FDA in collaboration with Columbia University began to study the existing random controlled trials of antidepressants. At the time of this investigation, there were nine antidepressants that had been studied in 24 different studies, although not all of the studies were to assess the medication for depression. The investigators assessed the number of spontaneously reported suicidal ideations and behaviors. The suicide adverse event analysis showed an overall increased risk of suicidal ideation and suicidal behavior when the participants were treated with antidepressants. Despite the increase in the report of suicidal ideas, there were no suicide completions in the studies. After complex statistical measures were applied, it was reported that 11 times more youth will respond positively to an antidepressant than will spontaneously report suicidal thoughts (Bridge et al., 2007). It remains unclear if there are potential identifiers to help predict which youth might have an adverse response.

A final potential concerning side effect is that an antidepressant can cause an individual with depression to "switch" to mania. This mood change must be differentiated from the side effect of behavioral activation. If a mania occurs, the individual is more likely to develop bipolar disorder.

When an antidepressant is used in children or adolescents, a small starting dose is appropriate. The dose needs to be gradually titrated based on response, and there is some support to the fact that youth might need similar dosages to adults (Findling et al., 2006). It is believed that many antidepressants are metabolized more quickly in younger children. Therefore, it is possible that children can experience withdraw effects if the medications are given once daily. Withdraw effects can include pronounced irritability or agitation, headache, nausea, or in extreme cases an experience of "shooting nerve pains."

Antidepressants take 2 to 4 weeks to show benefit, so the dose might need to be titrated every 4 weeks based on response. It is also recommended that there be frequent monitoring for the emergence of suicidal thinking. The FDA has recommended weekly monitoring of suicidal thoughts during the first 4 weeks of treatment and then bimonthly monitoring after that. Also there should be weekly monitoring with each increase in dose.

If side effects are significant enough to warrant the discontinuation of the medication, it is recommended that this be done slowly to prevent withdraw side effects. Withdraw effects can begin as soon as 24 to 48 hours after discontinuation of the medication. These withdraw effects can include the appearance of a relapse of symptoms, tiredness, irritability, and somatic symptoms. Fluoxetine might be the exception to this rule. Because of its long half-life, this medication gradually self-tapers over 2 to 3 weeks.

Medications begin to improve depression within 2 to 4 weeks. Depending on the individual and depressive episode, there can be ongoing reduction in depressive symptoms for several months. When the individual identifies that the baseline has returned, it is recommended that medications be continued for 6 to 9 months to ensure a remission.

Clinical Case

Cindy was a 15-year-old female when she presented for a psychiatric evaluation in January. At the time of presentation, she had been refusing to attend school and had missed 25 days of school. She complained frequently of abdominal pain. She reported constant nausea and decreased appetite. Eating caused further distress. The family had pursued an extensive gastrointestinal work-up including endoscopy, and no physiological problem was identified. Despite this positive news, Cindy continued to have frequent abdominal distress. After Cindy's ongoing school refusal and unexplained somatic complaints, her pediatrician referred her for the evaluation.

A review of symptoms revealed that Cindy had become more isolated from peers before her nausea. She was also spending more time isolated in her room listening to what her parents called "dark" music. She was able to describe feeling sad, hopeless, and guilty. Significant stressors included Cindy's older sister moving to college shortly before Cindy's symptoms began and a breakup with her boyfriend over the summer. Her grades were poor, which was causing her distress because she was hoping to attend college. There was a family history of significant depression in her maternal grandmother and a maternal aunt.

Her mental status examination was consistent for appearing disheveled. She was attired in pajamas, having refused to dress for the appointment. She initially did not make eye contact and showed some mild psychomotor retardation. Her speech was normal in rate but quiet in volume. She described her mood as "miserable," and her affect was mood congruent and full ranged. Her thought form was clear and organized. There were no hallucinations or delusions. She expressed significant guilt and hopelessness. She endorsed frequently wishing she would die to escape the "pain of living" but denied any intention to harm herself.

I assessed that Cindy met criteria for a single episode of major depression, moderate. Because of the high degree of distress and functional impairment as seen by extensive school refusal, she and her parents opted to begin treatment with both medication and individual CBT. Fluoxetine 10 mg was initiated and well tolerated. Cindy began to explore her pattern of "all or nothing" thinking in CBT, and as she was able to modify her high expectations of herself, her guilt began to improve. Behavioral interventions included her parents encouraging her to socialize with peers on a weekly basis. A school intervention occurred to help Cindy gradually return to a full day of school over a 2-week time. One of her honor classes was replaced with an academic class, which she found helpful. Within 1 month of presentation, she reported that her symptoms were nearly fully resolved.

BIPOLAR DISORDER

Types and Characteristics

Just as depressive disorders exist on a spectrum, the same is true for bipolar disorder. The number of youth who have been diagnosed with bipolar disorder has increased over the past decade. Historically, bipolar disorder was thought not to exist in childhood and only rarely in adolescence. Some debate remains in the field of child and adolescent psychiatry as to the identification of juveniles with bipolar disorder. It is not yet clear if the childhood version of bipolar disorder is a separate diagnostic entity or if children who are diagnosed will continue to have symptoms in adulthood. However, over the past few years, there has been increasing consensus on the diagnosis of bipolar disorder. Currently, the criteria for diagnosing adults are applied to children and adolescents.

Bipolar disorder, Type 1 is the most severe illness within the bipolar disorder spectrum. To reach diagnostic threshold, the individual must have had one episode of MDD that lasted 2 weeks and one episode of mania that lasted 1 week. Mania is described by a distinct period where there is a persistent abnormality in mood. This mood abnormality can appear as elevated, expansive, or irritable mood. In addition to the mood change, there must be at least three of the following symptoms present for an individual to be diagnosed with mania: inflated self-esteem or grandiosity, decreased need for sleep, pressured speech, flight of ideas, distractibility, increased involvement in goal-directed activities or psychomotor agitation, and excessive involvement in pleasurable activities with a high potential for painful consequences (APA, 2000, p. 357). The elevated mood can initially be pleasant and productive, but over time it often becomes uncomfortable.

Moving down the spectrum is bipolar disorder, Type 2, which is less severe. This type of mood disorder is defined by at least one episode of major depression that lasted for 2 weeks and a 4-day period of hypomania. An episode of hypomania has similar symptoms as mania, but the disturbance is less severe and does not result in hospitalization (APA, 2000).

Adults with bipolar disorder tend to have episodes of depression and mania along with having a normal mood state. If more than four distinct episodes of depression exist in 1 year, then the individual is diagnosed with a rapid cycling variant of bipolar disorder. Another classification of the type of bipolar disorder is "ultra rapid cycling." This term is applied to individuals with more sudden changes in mood state. These individuals might not have 1 week of mania and 2 weeks of depression, as there can be rapid fluctuation between these two extreme mood states. A mixed episode is characterized by a week time during which criteria are met for both mania and depression nearly every day. Frequent agitation, insomnia, appetite dysregulation, psychotic features, and suicidal thinking are prominent. A person who has a mixed mood state tends to feel dysphoric and uncomfortable. Mixed states can occur spontaneously, or they can come at the end of an episode of mania or depression.

Another bipolar mood disorder on the spectrum in cyclothymia. In this type of mood disorder, there are distinct periods of dysthymia and distinct periods of hypomania. There is no time specified for either the dysthymic symptoms or the hypomanic symptoms, but the person must have never met criteria for an episode of major depression or mania (APA, 2000).

The least severe on the spectrum is bipolar disorder, NOS. It is the term that is used for subsyndromal changes in mood. It can be used when there is definite variability in mood but if there are not sufficient criteria to suggest a full-blown episode of MDD or mania. Many children are initially diagnosed with bipolar disorder, NOS, as childhood symptomatology often appears different in children than in adults.

Children and Adolescents

Juveniles are now recognized as having bipolar disorder. However, the characteristic pattern of the illness is slightly different. It is uncommon especially before puberty for there to be a sustained episode of mania that lasts 1 week. There might not be distinct episodes of depression or mania. Mania in childhood is characterized by more irritability, belligerence, and mixed states. Children with bipolar depression tend to have more anger, dysphoria, and conduct problems. Essentially, youth with bipolar disorder have constant difficulty regulating mood and behaviors. Children commonly have shorter times without mood symptoms, and in contrast to adults they more rarely display normal mood periods.

Bipolar disorder likely has a strong genetic component. There is an estimated four to six times higher chance of developing bipolar disorder if one family member has the same illness (Nurnberger & Foroud, 2000). In fact the understanding of juvenile bipolar disorder originated from surveys of adults with bipolar disorder who described mood shifts and behavioral dysregulation as children. However, caution must be taken not to assume that disruptive behavior in a child with a parent with bipolar disorder automatically has the same diagnosis.

Epidemiology and Comorbidity

It is estimated that the lifetime prevalence of bipolar disorder, Type 1 is 0.4% to 1.6% (AACAP, 2007b). However, broadening the bipolar disorder spectrum to include bipolar disorder, Type 2 and bipolar disorder, NOS, then the prevalence could increase to 6% (AACAP, 2007b). When questions were asked of adults with bipolar disorder, many adults identified mood symptoms in childhood. The majority of these symptoms were depression and irritability.

There is a high rate of comorbidity between bipolar disorder and behavioral disorders. ADHD and oppositional defiant disorder are also present and could have been the initial diagnosis identified. The diagnosis can be difficult, as medications to treat ADHD can cause irritability and explosiveness, which can mimic symptoms of mania.

If an individual presented first with an episode of depression such as MDD and subsequently developed a mixed state or a mania, the diagnosis changes to bipolar disorder. A person cannot be diagnosed with both a depressive disorder and a bipolar disorder.

Adolescents with bipolar disorder have a high risk of comorbid substance abuse. The use can be done to indirectly help stabilize moods, but the use often exacerbates the underlying mood shifts.

Evaluation

A psychiatric evaluation should routinely screen for symptoms consistent with mania and depression. Specifically, there should be an assessment of mood changes and mood dysregulation. It is important to inquire about sleep changes and psychomotor agitation during times of mood changes, as this can be the clinical picture of a youth with bipolar disorder. The illness is a distinct change from the person's baseline functioning and must be present in all areas of life. If the explosiveness and irritability occur only at home, this is less likely to be a true mood disorder and more likely represents a behavioral disorder.

The term bipolar disorder, NOS should be used as a diagnosis if there is evidence of mania but the duration is shorter than 4 days. In addition, this diagnosis should be used if the child has chronic manic-like symptoms as a baseline.

When bipolar disorder is suspected, there should be a careful assessment for comorbid difficulties. Adolescents particularly should be carefully screened for a substance abuse disorder. Medical problems should be considered. In addition, it should be carefully evaluated if the symptoms of mania have been induced by a medication, particularly an antidepressant.

The diagnostic validity of bipolar disorder has not been determined in preschool children, so there should be very careful consideration when using this diagnosis in very young children.

The Young Mania Rating Scale is an instrument used to assess the severity of mania in children ages 5 to 17 years. This scale is not meant to be a diagnostic tool alone, but it can often be useful in helping other clinicians determine if a psychiatric evaluation is needed. In addition, there is a parent version of this scale where the parent is asked 11 questions that help to clarify the child's mood state. This is another good screening tool, but it is associated with a high rate of false positives. In other words, elevated scores are not always consistent with a diagnosis of bipolar disorder (see accompanying CD: 6.4).

Psychotherapy Treatment

When mania is present the primary treatment should include medication. However, supportive psychotherapy is an important component in the treatment of early onset bipolar disorder. The first goal of this intervention is to provide psychoeducation to both the parents and the youth. There should be a clear description about the chronic course of this illness. Understanding how poorly regulated mood states can lead to poorly regulated behavior is helpful for parents to understand. Educational support might be needed, as irregular mood states can have an implication on learning. It is important for all individuals with a diagnosis of bipolar disorder to share this information with schools to allow appropriate supportive services.

The next focus of supportive therapy is on relapse prevention. The importance of compliance with medication is stressed. In addition, understanding the stressors that can trigger mood dysregulation should be explored, and alternative strategies to handle difficult situations with these stressors should be emphasized.

As with the treatment of depressive disorders, CBT and IPT are the most commonly used individual therapeutic strategies. There is increasing exploration into family therapy for another treatment intervention. There have been a few preliminary positive studies that have used a combination of individual and family CBT.

Medication

The use of medication in juveniles with bipolar disorder has several considerations. If acute mania is present, a mood stabilizer is indicated. If depression is present in the context of an individual with known bipolar disorder, there can be consideration for the addition of a very low dose of an antidepressant. This should be carefully monitored to ensure that it is not triggering a mixed or manic state. If ADHD is comorbid with bipolar disorder, a stimulant can be considered after it is certain that the mood has been stabilized with an antidepressant.

The mood stabilizer with the longest history is lithium. Lithium has been a known treatment for mania in adults since the 1950s. In its natural state it is an element with properties similar to those of sodium. Its mechanism of action is to disrupt the sodium channels of the neurons, which has in indirect effect on serotonin and tryptophan.

Common side effects of lithium include drowsiness, fine hand tremor, dry mouth, gastrointestinal distress, and weight gain. Lithium is associated with a narrow therapeutic margin. The blood levels must be carefully monitored because there is a small difference between too little and too much of this medication. Dehydration must be avoided, as this can increase the blood concentration of lithium. If the amount of lithium becomes too high, significant toxicity can occur. Signs of toxicity include confusion, unsteady gait, extreme fatigue, severe diarrhea, seizure, and coma. Lithium can also be lethal in overdose. Another potential long-term side effect of lithium is the development of thyroid problems (see accompanying CD: 6.5).

Lithium is approved in children over the age of 12 years. There have been a few randomized controlled studies of lithium conducted that support that it is effective for reducing the symptoms of mania in juveniles. Lithium is an effective medication. However, unless the family system is stable and can be involved in monitoring this medication, it should be avoided because of its potential toxicity and lethality.

A second category of mood stabilizers in adults was first designed to treat seizures. Common medications in this class that are used in adults are valproic acid, carbamazepine, lamotrigine, and gabapentin. As with the pharmacologic treatment of child and adolescent depression, the research support for mood stabilizers is less advanced than the support for treating adults with medication.

Today, there no randomized controlled trials of valproic acid in juvenile mania. However, a number of studies have shown this medication to be helpful particularly in combination with other medications. However, there is support through open trials and case review that it is effective. Valproic acid has significant side effects, but it is considered safer medication than lithium because it has a wider therapeutic margin. Valproic acid is associated with minor side effects including diarrhea, dizziness, drowsiness, and ringing ears. It has also been associated with hair loss, a side effect that can sometimes be countered by the ingestion of zinc. Potentially more serious side effects include bleeding problems, chest pain, and liver abnormalities. It is recommended that liver function and blood counts be monitored regularly. In addition, females exposed to Depakote in childhood and teen years can experience menstrual irregularities or polycystic ovary disease (see accompanying CD: 6.6).

Another antiepileptic drug, lamotrigine, can be helpful in treating adolescent depression associated with bipolar disorder according to preliminary research. This medication also has a potentially serious side effect, which is the development of a severe rash called Stevens–Johnson syndrome. This side effect is known to occur more commonly in individuals under the age of 16 years. It can also occur if the starting dose is too high or if the dose is escalated too rapidly. Other less concerning side effects include dizziness, headache, drowsiness, diarrhea, and nervousness.

Carbamazepine is another antiepileptic drug that is helpful in treating adult bipolar disorder. It is occasionally used in youth. Its use is complicated in part by its effect on the liver, which causes interactions with other medication that can be used. Like lamotrigine it is associated with a potential rash, which can be severe. In addition, it can suppress a person's bone marrow, which can be life threatening.

The atypical antipsychotics are another category of mood stabilizers, and there is emerging evidence that they also are effective in adults. Clinically, this class of medications is commonly used in children despite little research support. There have been open trials of Risperdal and olanzapine used in juveniles with good success. One double-blind study showed that mania symptoms improved when quetiapine was added to valproic acid. This class of medications will be covered in more detail in the chapter on psychotic disorders.

Clinically, it is recognized that juveniles do better on a combination of mood stabilizers than on one medication alone. Common combinations can include lithium combined with an antiepileptic medication, two antiepileptic medications, and lithium or an antiepileptic medication combined with an atypical antipsychotic. In addition, medications might need to be adjusted or changed frequently to maintain effectiveness, particularly early in treatment. It is also clear that most of the mood stabilizers have potentially serious side effects. As a class these medications need to be used when clinically indicated, but they must be monitored very closely. In addition, in the spring of 2009, the FDA stated that all antiepileptic drugs must also come with a warning that they can contribute to increased thoughts of suicide.

Mood stabilizers do a poor job of ameliorating symptoms of depression. Antidepressants can be added to the pharmacologic regimen once the person is no longer in a manic or mixed mood state, although this should be done cautiously. This needs to be done with close observations, as antidepressants can trigger a mood switch to mania. It can be prudent to discontinue the antidepressant once the depression has cleared to minimize the risk of this mood switch.

The treatment of bipolar disorder and ADHD has been controversial. Some preliminary studies suggested that boys with ADHD who were later diagnosed with bipolar disorder did not show a different response to treatment with stimulants (Carlson, Loney, Salisbury, & Kramer, 2000). Other studies and case reports that have subsequently been conducted suggest that stimulants can trigger mania and should be avoided until the youth's mood has been stabilized with a mood stabilizer. In addition, it was found that stabilizing a mood with valproic acid was beneficial prior to initiating stimulants (Scheffer & Niskala Apps, 2004).

Clinical Case

Jack was a 6-year-old boy who was referred for a psychiatric evaluation by his school district. Jack was completing kindergarten and had had a very difficult year. His parents described that he was a generally happy and compliant preschool child. He interacted well with peers and was noted within his day care setting to be advanced in his learning and interactions with others. For the first few weeks of kindergarten, Jack did well. However, he began to become increasingly explosive. Some days he would enter the classroom smiling and interacting well with peers. Other days he entered the building in what appeared to be an irritable mood. On the irritable days, any small trigger would cause verbal and physical outbursts. The classroom needed to be cleared on several occasions because of Jack's throwing large items around the room.

His parents reported that over the past 8 months, Jack was increasingly irritable at home. He would cry quickly. He was less cooperative with parental requests. In addition, he would have times of prolonged energy where he would run without stopping. He was not sleeping as well as before, and on two occasions he did not sleep during the night. His parents also described that for several days, he would "seem back to himself" but then without a clear precipitant he would become aggressive and irritable. They were increasingly reluctant to take him places, as his responses were so unpredictable.

There were no medical problems identified. The family unit was intact and appeared to be functioning well. There were no acute stressors identified. Jack's father and paternal aunt had both been diagnosed with bipolar disorder. Jack's paternal grandmother had been institutionalized with an unknown mental illness, but there was a belief that she too had bipolar disorder.

Jack's mental status examination was significant for a neatly groomed young boy who appeared his stated age. He was in constant motion during the interview, often rolling from one side of the room to the other. With prompting he was able to sit still for a few moments. His speech was rapid and at times difficult to understand because of its speed (pressured). He described his mood as "awesome." However, his affect was labile, shifting from silliness to sullenness in a way that was mood incongruent. He denied wanting to die and stated "I'm going to live forever" in response to this inquiry.

Because of Jack's pressured speech, decreased need for sleep, grandiosity, and irritability, a diagnosis of bipolar disorder, NOS was given. That this represented such a distinct difference from his earlier functioning helped.

Jack's father had been stabilized for 5 years on Depakote. After reviewing potential treatment options, the family elected to have Jack participate in a partial hospitalization program to initiate this medication under close observation. He was started on Depakote, and the dose was gradually increased to a therapeutic level. Educational recommendations were forthcoming from the program and included having Jack participate in a therapeutic emotional support classroom where he could continue with more intensive therapeutic services.

I saw Jack the following fall in first grade. Although his mood is occasionally irritable and he occasionally became excessively angered, there was a dramatic improvement in his mood and behavioral regulation.

MOOD DISORDERS: EDUCATIONAL IMPLICATIONS

Students with mood disorders can present with interesting educational challenges. Typically, either depression or mania represents a distinct change in the student's mood state. Either mood state can be associated with irritability, tears, poor concentration, and lowered frustration tolerance. Mania can be associated with grandiosity and reckless behaviors. When a student presents in an altered mood state, attending to the details of academic work can be difficult.

Students with depressive disorders can have difficulty attending school. There are often somatic complaints that occur and can be used as the reason to miss school. There can be significant social withdraw and severe difficulty completing tasks. Students with depressive disorders need encouragement to stay engaged with others and need gentle but firm support from adults. Teachers must balance academic demands with reasonable expectations. A student with depression should not be allowed to avoid work, but a high intensity of academic pressure can worsen the depressive symptoms. Offering support through teachers or the guidance office can naturally help the symptoms, as support and reflective listening are helpful therapeutic interventions.

Students with bipolar disorder tend to cause more behavioral disruptions. The mood states change more frequently, and there is a higher likelihood of significant behavioral problems associated with this disorder. In addition, as bipolar disorder is more often a chronic mental illness, the educational difficulties can be more pronounced and longer lived. These students often need intensive educational supports and an individualized education program may be necessary to provide a high level of educational and therapeutic supports.

MOOD DISORDERS: SUMMARY

Children and adolescents can have mood disorders. These disorders have characteristics similar to those of adult mood disorders but can cause significant delay in development and significant social impairment. There are biological contributors through temperament and genetics that can predispose the person to this illness. Psychological and social stressors can then contribute in such a way that the mood symptoms occur. They can be helped with supportive therapy or other more intensive therapeutic interventions. In addition, medication management can be critical in further resolving the symptoms.

Seven

Anxiety Disorders

ANXIETY DISORDERS: INTRODUCTION

Fear and worry are common in children. For fear to be considered a clinical disorder, its intensity must be greater than what would be expected for a child of a similar developmental level, and there must be noted impairment because of the fear. The nature of an anxiety disorder is that the fear is irrational. However, children with anxiety disorders often do not realize that their fears are out of proportion or irrational. Somatic complaints such as headache or nausea are frequent in children who are excessively anxious. Anxiety disorders can cause behavior problems and physical problems. Intense fears can cause a child not to engage in an activity or can cause a tantrum so the behavior can look oppositional when the true cause for refusal is the internal fear. Anxiety disorders disrupt normal psychological development. They can prevent normal periods of separation from family members. They can have significant associated morbidity. There can be severe social or academic impairment associated with the fears. Typically, poor social skills and a negative self-concept develop (American Academy of Child and Adolescent Psychiatry [AACAP], 2007a).

The development of anxiety disorders is complex. Anxiety disorders are known to cluster in families. This is related to both a genetic component and an environmental component. A child may observe a parent have an anxious response to a particular situation and then model it. In addition to genetic and familial factors, temperamental characteristics are also a factor. Children who are more temperamentally inhibited are more likely to develop anxiety. Attachment and parenting styles can also heighten the risk or minimize the risk. Children who are insecurely attached to a parent may not develop resources to solve problems with fears. An overly strict, excessively protective, or controlling parenting style can contribute to anxiety.

Several of the anxiety disorders have common presentations and will be reviewed together. These include generalized anxiety disorder, separation anxiety disorder, social phobia, specific phobia, and panic disorder. Each of these disorders will be described separately, but because of common patterns, the evaluation and treatment for these will be summarized together. Two distinct anxiety disorders are obsessive-compulsive disorder and post-traumatic stress disorder. Because of the unique features of both disorders, these two disorders will be reviewed separately from the others for the purpose of this book.

There are two additional diagnoses that are not technically considered anxiety disorders according the *DSM-IV-TR* but are often considered to have some component of anxiety. These are selective mutism and trichotillomania. Selective mutism is recognized by an individual's failure to speak in specific social situations. This causes interference with academic functioning and occurs for more than 1 month. The inability to speak is not due to a lack of knowledge or comfort with the language (American Psychiatric Association [APA], 2000, p. 127). Children who have a diagnosis of selective mutism can also be excessively shy and clingy and demonstrate controlling behavior at home. This is generally recognized as an uncommon disorder, and although it is not considered an anxiety disorder by description, it is thought the reason behind the failure to speak is fear. Treatment interventions are similar to those of other anxiety disorders.

Trichotillomania, according to the *DSM* system, is classified as an impulse control disorder. This disorder is described as a recurrent pattern of an individual pulling out his or her hair. Many children and adolescents who engage in this behavior are noted to be anxious, and the act of pulling out hair can be self-soothing. Treatment interventions for anxiety disorders can help with the reduction of behavior.

GENERALIZED ANXIETY DISORDER

Characteristics

The core feature of generalized anxiety disorder (GAD) is excessive worry that occurs for more days than not for at least 6 months. The worry is about a number of events or activities, and the person finds it difficult to control the worry. There must also be one of the following symptoms present in children: being restless, being easily fatigued, having difficulty concentrating, being irritable, having muscle tension, or having disturbed sleep (APA, 2000, p. 476). In prior editions of the *DSM*, there was a separate diagnosis called overanxious disorder of childhood, but with the *DSM-IV* this diagnosis was made similar to GAD.

Children with GAD worry about a variety of areas such as relationships, upcoming events, money, performance in activities, or the future. The worry is persistent and difficult to control. Children with GAD are perfectionistic and frequently seek reassurance. They can also be inhibited and fearful to try new things.

This diagnosis should be made cautiously in children after being certain that no more specific anxiety disorder is present. The feature that distinguishes this anxiety disorder from the others is that there are numerous fears and worries, and these can change frequently depending on the situation.

Course

GAD has a chronic and fluctuating course. It can present at any age, and the history often suggests that children with GAD were inhibited and fearful from toddlerhood. It is also common for this disorder to worsen in times of stress. This disorder can cause significant impairment in all areas of functioning, as the child or adolescent can become reluctant to engage in activities.

SEPARATION ANXIETY DISORDER

Characteristics

Youth with separation anxiety disorder (SAD) experience excessive anxiety about separation from the home or from those to whom they are attached. This fear must last for at least 4 weeks and cause clinically significant distress in areas of functioning. When the individual must separate from an attachment figure, he or she often needs to know the adult's exact whereabouts. The individual becomes excessively homesick and becomes preoccupied with reunion (APA, 2000, p. 125).

Children and teens with SAD have difficulty thinking about things other than their fears that something negative will happen to them or their parents when they are separated from them. They might be unable to leave the home, particularly if not in the presence of a parent. This fear can first become apparent as school refusal. Children are unable to stay at another person's home. The distress can be present even in their own home if the parent is not in the same room, and children might follow the parent throughout the house. Simple reassurance that no harm will happen does not provide relief. This particular anxiety disorder can cause significant academic difficulties, particularly when school refusal is a piece of the clinical presentation.

Course

SAD can develop after life stress such as serious illness, a move, or death. It can be present as early as preschool age or at any time through childhood. It is uncommon to present as a new onset by late adolescence (APA, 2000, p. 121).

In young children the fears are more commonly nonspecific and difficult to articulate. Most often they simply say, "I'm scared." With children's increased age, the fear becomes more focused. Children might report they are afraid the parent might die or be kidnapped. Adolescent fears are also specific and more complex. Many children with SAD are able to be anxiety free in adulthood. However, some youth with SAD can develop panic disorder with increased age (AACAP, 2007a).

SOCIAL PHOBIA

Characteristics

Social phobia is characterized by an individual's feeling uncomfortable and scared in social settings or performance situations. The worry is related to the fear of doing something embarrassing. Exposure to a social or performance situation provokes an immediate anxiety response. Significant efforts are made to avoid the anxiety-provoking situation. Sometimes the refusal can be subtle, but other times dramatic opposition can appear. Children do not need to recognize the fear as excessive, but a criteria for adolescents and adults is that the worry is recognized as greater than the situation should warrant (APA, 2000, p. 456).

These children might be unable to speak in front of the class and avoid raising their hands. They can be reluctant to talk to adults or peers. Young children can appear excessively timid or shy in social situations. They might cry, freeze, have tantrums, or cling to a known person in an unfamiliar setting. To have a social phobia, children must demonstrate anxiety with peers and adults. However, they must demonstrate an ability to form relationships with others, which is an important distinction between social phobia and a pervasive developmental disorder. This is differentiated from SAD, as individuals with SAD fear separation, whereas individuals with social phobia fear embarrassment and being in the center of attention.

Course

The most common age of onset for social phobia is the mid-teen years, although there can be a childhood history of social shyness beginning in early childhood. Without treatment the course of social phobia is chronic. With the individual's advancing age, it can cause significant impairment in interacting with other people. As with other anxiety disorders, social phobia worsens during times of stress.

SPECIFIC PHOBIA

Characteristics

A specific phobia is similar to social phobia except the feared object is not a social or performance situation. Significant efforts are made to avoid the phobic object. Children can express the anxiety by crying, having tantrums, freezing, or clinging. If there is contact with the feared object, there is significant anxiety and worry. In adolescents there is a recognition that the fear is excessive. Some examples of phobias include animals (dogs), the natural environment (storms), blood, or a specific situation (pool) (APA, 2000, p. 449).

Course

To make a diagnosis of a specific phobia, the clinician must be certain that the fear is more than what can be expected for the developmental age. For example, young school-age children can be afraid of the dark or insects, but if this fear is not interfering with functioning or causing significant distress, the diagnosis should not be given.

Depending on what object is feared, there can be either small or significant functional impairment. The intensity of the feared object can diminish with age. In subtle cases there might not even be an awareness that the person has a phobia.

PANIC DISORDER

Characteristics

A panic attack is a discrete episode of an excessively anxious response. There are four or more somatic symptoms that develop abruptly and reach a peak within 10 minutes. These symptoms include heart palpitations, sweating, trembling, shortness of breath, feeling of choking, chest pain, nausea, dizziness, derealization, fear of losing control, fear of dying, paresthesias, and chills or hot flushes. A panic attack can occur in response to exposure to a specific event, or it can occur without any warning. During the brief time it is present, the intensity is quite high (APA, 2000, p. 432).

Panic disorder is diagnosed when there are both recurrent panic attacks and a fear that a panic attack will occur again. The duration of the fear must be 1 month. Individuals with panic disorder also report a general high degree of anxiety that is not associated with the fear of a recurrent panic attack, although this is not diagnostic. In addition, because of the intensity of physical symptoms, individuals with panic disorder often believe that there is an unrecognized medical illness that is responsible for these bodily symptoms (APA, 2000, p. 440).

Course

Panic disorder becomes more common after puberty. It can be related to exposure to a single stressor, or the first panic attack can occur out of the blue. In some cases the course is very severe and can result in agoraphobia, where the person is afraid to leave the house because of a fear of experiencing a panic attack in a place from which escape is not possible.

ANXIETY DISORDERS

Epidemiology and Comorbidity

It has been difficult to establish the true prevalence of each of the above anxiety disorders. However, as a group these anxiety disorders have a prevalence of 6% to 20% over several large epidemiological studies (Costello, Egger, & Angold, 2004). Girls are more likely than boys to identify symptoms of anxiety.

Many of the anxiety disorders exist with each other, and the presence of one anxiety disorder in childhood can increase the likelihood of the development of another later in life. For example, many late adolescents who have panic disorder may have had SAD as a child. Clinically, it is not uncommon to see an increase in anxiety as puberty approaches. Following the completion of this phase of life, the anxiety can decrease.

Each of the anxiety disorders can also be present with mood disorders. In some situations the mood disorder is the reason for the initial clinical referral, and during treatment for the mood disorder, an anxiety disorder is found. Treatment of the anxiety disorder increases the success for treatment of the mood disorder.

Anxiety disorders can also be diagnosed during the assessment of a behavioral disorder or attention-deficit/hyperactivity disorder (ADHD). Children can be disruptive or appear inattentive when they are really preoccupied with internal anxiety. Anxiety disorder is common in children with ADHD. The MTA Cooperative Group (2001) found that as many as one third of children with ADHD have co-occurring anxiety disorders. Anxiety is a difficult symptom for adults to recognize, as with many of these disorders, there is a need to appear perfect, and the children can work very hard to keep the symptoms masked.

Evaluation

It is a clinical standard of care that all children and adolescents who are undergoing a psychiatric evaluation be screened for anxiety disorders. This screening can occur with questions to elicit fears, worries, or phobias. Alternatively, some clinicians prefer to use screening questionnaires to learn the same information. Two examples of these screening tools are the Hamilton Anxiety Scale, and the Screen for Child Anxiety Related Disorders (SCARED). However, these tools like other screening tools are useful sources of information but should not be the only source provided. If there seems to be a high level of anxiety, there should be more thorough investigation of the type, nature, and duration of the fears.

Parents can provide information regarding behavior and observation of the reaction when the child is exposed to a fear. Parents are often better informants regarding the impact the fears have on daily life. The child or adolescent is the person who must be able to provide the most information regarding internal thoughts. Children are often able to better express their fears by playing, and if anxiety is highly suspected in younger children, a play assessment can provide much more useful clinical information. In addition, helping the child to rate the fears subjectively on a scale of 1 to 10 can provide more insight into the amount of distress that is experienced. When anxiety is present, there should be a careful assessment of any underlying trauma that might have triggered the response.

There should also be a careful review for the presence of other psychiatric disorders, and it should be ensured that there are no other disorders present that can mimic anxiety. For example, individuals with Asperger's disorder are socially awkward and often withdrawn, but the core of this difficulty is not fear. There can be a consideration to screen for medical disorders such as hyperthyroidism, migraines, and caffeine intoxication, which all have symptoms that can mimic anxiety. In addition, some medications, particularly the stimulants that can be prescribed to treat ADHD, can exacerbate anxiety.

Therapeutic Principles

The treatment interventions for anxiety should be based on the type and severity of symptoms. Anxiety disorders that are causing little impairment might need reassurance, but those that are causing significant impairment might require a combination of medication and therapy. The combination treatment approach is needed to reduce anxiety in a severely anxious child. Additionally, the combination treatment approach can be used if there has been only a partial response to therapy alone. In addition, the presence of anxiety with a comorbid condition can require a combination approach.

Psychoeducation is often a critical part of the treatment. Both the youth and the family must understand that anxiety is the primary problem and must understand the youth's symptoms of anxiety. Reassurance that there are no underlying physical illnesses can be helpful. This must be explained in a way that does not place more blame on the youth for the problem. It is also helpful for the parents to understand that rational explanations for why the fear will not come true do not promote a permanent relief of anxiety.

Psychotherapy Treatment

For the general psychotherapeutic treatment of anxiety disorders, exposure-based cognitive behavioral therapy (CBT) has the most research support (Compton et al., 2004). Numerous double-blind studies have shown it to be more effective than wait-list control groups, but to date there are no randomized controlled treatment studies comparing CBT to other therapeutic interventions. However, most clinicians believe that CBT is the most effective therapeutic intervention. Some predictors for less robust benefit from CBT include a high severity of anxiety symptoms and older age at presentation (Barrett, Dadds, & Rapee, 1996).

There are five strategies that are used in CBT to treat children with anxiety disorders. The first step is psychoeducation. Both the parent and the child are taught about the illness, and steps are introduced to externalize the illness. The second step involves teaching skills to reduce the somatic symptoms. These skills include relaxation strategies, deep breathing, and self-monitoring. Next, cognitive restructuring techniques are taught and practiced. This includes challenging negative thoughts and modifying negative self-talk. The fourth step includes gradual exposure to the feared item. This initially occurs by imaginative exposure and moves to full exposure while using the relaxation strategies. The final stage of CBT includes relapse prevention, which can require booster sessions to review the strategies (Albano & Kendall, 2002).

Sessions using CBT are a combination of individual sessions and parent sessions. The parents are taught the same skills so they can help the child practice the steps at home. Depending on the specific type of anxiety, different components are emphasized.

Many clinicians use CBT strategies in a flexible way to treat anxiety disorders. When this approach is taken, there can be gradual modifications for the individual need of the child and family. However, there are also manualized versions of CBT that can be more effective for some individuals. One version, called the Coping Cat Program, has received empirical support (Kendall, 1990) to treat SAD, GAD, and social phobias (see accompanying CD: 7.1).

CBT has also been shown to be helpful in treating school refusal associated with SAD. However, the combination of CBT and educational supports are often more successful than CBT alone.

When treating specific phobia, CBT is the preferred treatment method, but there is much more emphasis placed on the gradual exposure to the feared object. Children do not respond well to abrupt exposure. For example, if the feared item is a dog, the clinician will first practice relaxation strategies while the child imagines a dog. If this is well tolerated, the next step can be to look at a cartoon dog, followed by looking at a picture of a dog, followed by watching a dog on TV, followed by viewing a service dog from a distance, and continuing to gradually move to petting a dog.

Treatment of social phobia is similar to the other CBT treatment principles, but there should also be emphasis on social skills. Individuals who are socially anxious might not have developed appropriate tools to initiate and maintain a conversation with others, and increased comfort with these skills can also help to lower the anxiety.

When CBT is used to treat panic disorder, there is more emphasis on relaxation strategies and self-monitoring. When the individual begins to perceive that there are good resources for managing the somatic symptoms of a panic attack, there may be less fear of a recurrent attack.

CBT is an effective intervention for both the acute reduction of symptoms and longer term symptom resolution. However, structured CBT programs may not be available in all communities. Many therapists can initiate the CBT principles, and this may be effective. As described above, if there are numerous anxiety symptoms present, CBT alone may be ineffective. In these situations, using some CBT principles in conjunction with other therapeutic interventions may be more helpful.

Alternatively, some clinicians prefer to use psychodynamic therapy to reduce anxiety. In psychodynamic theory, anxiety is understood as an internal signal of distress and conflict. The goal of treatment is to return the anxiety to a functioning level. The clinician works with the child to understand the underlying psychological conflicts, and the awareness of these conflicts reduces anxiety. There has been some support for the effectiveness of this treatment, but it is more difficult to consistently implement and has not been as rigorously studied (Lis, Zennaro, & Mazzeschi, 2001).

The involvement of the parents in the treatment of anxiety disorders is very important. As described earlier, there are genetic and parenting factors and patterns of interactions that may be maintaining the symptoms of anxiety. Parents are used in CBT approaches. However, a broad family therapy approach can also be a helpful therapeutic treatment. When family therapy is used, the emphasis is taken off the child, and the focus becomes the family interactions and how these may be contributing to the symptoms.

Medication

When medications are indicated, the preferred class is the SSRI antidepressants (see accompanying CD: 6.2). There have been randomized placebo-controlled trials that support the efficacy of SSRIs for selective mutism with social anxiety (Black & Uhde, 1994), GAD, social phobia, and SAD (Birmaher et al., 2003; Research Units on Pediatric Psychopharmacology Anxiety Study Group, 2001; Rynn, Siqueland, & Rickels, 2001; Wagner et al., 2004).

Generally, this class of medications is well tolerated in children and adolescents. However, the same concerns exist when SSRIs are used for anxiety as when they are used for the treatment of depression. There must be caution and close monitoring to ensure that suicidal thoughts are not emerging early in treatment. These medications are ultimately helpful at reducing the symptoms of anxiety. However, early in treatment if the dose is not started very low and increased in small increments, there can be a worsening of the anxiety symptoms.

As with the treatment of depression, the benefit to the SSRIs can take several weeks to recognize. The child and family must look for small improvements gradually, or there will be frustration and a lower likelihood of compliance.

Other antidepressants such as venlafaxine or clomipramine have shown some benefit in treating adolescent anxiety disorders, but there is less research support, and these medications have similar potential side effects.

Adults benefit from short-term use of a class of medications called the benzodiazepines. Some common examples of benzodiazepines include lorazepam (Ativan), alprazolam (Xanax), and clonazepam (Klonopin). These medications work quickly with the first dose of medications. There is no support for the long-term use of these medications in children and teens, although in some clinical situations, using these medications briefly while waiting for the SSRI to work can be indicated. There must be caution used when these are prescribed, as they can be associated with misuse and dependence. In addition, younger children can have an idiosyncratic response and become disinhibited and hyperactive when given this class of medication.

There is a nonbenzodiazepine medication called buspirone (Buspar) that is approved to treat GAD in adults. This medication primarily reduces anxiety after it has been taken consistently for several weeks. It can sometimes be used in children and adolescents, but with additional other SSRI antidepressants, it is less commonly used than it was in the past.

POST-TRAUMATIC STRESS DISORDER

Characteristics

Individuals who are diagnosed with post-traumatic stress disorder (PTSD) have developed a characteristic pattern of symptoms following exposure to an extreme stressor. By definition the stressor must involve direct personal exposure to a threatened serious injury; threat to physical integrity; witnessing an event that involves death, injury, or threat to another person; or learning about the violent death of someone else. The response following the stressor involves fear, helplessness, or horror. In children the response may be recognized as disorganized behavior. There must be a pattern of reexperiencing the trauma such as intrusive memories, flashbacks, or nightmares. There must be avoidance and a pattern of numbing of responsiveness when thinking about the event. This can be recognized as the avoidance of activities that cause memory of the trauma and inability to recall important aspects of the trauma, detachment from others, and a sense of a foreshortened future. Finally, there must be symptoms of increased arousal such as difficulty falling asleep, irritability, difficulty concentrating, or hypervigilance. These full symptoms must be present for 1 month (APA, 2000, p. 463).

Frequently, the individual experiences guilt about surviving, particularly if other individuals died in the event. There can be impaired regulation of mood and self-destructive behavior. Some examples of self-destructive behavior can include cutting or putting oneself in dangerous situations. Mood difficulties are most often seen by rapid shifts in mood and a sense of general unhappiness. Internally, the youth may experience shame, despair, and hostility. It is not uncommon that the individual who has PTSD has impaired relationships with others.

PTSD became recognized as a clinical entity in the 1980s, although there is a long history of case reports with similar symptoms. Freud used the term "hysterical neurosis" to imply a similar cluster of symptoms. The first modern-day recognition of these symptoms came from military personnel who fought in the Vietnam War. Initially, it was not believed that children could be affected with PTSD, as children tend to repress negative memories. However, many individuals contributed information to describe that children can experience PTSD symptoms, but the disorder can appear different. The *DSM-IV-TR* now notes that children can initially show disorganized or agitated behavior in response to a traumatic event. Children can demonstrate persistent reexperiencing of the trauma by repetitive play, through nightmares of unrecognizable content, or through trauma-specific reenactment (APA, 2000, p. 468).

Epidemiology and Comorbidity

There is believed to be a lifetime prevalence of PTSD of 8% (APA, 2000, p. 466). However, this statistic is difficult to understand, and it might be more helpful to determine what percentage of individuals who are exposed to a traumatic event develop PTSD. Studies of children who have been exposed to trauma suggest prevalence rates from 3% (Garrison et al., 1995) to 100% (Frederick, 1985).

There are three factors that are associated with the development of PTSD in children. The severity of the trauma is likely to be a significant factor, with a more severe experience being more likely to develop PTSD. The worse the stressor, the more likely one is to develop PTSD. The parents' response to the trauma and any distress they may experience from the event is also important. If the parent is also experiencing fear, guilt, or distress, the child is more likely to develop symptoms. Finally, the closer to the event, the more likely a child will have PTSD (Foy, Madvig, Pynoos, & Camilleri, 1996).

It is estimated that 50% of children who have been physically abused will develop PTSD (A. H. Green, 1985). In addition, it has been found that 44% of sexually abused children met full criteria for PTSD (McLeer, Deblinger, Henry, & Orvashal, 1992).

PTSD can occur in conjunction with other anxiety disorders. There is some belief that temperamentally highly anxious children may be more susceptible to developing PTSD. In addition, a high percentage of youth with PTSD can also have depressive disorders.

Interestingly, there is an overlap between ADHD and PTSD. Individuals with PTSD may first be diagnosed with ADHD because of disruptive and aggressive behaviors that can really be the reexperiencing symptoms. It is also possible that children with ADHD are more difficult to parent and thus can be at an increased risk of being mistreated, which can result in PTSD. Particularly for new onset ADHD symptoms, a very careful history may distinguish the two.

Finally, there is comorbidity between PTSD and borderline personality disorder. Some individuals who have been abused may develop borderline personality disorder as recognized by a pattern of instability of relationships, self-image, and marked impulsivity. Not everyone who has been abused develops borderline personality disorder, and not all individuals with borderline personality disorder have been abused, but there is a high degree of comorbidity between the two.

Course

There must be a clearly recognizable traumatic event for an individual to be diagnosed with PTSD. This event must be outside of normal childhood experiences. For example, physical abuse and sexual abuse are both considered significant stressors. In addition, witnessing horrific violence is a significant stressor. Experiencing a sad event, like the nonviolent death of a family member or divorce, would not qualify for this disorder, as these are not considered traumatic. If there is an anxious reaction to sad events, the diagnosis of adjustment disorder, anxious type is given.

PTSD symptoms typically begin within the first 3 months of the trauma. If the symptoms occur within the first month, a diagnosis of acute stress disorder is given. Once started, the symptoms can continue for a few months, but depending on the nature of the trauma, reexperiencing symptoms can have a chronic course.

Evaluation

Careful history must be gathered from a number of sources to make a diagnosis of PTSD. Parents can report the traumatic event and are often helpful in describing the child's initial response to the stressor. They can also provide information regarding the reexperiencing symptoms that may be evident as seen by nightmares and repeated play of the trauma. The child must also be evaluated individually. In this section of the evaluation, the examiner must have the child explain in his or her words what was seen. Although this might not be able to be done in the first evaluation session, there should be efforts made to have the child tell the story to ensure that the child does not have memories that others do not believe he or she has. The child should also be allowed access to dolls or toys to use in telling the story. There should be careful observation of the way in which the story is told and the affect that the child displays.

There can be a tendency to overdiagnose PTSD in children and teens. Sometimes the diagnosis can be given if a youth is acting in a negative manner after having been exposed to a disturbing event. The clinician should make sure that there are symptoms consistent with reexperiencing, numbing, and hyperarousal before the diagnosis is given.

Therapeutic Principles

There is less robust literature to support interventions for youth with PTSD. Acute traumatic events such as earthquakes or hurricanes can lead to a larger population to assess and treat. However, this type of event can have a different treatment course when compared to a chronic stressor such as repeated sexual or physical abuse.

Some basic premises are believed to be important to the treatment of PTSD. Direct exploration of the trauma such as allowing the child to retell the story is believed to be a useful intervention. Teaching relaxation and coping strategies to manage the reexperiencing symptoms is also important. Parental support is instrumental, and depending on the nature of the stressor, the parent may also need treatment.

Psychotherapy Treatment

As with other anxiety disorders, many of the principles of CBT can be applied and used in the treatment of PTSD. A number of randomized controlled studies show that this type of treatment is effective at reducing the distress when compared to wait-list controls.

One study (Deblinger, Lippman, & Steer, 1996) used CBT with a trauma focus to treat 100 sexually abused children. In this study the treatment arms included child only CBT, parent only CBT, and child and parent receiving CBT or community treatment. All four groups improved, but the benefit was greater when the child received CBT either alone or with the parent.

The therapist must be prepared to discuss the trauma for the symptoms to improve. Play techniques can be a useful start to a younger child telling the story. Efforts should be made not to force the youth to tell all details in one setting, but helping the event be articulated is very important. Depending on the nature of the trauma, there can be some reluctance to have a victim of sexual abuse retell the story until there has been legal intervention. There is concern that children's memory is suggestible, and with therapeutic intervention the details can be altered. However, a savvy clinician is aware of this and will encourage the child to tell of the event in his or her own words without suggesting any information.

It can be important for the clinician to teach some CBT skills before beginning to have the youth talk about the trauma. Deep breathing and progressive muscular relaxation can be useful tools that the child can use when talking about the trauma to reduce acute anxiety. Thought-stopping techniques can also be helpful to prevent the memories from returning too abruptly.

Parents are important in the treatment as well. They should be taught the same CBT techniques to help the child if the anxiety becomes heightened at home. They can benefit from instruction to allow the child to talk about the event at his or her pace and not to change the subject if the child begins to speak about the event.

Another newer therapeutic technique for the treatment of PTSD in adults is eye movement desensitization and reprocessing (EMDR). This treatment combines cognitive therapy components with directed eye movements. Some preliminary studies are showing that this technique can be modified to a child's developmental level, and it can be a helpful treatment intervention (Ahmad & Sundelin-Wahlsten, 2008). This intervention is most successful at reducing the reexperiencing symptoms.

Medication

The SSRI antidepressants are helpful medication interventions for adults with PTSD. There may be some benefit in children and adolescents with this medication strategy. However, medications are generally believed to be less helpful than psychotherapeutic interventions. The main benefit of the medications can be to reestablish sleep patterns and reduce the hyperarousal. Often individuals with PTSD are also anxious apart from their PTSD symptoms. If this is the case, there can be benefit from the SSRI class of antidepressants.

Inderal, a beta-blocker antihypertensive medication, has been shown to reduce the reexperiencing symptoms that can be associated with the disorder. In addition, the alpha-2 antagonist clonidine may be helpful in improving sleep and reducing the hyperarousal, particularly if ADHD is comorbid.

OBSESSIVE-COMPULSIVE DISORDER

Characteristics

An obsession is a recurrent intrusive thought, impulse, or image that is distressing. A compulsion is an action such as a repetitive behavior or mental act that is meant to reduce distress or prevent a negative outcome. For an individual to be diagnosed with obsessive-compulsive disorder (OCD), either or both obsessions or compulsions must be present and cause marked impairment in distress or functioning. As a guide these actions can encompass 1 hour or more a day. These events must be differentiated from normal developmental rituals of childhood.

The most common obsession for children is a contamination fear. Children with obsessions frequently worry that germs will contaminate them. Obsessive worries about parents can also be present, and if this is the only obsession, there must be careful consideration to determine if SAD is not a more accurate diagnosis. Another common obsession in children is a worry that one has caused harm to another. A very common compulsion is hand washing. Along with hand washing, other common compulsions are repetitive checking, counting, and rearranging of objects.

For an individual to meet *DSM IV TR* (APA, 2000, p. 462) criteria for OCD, there must be either obsession or compulsion. The obsessions are recurrent and persistent thoughts, impulses, or images that are intrusive, inappropriate, and cause anxiety. These thoughts are not excessive worries about real-life problems. The person must attempt to ignore or suppress the thoughts or neutralize them with another thought or action. The person recognizes that the obsession is a product of his or her own mind. A compulsion is defined as a repetitive behavior or mental act that a person is compelled to perform. The behavior or mental acts are to prevent or reduce distress and are not connected in a realistic way to the obsession.

Epidemiology and Comorbidity

Community sample studies suggest a childhood incidence of OCD between 1% and 3% (Apter et al., 1996). It is also believed that there may be more individuals with OCD who are better able to mask their distress and symptoms. Boys are more likely to be diagnosed with OCD before puberty, and girls are more commonly diagnosed after puberty. In childhood the ratio of male to female is 3:2 (Swedo, Rapoport, Leonard, Lenane, & Cheslow, 1989).

There is a high rate of comorbidity with tic disorders, particularly Tourette's disorder. It is estimated that 50% of children with Tourette's disorder will also be diagnosed with OCD (Leckman, Walker, & Cohen, 1993).

Many children with OCD have another anxiety disorder as well. There can be a past history of SAD. In addition, the depressive disorders are also common.

There can be clinical confusion at times when differentiating Asperger's disorder, a pervasive developmental disorder, from OCD. In both conditions there can be ritualistic behaviors. The lack of social skills can be one factor that helps to distinguish these two.

Course

OCD can occur in children as young as 5 years old. Many studies of adults with OCD have reported that one third to one half experienced symptoms before the age of 15 years (Pauls, Alsobrook, Goodman, Rasmussen, & Leckman, 1995).

Individuals with an earlier onset are more likely to have a family history of OCD. Boys are also more likely to have tic disorders. OCD is thought of as a chronic condition that has periods of exacerbation and remission.

Disruptive behavior disorders can predate the development of OCD. Young children are more likely to be excessively irritable, and they may have difficulty articulating their distress. Children with OCD are not commonly neat and perfectionistic. Tantrums can occur if a compulsion is stopped.

Evaluation

Routine screening questions about obsessions and compulsions should be asked in all psychiatric evaluations. There should be additional time spent on eliciting these symptoms if there is an indication that the child is highly anxious. It is not uncommon for children to initially try to hide the rituals, and there can be denial about their existence. The parents should be asked about the specificity of routines or compulsive behaviors like hand washing. The child should be asked about intrusive and unwanted thoughts or images. Sometimes describing some common obsessions or compulsions can allow the child to be more forthcoming with symptoms. Children and families may have developed their own words to describe the symptoms, and for younger children these words should be used.

The evaluation should also include an understanding as to the time involved in the rituals. There should be a review of what strategies have been tried to prevent the obsession or compulsion. As with other anxiety disorders, the perceived distress is best based on the child's report, but the degree of functional impairment is best described by the parent.

The evaluation should also include an assessment of comorbid conditions. For OCD there should also be a more thorough medical history. There is a subset of children who develop OCD as a postinfectious sequelae of streptococcus infection or after exposure to certain medications. A family history can reveal someone with OCD or Tourette's disorder.

There are useful measures to help define the amount of distress and time of disorder that can be useful once the diagnosis has been made. Specifically, the Yale-Brown Obsessive Compulsive Scale (Y-BOCS) and Children's Yale-Brown Obsessive Compulsive Scale (CY-BOCS) can serve this purpose. These screening tools are used by clinicians to help gauge the intensity of symptoms at presentation, and subsequent administration can be done to show treatment response in a concrete fashion.

Therapeutic Principles

The first line of therapeutic intervention involves a strong psychoeducational piece. There must be an understanding that this is a brain-based illness that is beyond the individual's control. The child is not necessarily being stubborn or difficult when behaviors are compromised as a result of the compulsions. It is important that the child and family understand that there should not be guilt or shame associated with OCD.

OCD has perhaps the strongest studies supporting treatment efficacy. There is extensive support for benefit from CBT and SSRI medication.

Psychotherapy Treatment

CBT has been consistently shown to be an ideal treatment intervention for OCD (Leonard, Swedo, Allen, & Rapoport, 1994). There are three steps that are taken in the treatment. The first is the gathering of information. This is needed to understand the obsessions and compulsions. After the details of the symptoms are known, the therapist can assist with exposure and response prevention. Repeated exposure is believed to reduce anxiety across trials until there is no longer fear of contact. As with other treatment strategies, the exposure to the feared stimulus is gradual. Finally, homework assignments are used to practice the techniques at home.

There should also be ongoing education and cognitive retraining to help the child recognize the symptoms of the illness.

Relaxation strategies can also be taught, not to reduce the obsessions or compulsions but to generally help the child feel better.

Both the child and the family have to be involved, but it is important to find the balance of time spent with both. Parents need to reinforce the new thinking patterns at home. Also parents may have inadvertently been pulled into the compulsion if the child is repetitively seeking their reassurance. They must be able to recognize this pattern and help make certain that this behavior is noted.

Medication

The decision to use medication to treat OCD is difficult. It may be wise to begin CBT to treat a case of mild or moderate OCD where there are no comorbid diagnoses. If there is an inadequate response to CBT, then there can be a trial of medication. In addition, if there are other mental health symptoms identified at the time of presentation, such as depression or other anxiety disorders, there could be an earlier start to medication.

The SSRI medications are the recommended first-line medication for OCD. These medications are effective at reducing the intensity of the obsessions and compulsions. Numerous studies have shown that this class of medication is particularly helpful at reducing OCD (March, Biederman, Wolkow, Safferman, & Group, 1997). This class of medication can help to "break" the recurrent thought loop that occurs during the time of obsessive thoughts.

Similar side effects and black box warnings exist with these medications, and caution needs to be used when initiating or changing the dose. The time to notice response from medication is long. In some cases no benefit is noted for the first 6 to 10 weeks of treatment (Greist, Jefferson, Kobak, Katzelnick, & Serlin, 1995). The response curve also shows that there can be ongoing improvements after 3 months of medication. If one medication is not effective after several months, there should be a consideration to switch to a different SSRI.

It is recommended that the medication be continued for 12 to 18 months before there is a consideration to taper or discontinue its use (March, Frances, Carpenter, & Kahn, 1997). Changing the medication sooner than that time increases the likelihood of relapse.

If the OCD symptoms occur in conjunction with streptococcus infection, the recommended treatment strategy is antibiotic treatment.

ANXIETY DISORDERS: EDUCATIONAL IMPLICATIONS

Anxiety disorders can cause a number of significant educational problems. Most commonly, anxious children work very hard to mask their symptoms and work very hard to reach perfectionistic standards. In this pattern the anxiety might not be evident in school. However, these students typically struggle excessively at home. For example, a student with OCD may be able to tolerate a school day without engaging in compulsions, but on arrival home there can be an extended period of ritualized behavior to compensate for the internal distress that has been experienced all day. The anxiety can then interfere with studying and the completion of homework, which worsens the anxious response pattern the next day.

Another common educational implication of anxiety is school refusal. School refusal is important to address promptly, because the longer this behavioral pattern continues, the more difficult it becomes to change. Children with SAD and panic disorder often attempt to avoid school, preferring the familiarity of their home. Initially, there can be many somatic reasons given for the school refusal, and it can take several days or weeks to recognize that the reason for absence is psychological not medical. Once an anxious child has missed school, it is very difficult to return in large part because of the fear that others will ask about the absence. In addition, falling behind in schoolwork further increases the anxiety. It takes close communication between the treatment provider and the educational team to support the child's return to school. Efforts should be made to allow the student some time to make up missed assignments. Returning to school for a portion of the day with increased time spent at school each week can help with the transition in many severe cases. If anxiety is present, all efforts should be made to avoid homebound instruction. Receiving a doctor's note requesting an extended period of absence further increases the school refusal. Remaining at home often results in a significant reduction in anxiety. When the time ultimately comes to return to school, the child's anxiety magnifies, and there are no strategies or supports in place to help.

Individuals with anxiety can be so perfectionistic that they are unable to complete work. Academic performance can begin to decline, as the student is unable to finish an assignment. Anxiety can prevent some students from attempting to take classes or engage in activities because of fear of failure.

When anxiety disorders are present and being treated, it is helpful for the clinician to communicate with the school. Some families and students are reluctant to have this occur because of fears of stigmatization. Others are reluctant to discuss this with school personnel, as they do not believe the symptoms are causing educational impairment.

In some cases the school can be the first site where the anxiety is recognized as problematic. When school personnel recognize the presence of anxiety, this topic must be discussed gently with the parents and students. Very frequently when an anxiety disorder is present in a younger child, at least one family member is also experiencing the same. Using nonclinical terms such as *fear* and *worry* can help parents hear and understand the concern better than the term *anxiety.*

ANXIETY DISORDERS: SUMMARY

The anxiety disorders are a diverse group of problems that are associated with fears and worries. Inappropriate mechanisms exist to help manage the worries, and severe problems in functioning can occur. This class of disorders can be more difficult to recognize, as efforts are made by the child to keep the symptoms hidden. In addition, families can inadvertently increase the secretiveness of the disorder, as they can perceive that it is the child's fault.

Interventions such as therapy, medication, and educational support are useful in restoring the child's functioning to a normal level. However, there is a likelihood that these disorders will continue throughout life, in a waxing and waning course.

Eight

Psychotic Disorders

PSYCHOSIS: DEFINED

Over the history of psychiatry, the term *psychosis* has had a number of different definitions. Currently, the most restrictive definition of this term implies the presence of delusions or prominent hallucinations where there is a lack of insight into the pathological nature. A delusion is described as a permanent and false belief. This belief cannot be changed by any logical argument, and the person does not recognize the belief as untrue. A hallucination is when a person believes he or she is experiencing a sensory input when there is none present. This can include the sense of sight, hearing, smell, or touch. Most commonly in psychotic illnesses the hallucinations are auditory (hearing) or visual (sight). In other words people who have psychotic symptoms have a difficult time differentiating reality from fantasy.

Psychosis can occur as the primary symptoms in an illness. Examples of this include schizophrenia or schizophreniform disorder. Psychosis can also occur in the midst of a mood disorder such as major depression with psychotic symptoms or bipolar disorder with psychotic symptoms. Psychotic disorders can be caused by a substance such as an illicit drug or prescribed medication. In addition, although not reviewed in this book, psychosis can occur in older individuals who are suffering from dementia.

The most serious of the psychotic disorders is schizophrenia. Closely related to this illness is schizophreniform disorder, which is similar but is used as a diagnosis if the symptoms have been present for fewer than 6 months. Another psychotic disorder is brief psychotic disorder, which is the presence of one of the psychotic symptoms (delusions, hallucinations, disorganized speech, or grossly disorganized behavior) for more than 1 day but less than 1 month (American Psychiatric

Association [APA], 2000 p. 332). A final common diagnosis is psychotic disorder, not otherwise specified, which implies some psychotic symptoms, but the symptoms do not meet full criteria for any other psychotic illness.

The first section of this chapter will focus on illnesses where psychosis is the primary problem. The second and third sections will focus on psychosis in the context of a mood disorder, and the fourth section focuses on psychosis in the context of a substance abuse disorder.

SCHIZOPHRENIFORM DISORDER AND SCHIZOPHRENIA

Characteristics

The primary distinction between schizophreniform disorder and schizophrenia is the time the symptoms have been present. A person is first diagnosed with schizophreniform disorder when the psychotic symptoms have been present for 1 month but fewer than 6 months. After 6 months if the symptoms persist, the diagnosis changes to schizophrenia.

Two or more of the characteristic symptoms must be present for either illness: delusions, hallucinations, disorganized speech (also termed thought disorder), grossly disorganized or catatonic behavior, or negative symptoms such as affective flattening, alogia, or avolition. The symptoms must cause significant functional impairment and cannot occur exclusively during a mood disorder or be a direct result of a substance (APA, 2000, p. 310).

The term *formal thought disorder* can be used when discussing the psychotic symptoms in schizophrenia. When an individual has a thought disorder, there is a lack of connection with the words and thoughts that the person expresses. A person with schizophrenia can have disorganized thoughts where there is no connection between the words in the sentence. In the most severe form of schizophrenia, the term *word salad* can be used to describe the thought form. A word salad can be quite obvious in a person who is experiencing disorganized thoughts. More subtle variations of disorganized thinking can be apparent through writing (see accompanying CD: 8.1).

The symptom clusters of schizophrenia are described as either positive symptoms or negative symptoms. The positive symptoms consist of hallucinations, delusions, and thought disorder. Children with schizophrenia can commonly present with loosening of associations and illogical thoughts. Positive symptoms are increasingly likely to occur with increasing age. The negative symptoms consist of flat affect, paucity of thought, and anergy. These symptoms are more rare in children and adolescents.

It is important to clarify that not all children who experience hallucinations are psychotic. In children hallucinations can also be symptoms of anxiety. In adolescents hallucinations can occur with the ingestion of some illicit substances. In addition, the phenomenon of a person hearing his or her name called can be a normal experience that does not imply any pathology. When the clinician is assessing hallucinations, it is important to inquire about the content of the voices, the way in which the hallucinations are heard, and the person's perception of the experience. In addition, approximately 60% of children and adolescents experience hallucination upon falling asleep or immediately upon awakening.

There are several recognizable stages in schizophrenia or schizophreniform disorder. The first is the prodromo stage. During this phase there is a deterioration in functioning as seen by social isolation, bizarre thoughts, declining academic performance, and self-care. However, during this phase there are no overt psychotic symptoms identified, so the diagnosis of schizophreniform disorder should not be given. This is followed by the acute phase of illness where the psychotic thoughts become present, and there is ongoing functional deterioration. During this phase there are active hallucinations, delusions, or disconnections from reality. The recovery phase may follow, where there are few active psychotic thoughts, but there can still be ongoing deterioration in functioning. This phase can be associated with dysphoria. The residual phase may follow, where prominent negative symptoms remain. Schizophrenia in particular is characterized as a chronic illness.

Epidemiology and Comorbidity

Schizophrenia has been observed worldwide. For adults the prevalence of the disorder is estimated to be between 0.5% and 1.5% (APA, 2000, p. 308). Early onset schizophrenia is defined by the development of psychotic symptoms before the age of 18 years, and very early onset schizophrenia is defined by the development of symptoms before the age of 13 years (American Academy of Child and Adolescent Psychiatry [AACAP], 2001). Very early onset schizophrenia is rare, but there is believed to be a twice-greater likelihood for boys to be affected compared to girls (W. H. Green, Padron-Gayol, Hardesty, & Bassiri, 1992; Werry, McClellan, & Chard, 1991).

The likelihood of schizophrenia increases with age, and most commonly, symptoms can begin to occur around age 15 years. It is very rare for individuals over the age of 30 years to be diagnosed with schizophrenia. With increasing age the ratio between males and females begins to equalize.

When a person has schizophrenia, there cannot be a mood disorder present. If a mood disorder is present in the context of psychotic symptoms, the diagnosis becomes either major depression with psychotic features or bipolar disorder with psychotic features. It is not uncommon for juveniles to be first diagnosed with mood disorders or anxiety disorders until the acute psychotic symptoms present. Once the psychotic symptoms are identified, there must be an assessment to determine if the mood or anxiety symptoms remain a part of the clinical presentation. The anxiety can be related to the delusions, but once it is clear that delusions are present, the anxiety disorder is no longer considered primary.

Individuals with schizophrenia are more likely to abuse substances. One particular substance that is commonly used by individuals with schizophrenia is nicotine. There is a belief that individuals with schizophrenia are more violent than the normal population, but this is not supported.

This illness is differentiated from pervasive developmental disorders by the onset of symptoms at an older age. It is not uncommon that adolescents with schizophrenia struggle with social interactions, but this problem has not been present from a young age as is necessary for the diagnosis of a pervasive developmental disorder. In addition, it is uncommon for youth with a pervasive developmental disorder to have overt hallucinations and delusions, whereas these are common in youth with psychotic disorders.

Course

Schizophrenia is conceptualized as a neurobiological illness. It is theorized that there is disruption in the neural development and differentiation that occurs during the second trimester of pregnancy (Akbarian et al., 1993). There are subtle brain changes seen on MRIs in adults with schizophrenia, but the neuronal problems likely begin very early in life.

There is some support that individuals who eventually develop schizophrenia have a higher rate of childhood social, motor, and language impairments, although these are not needed for diagnosis. There is no evidence that psychological or social influences are related to the development of schizophrenia. However, social stressors can play a role in the timing of the presentation of symptoms. There is likely a genetic role, as first-degree relatives of individuals with schizophrenia have a risk for the same illness that is about 10 times greater than that of the general population (APA, 2000, p. 309).

Schizophrenia tends to be a lifelong disorder. In some individuals there are long periods of remission, whereas others have more chronic, acute psychotic symptoms. There is a significant mortality associated with schizophrenia. Individuals with schizophrenia have a higher incidence of suicide than average. Suicide tends to occur early in the illness and can occur when insight into the severity of the illness occurs. In addition, some deaths can occur unintentionally as a result of psychotic thinking (Werry et al., 1991).

Evaluation

A psychiatric evaluation should routinely screen for psychotic symptoms. During the mental status portion of the evaluation, questions are asked to elicit information about hallucinations and delusions. The family can provide information regarding atypical behavior and unusual thought preoccupations. The mental status of the youth is critical in identifying psychotic symptoms. The thought form can be significant for disordered thinking, loosening of associations, or word salad. If the thought form is disordered, then the individual more likely has schizophrenia. If hallucinations and delusions are identified, this must raise the threshold of investigation. If the psychotic symptoms exist without any mood symptoms and not in the context of substance use, then there should be understanding of the length of time the symptoms have been present.

If hallucinations or delusions are found in the context of a normal thought form, there must be further investigation of mood and anxiety symptoms. In other words if the psychotic symptoms are present in the context of a mood disorder, then the diagnosis cannot be schizophrenia. If there is a history of substance use, there must be a better understanding of the timing of symptom presentation.

It is very important to remember that not all children who report hallucinations are psychotic. Hallucinations in childhood can be a sign of anxiety. If hallucinations are identified, it is important to understand the nature of these experiences.

If the hallucinations are described as "commanding" or instructing the youth to do something, there is a higher likelihood that psychosis is present. Simple name-calling or even calming voices may be less likely to be psychotic.

The diagnosis of schizophrenia in youth is one that should be made only after there is very clear evidence of psychotic symptoms without other mental disorders over the course of 6 months. There can be a likelihood to overdiagnose this illness. There was recruitment to a national study of individuals with early onset schizophrenia, and a large number of referred participants did not meet the clinical criteria. These individuals showed a mixture of subclinical psychotic symptoms with developmental delays and mood lability (McKenna et al., 1994). Because of the continuity with adult schizophrenia and the chronicity of the illness, caution should be taken.

There are no blood tests or imaging studies that can be done to make a clinical diagnosis of schizophrenia. However, these may need to be completed if there are suspicions of underlying medical problems, for example, if there is a seizure disorder that can be associated with hallucinations. If the history of hallucinations is consistent with this type of seizures, an EEG may be indicated. Infectious diseases, in particular HIV infection, can also present with features similar to schizophrenia, and if infectious diseases are indicated, testing should occur.

One particular rating scale called the Brief Psychiatric Rating Scale (BPRS) can be used clinically to monitor psychotic symptoms and their treatment. This instrument rates 18 different scales including hostility, hallucinations, and suspiciousness. The items are rated on a scale from 1 to 7 based on the rater's assessment of severity. This instrument does not help with diagnosis but can be useful to assess response.

Therapeutic Interventions

Early supportive therapeutic interventions for schizophrenia should include psychoeducation. Both the juvenile and the family must understand the meaning of this illness, as there is continuity between early onset schizophrenia and the adult form of the illness. The various phases of illness should be described, and the medication treatment should be supported. It is also helpful for the family to not confront the delusions directly, but they should not encourage the delusions either. Often the approach of "agree to disagree" about the belief is the most effective approach for the family to take.

Along with the acute psychotic symptoms, individuals with schizophrenia often have social deficits. Therapeutic interventions that can improve these difficulties are often helpful. This can include focusing on verbal skills such as understanding the meaning, content, and context of what a person says. Alternatively, improving strategies to deal with interpersonal conflict and discussing another person's emotions can be beneficial.

Individual and family interventions can often be combined for the best success. However, along with therapy individuals with early onset schizophrenia may benefit from case management services. A case manager can be crucial in connecting the family with treatment interventions, community support, and in-home services. A multidisciplinary approach can be very useful, as this is a chronic illness.

There is no evidence that cognitive behavioral therapy, interpersonal therapy, or psychodynamic therapy is helpful in the treatment of schizophrenia. The primary individual therapeutic intervention is providing education and support and addressing social skills. The family needs education and support as well.

Medication

There is a long history of medication treatment in adults. There have been a few randomized controlled studies of antipsychotic medications in youth. For adults these medications are effective at reducing acute psychotic symptoms and improving overall functioning. There are two primary classes of antipsychotic medications that are used: neuroleptics (traditional antipsychotics) or atypical antipsychotics (see accompanying CD: 8.3).

Neuroleptics were first identified as being helpful for treating psychosis decades ago. Their primary mechanism of action is on dopamine. They act primarily as dopamine antagonists at the D2 receptor. Within this class of medications, there are high-potency agents like haloperidol (Haldol) and low-potency agents like chlorpromazine (Thorazine). The low-potency agents are associated with anticholinergic side effects like constipation, dry eyes, and dry mouth. They are also associated with sedation. If agitation is present, there is an advantage to choosing a sedating agent.

High-potency medications have fewer anticholinergic side effects, but they have an increased incidence of neurological side effects, called extrapyramidal side effects (EPS).

Children and adolescents may be more likely to experience EPS compared to adults. Common EPS include dystonia, parkinsonism, and akathisia. When dystonia occurs it is a sudden spastic painful contraction of a distinct muscle group. It commonly occurs in the neck, eyes, or torso. It is a frightening experience, but it is one that is rapidly treated if medical treatment in sought. Dystonia is likely to occur with medication initiation or rapid dose escalation. Parkinsonism consists of mild tremor, rigidity, and slowing of movements. This causes less distress, but if it becomes severe it can cause impairment of fine motor activities. Akathisia is an internal sense of restlessness that is noted by pacing, agitation, and an individual's sense of wanting to jump out of his or her skin. There are medications that can be given to combat the emergence of these side effects.

Another potential side effect of these medications is an elevation of prolactin levels. This can cause menstrual abnormalities and galactorrhea (fluid leakage from the breast) in females. In addition, elevated prolactin levels can cause gynecomastia (breast enlargement) in males. These side effects can be particularly concerning for adolescents.

All neuroleptic medications can be associated with the development of a delayed neurological side effect called tardive dyskinesia. This is characterized by involuntary movements on a regular basis of fine muscle groups. It often is noted in the area around the mouth but can occur in any region of the body. It can appear as a subtle puckering movement. At times it can be a permanent side effect even when the medication is discontinued. At other times it can be minimized or stopped with lowering the dose of medication. There is a second type of dyskinesia that can also occur with withdraw from the medications (withdraw dyskinesia), particularly if they are rapidly discontinued. If a juvenile is started on a traditional neuroleptic medication, there should be routine follow-up and assessment for the emergence of tardive or withdraw dyskinesia. The Abnormal Involuntary Movement Scale is one instrument that can be used to help monitor this side effect. These medications are clearly associated with what may be lifelong side effects. However, the severity of schizophrenia often shifts the risk–benefit balance to support initiation of treatment.

Neuroleptic malignant syndrome is a rare reaction that can occur at any time during treatment with an antipsychotic medication. It is considered a medical emergency. It is characterized by a high fever, severe rigidity, and confusion. The affected person's vital signs are unstable, and a specific body enzyme, called creatinine phosphokinase, is elevated (see accompanying CD: 8.2).

The second and newer class of medications that is used to treat psychotic symptoms is the atypical antipsychotics. This class of medications is characterized by the medications' activity at specific receptors for dopamine and serotonin. Some examples of the medications in this class are risperidone (Risperdal), olanzapine (Zyprexa), quetiapine (Seroquel), ziprasidone (Geodon), and aripiprazole (Abilify). Risperidone and aripiprazole are approved by the FDA to treat schizophrenia in children as young as 13 years. There is research support for the use of risperidone, olanzapine, and quetiapine for use in the treatment of early onset schizophrenia (see accompanying CD: 8.3).

Because these medications are less potent dopamine antagonists, this class is less likely to be associated with neurological side effects, although EPS and neuroleptic malignant syndrome have been reported. The most concerning side effect is weight gain. Some studies have supported that over half of the juveniles treated with this medication have a significant increase in BMI. This can lead to other potentially serious health effects including high cholesterol, hypertension, and Type 2 diabetes mellitus. Weight gain occurs significantly more often in children and adolescents than in adults. In addition, there can be cardiac side effects because slight changes in cardiac conduction are possible. There also can be blood count changes with a decrease in white blood and increases in liver enzymes. Sedation and dizziness can also occur (see accompanying CD: 8.4).

There can be negative interactions when combining antipsychotic medications with other central nervous system depressants. Specifically, this includes alcohol, sedatives, antihistamines, and opiates. These combinations can cause more significant sedation and lethargy. There should be caution when prescribing an antipsychotic with an antidepressant, as the antidepressant level can be increased. Some combinations of antidepressants and antipsychotics increase the chance of the individual developing neuroleptic malignant syndrome. This is more true with both the traditional antipsychotics and the tricyclic antidepressants.

A study conducted in 2008 (Sikich et al., 2008) compared the effectiveness of two atypical antipsychotics, risperidone and olanzapine, to molindone, a traditional neuroleptic, for 8 weeks. All three medications had a similar response rate of 40% to 50%. Molindone was associated with more neurological side effects. Olanzapine in particular was associated with a high rate of weight gain and other associated metabolic abnormalities. It is concerning that over the short length of this study there was not a more robust benefit from the medications.

One medication, clozapine, in particular should be considered for treatment-resistant schizophrenia. This medication was the first of the atypical antipsychotics to be developed. However, there are significant safety concerns with this medication, as it can seriously lower one of the white blood cell counts, the neutrophils. This can lead to death as the body becomes unable to fight infection. To prevent this from occurring, the clinician can have the patient use the medication if there is weekly monitoring of the patient's white blood cell counts.

The atypical antipsychotics are taken once or twice a day depending on side effects and the medication chosen. If sedation occurs, the patient can take the medication in divided dosages to minimize this problem. In addition, taking the larger dose in the evening can be helpful for promoting sleep. For an adolescent with schizophrenia, low starting dosages of the medication is indicated. Gradual titration is needed to minimize the occurrence of side effects and to monitor for symptom resolution. Efficacy to reduce acute psychotic symptoms can take several weeks. It is also known that continuing these medications for several months can also result in benefit for the social isolation and withdraw that can occur in this illness. Weight and laboratory studies are needed for monitoring side effects.

Clinical Case

Tom was a 14-year-old African American male who presented for a psychiatric evaluation at the request of his school district. He had recently started attending a large public high school where his unusual behaviors were quickly noticed. He would walk quickly through the halls, and at the intersection of two halls, he would stop and attempt to hide while looking at who was walking in his direction. He wore a hood over his head and obscured his eyes when sitting in class and walking in the halls. He would not talk to his peers, simply walking away when he was approached. He had turned in a paper in English class that was illogical, and the words within the sentences did not fit together. This was noted to be a dramatic difference when compared to previous writing samples.

Tom's family reported that beginning the summer before Tom started high school, he began to withdraw from all social interactions. He sat in his room for hours at a time without doing anything. His eating patterns changed. He would eat only food that was unopened, and when questioned about this, he made vague references to being poisoned. There was no significant past psychiatric or medical history. He denied use of any substances. There was an unknown mental illness in his father, who was no longer in contact with the family.

His mental status examination was consistent with a disheveled-appearing boy who wore his hood over his head throughout the interview. He answered questions in a very quiet voice. His thought form was organized when short answers were required; however, when he was asked open-ended questions, his thought form became disjointed. He admitted to a strong belief that "someone" whom he could not identify wanted him dead. He was certain he was going to be killed but was unsure if it would occur through poisoning, stabbing, or strangling. He admitted to auditory hallucinations of a specific male voice that continually repeated, "I am going to kill you." He reported significant distress about this concept.

As these symptoms had been present for 4 months, a diagnosis of schizophreniform disorder was given. Routine blood work was completed and was within normal limits. Treatment options were discussed, and his family elected to begin medication treatment with risperidone. Within 6 weeks of beginning treatment, Tom reported that he no longer had the hallucinations. He began to be able to describe alternative meanings to his suspiciousness. His family reported that he was eating food that had been opened, and he was able to go out to eat in restaurants. He became more interactive with other family members. After 3 months of treatment, he began to feel more comfortable at school and was able to eat in the cafeteria with large groups of people. He was able to walk appropriately in the hallways. His work products became more organized.

He began to struggle with consistency of medication, often wanting to discontinue its use. At one point after several months of being free of psychotic symptoms, he returned to darting quickly in the halls and began to skip lunch. When questioned about this return of symptoms, Tom initially refused the presence of paranoia or hallucinations. However, when his mother was doing laundry, she found 10 pills that had been stuffed into a plastic baggie in his jeans. She appropriately confronted him, and he agreed that he had stopped taking his risperidone. Within 2 weeks of restarting it, he again began interacting with others in a more appropriate way.

With consistency of medication and psychoeducational support, Tom has now been free of acute psychotic symptoms for 2 years. Right now he is not demonstrating significant negative symptoms of schizophrenia. The dose of his medication has been lowered every few months, and today he is on 0.5 mg of risperidone. The long-term outcome is unclear, but it is a positive sign that he has remained symptom free for this time.

MAJOR DEPRESSION WITH PSYCHOTIC FEATURES

Characteristics

Episodes of major depression are characterized as mild, moderate, or severe. If psychotic symptoms are present, then the episode is categorized as severe, although not all severe episodes have psychotic symptoms present. By definition an individual episode of major depressive disorder (MDD) with psychotic features must have either hallucinations or delusions (APA, 2000, p. 412). Most commonly, both of these presentations are mood congruent. In other words, the psychotic symptom matches the depressed mood. The delusions can have themes of guilt, being deserving of punishment, or somatic concerns. Hallucinations are usually transient and most commonly include voices that comment on negative characteristics of the person.

Course and Evaluation

The course of MDD with psychotic features closely mirrors the course of MDD. However, the presence of psychotic symptoms implies a more severe illness that can be suggestive of more frequent recurrences.

Routine evaluations for MDD should inquire about the presence of psychotic symptoms. In addition, if the presenting problem is psychotic symptoms, there should be inquiry into depressive symptoms. Frequently, it is easy to differentiate MDD with psychotic symptoms from schizophrenia, as the delusions and/or hallucinations are mood congruent. If there is difficulty making this distinction, one feature that should be carefully considered is the individual's thought form. If there is a dramatically disorganized thought form, the presenting illness is more likely to be schizophrenia.

Treatment

Because an episode of MDD with psychotic features implies a severe form of the depressive illness, rapid and intensive treatment is indicated. In other words, beginning with only supportive care is insufficient. Depending on the severity of presentation, a hospitalization or partial hospitalization program may be necessary. If there are suicidal thoughts along with the psychotic symptoms, hospitalization is likely necessary to ensure the person's safety.

Medications are indicated in the treatment. If the psychotic symptoms are mild or transient, it can be reasonable to begin treatment with an antidepressant and watch for response. The psychotic symptoms should resolve as the depression resolves. However, for more frequent and severe hallucinations or delusions, a combination of an antidepressant and atypical antipsychotic is clinically indicated. Because of the potential long-term effects of antipsychotics, once the psychotic symptoms have resolved, it may be appropriate to taper and discontinue this medication while continuing on longer term antidepressant therapy.

BIPOLAR DISORDER WITH PSYCHOTIC FEATURES

Characteristics

As in cases of MDD with psychotic features, if psychotic features are present during either mania or depression, this is considered a severe mood episode. The psychotic symptoms of bipolar disorder are also hallucinations or delusions. They are also most commonly mood congruent. For example, if an individual with bipolar disorder is manic, the delusions can be grandiose, such as "I have a special assignment to complete." The hallucinations can support this belief. If an individual with bipolar disorder is depressed, the mood-congruent themes are of persecution or guilt. Occasionally, the psychotic symptoms might not be consistent with the mood (mood incongruent). Some examples of this include delusions of thought insertion, thought broadcasting, and delusions of control. These features are associated with a poor prognosis.

Course and Evaluation

Some studies have supported the idea that if psychosis is present with mania, then the course of illness will be more chronic (Geller & Luby, 1997). In addition, the presence of psychotic symptoms implies more aggressive treatment is needed. Safety is important to consider, as there can be more significantly impaired insight and judgment when psychosis is present.

Just as the evaluation of depression should include a screening for hallucinations and delusions, the same is true when mania is the presenting problem. New onset mania in adolescents often presents with psychosis (McGlashan, 1988), and diagnostically these two entities can be initially difficult to differentiate. If an individual presents with acute psychotic symptoms, there should be careful screening for lack of sleep and affective instability. Each of these characteristics offers more support for bipolar disorder with psychotic features than for schizophrenia.

It is important to carefully consider the differences between bipolar disorder with psychotic features and schizophrenia. Although these two illnesses can look similar, episodically the course of illness is different. Schizophrenia is more likely to be a chronic and potentially deteriorating course, whereas bipolar disorder tends to have episodes of recovery that alternate with active illness states.

Treatment

If the psychosis is present in the context of a mania, the front-line treatment to be considered should be an atypical antipsychotic. This one medication can have the effect of both treating the psychotic symptoms and stabilizing the mood. Again because the presence of psychotic symptoms in the context of a mood disorder implies a more severe presentation of the illness, the individual may need to be placed on two mood stabilizers, and one of those medications should be an atypical antipsychotic.

If the psychosis is present in the context of depression, it is important to cautiously treat the depressive component. An antipsychotic is going to have to be strongly considered in the treatment regimen.

Clinical Case

Greg was an 18-year-old male who was referred for a psychiatric evaluation by his parents. A second opinion was requested, and ongoing medication management was needed. Two days after graduating from high school, Greg did not return home at the expected time. His parents received a phone call 3 hours later by a police officer in a town 2 hours east of their home. The police reported that Greg was parked on the side of a busy highway and was "not making sense." He was transported to a hospital where a crisis assessment found him to be acutely psychotic with grandiose delusions and confusion. A urine drug screen was negative. Greg reported on assessment that he was driving to his college (which was 2 hours to the west of his home) to be on the soccer team. He stated he had received a message from God that he was to play soccer for college although he had never played in high school.

Because of his confusion and unusual presentation, Greg was hospitalized following his crisis assessment. While in the hospital, he was given a diagnosis of schizophrenia. His parents questioned this diagnosis in large part because of the rapidity of symptom onset and high premorbid functioning.

Greg's parents reported that in the 2 weeks before graduation, Greg had not been sleeping, complaining of feeling overwhelmed with work. He stayed up very late for several nights making lists of what to pack for college at the end of the summer. He appeared excessively animated and energized. Greg had always been a quiet and reserved child, but during this time he became very animated, gregarious, and loud.

Greg was placed on risperidone in the hospital and discharged within 3 days of arrival. Greg came to my office 2 weeks after his discharge from the hospital. At the time of presentation, he continued to have grandiose delusions of playing soccer at college. He became agitated when the logic of his lack of skill was shared. He continued to believe that God wanted him to play soccer. Despite being on risperidone for 2 weeks, he continued to not sleep and was restless. His speech was fast, and his thought form showed flight of ideas. It was organized loosely but skipped quickly between topics.

There were no medical problems and no history of any substance use. There was no family history for any psychiatric illness or treatment. School records supported that he was a very good student who was somewhat quiet but well liked.

Because of Greg's grandiose delusions, flight of ideas, decreased sleep, and change in his baseline personality from quiet to very outgoing, I provided a diagnostic suggestion of bipolar disorder, manic with psychotic features. Because his mood had not stabilized with the use of risperidone, I added valproic acid and gradually titrated it to a therapeutic level. He continued on the risperidone. Within 3 weeks his mood was stabilizing. He was sleeping 6 hours a night, and he began to talk more slowly and returned to his quieter self. He began to recognize that God was not talking to him, and he recognized he could not play on his college soccer team. After

3 months without psychotic symptoms, Greg could be gradually taken off his antipsychotic medication.

Greg and his family requested a medical leave of absence from his college, before he even started. He remained living at home for the next year while he completed college courses at a community college. By the following summer his mood had remained euthymic, and there were no recurrences of psychotic symptoms. The following year Greg went away to college while continuing on valproic acid. For a brief time during his junior year, he had a mild depressive episode that was treated by his college counseling department and did not require a change in medication. During the past few years, he has continued to be free of all mood symptoms.

OTHER PSYCHOTIC DISORDERS

Characteristics

Psychotic disorders can occur in conjunction with substances. The essential feature of this disorder is the presence of hallucinations or delusions that are judged to be due to the direct physiological effects of a substance. This substance can be a drug of abuse, a medication, or a toxin (APA, 2000, p. 342). Many drugs of abuse are associated with hallucinations or delusions. A psychotic disorder is identified only if the symptoms are greater than what typically occur with the known substance. For example, hallucinations commonly occur with LSD during the phase of intoxications. Therefore, this would not be classified as a psychotic disorder.

Psychotic disorders can occur in association with the intoxication stage of alcohol, amphetamines, cannabis, cocaine, hallucinogens, inhalants, opioids, phencyclidine, sedatives, hypnotics, and anxiolytics. Psychotic disorders can occur during withdrawal from the following classes of substances: alcohol, sedatives, hypnotics, and anxiolytics (see accompanying CD: 8.5). Typically, the onset of symptoms closely mirrors either the intoxication or the withdrawal. The psychotic symptoms are typically persecutory and vivid. Often the symptoms clear when the offending substance clears the body, but there are situations when the symptoms persist (APA, 2000, p. 340).

Along with substances of abuse, the following classes of medications can also cause a substance-induced psychotic disorder: anesthetics and analgesics, anticholinergic agents, anticonvulsants, antihistamines, antihypertensive medications, antibiotics, antiparkinsonian medications, chemotherapeutic agents, corticosteroids, muscle relaxants, OTC medications such as pseudoephedrine, and antidepressant medications. Toxins such as carbon dioxide and volatile substances such as fuel, paint, and insecticides can also be associated with a substance-induced psychotic disorder (APA, 2000, p. 341).

Psychotic disorders can also occur in individuals with medical conditions. Some common medical conditions that can affect juveniles include epilepsy, migraines, or central nervous system infection. These are less likely to occur in adolescents, but they should be considered.

Treatment

If the psychotic disorder is related to a medication or substance, the first step of treatment is to identify and remove the offending agent. If the psychotic symptoms remain, treatment with a medication should be initiated. This should be done cautiously if the offending substance is unknown.

If the psychotic disorder is related to a medical condition, the first step of treatment is to identify and treat the condition. This will typically lead to a resolution of symptoms, but if not, treatment with a low dose of an antipsychotic medication should be considered.

PSYCHOTIC DISORDERS: EDUCATIONAL IMPLICATIONS

Schizophrenia and the other psychotic illnesses can cause significant impairment in a youth's educational performance. These illnesses are generally recognized as a distinct change in the individual's previous level of functioning. However, schizophrenia in particular rarely presents in a dramatic way, and the changing patterns of thought commonly develop over several years.

When acute psychotic symptoms are first recognized, there is an inability for the person to function in any domain. Often new onset psychotic symptoms can require an inpatient hospitalization for stabilization. However, it is equally possible that because of the insidious nature of the illness, a student can be psychotic for many months before it is recognized.

If school personnel are the first to become concerned that a student is psychotic, the first step should be to help the family obtain a psychiatric evaluation. In the short term, a crisis assessment may be needed to ensure that the student is safe, but for the full assessment of psychotic symptoms, a psychiatric evaluation is needed. A clue to determine if a student has psychotic symptoms would be observing the student appear internally preoccupied, such as darting eyes when nothing is moving or moving lips as if in conversation. Thought disorders can at times be noted in drawings and writings. Excessive suspiciousness can be a clue to emerging delusions.

If school personnel are working with a student with a known diagnosis of schizophrenia, anxiety can develop on the part of the staff. Support personnel can be utilized to provide appropriate education to staff about the nature of the illness. For example, it is a common misperception that schizophrenics are violent. Teachers need to understand that the person has an illness that causes him or her to not always be in touch with reality. Staff should not directly challenge the student's false beliefs. Staff must also be encouraged to talk to the person and attempt to engage the student in typical conversations.

Academics may need to be adjusted. For example, if a student's paper is disorganized in thought, this needs to be considered part of the illness, and the grade should not reflect significant penalty. On the other hand, the psychosis does not give the student the ability to stop attempting to do work and continue to receive credit.

If a student with schizophrenia is in the school system, there will need to be close communication with the outpatient psychiatrist who is providing care. School personnel may notice a student's return to psychotic thinking sooner than the family does. If there are concerns or questions about the return of symptoms, this should be clearly conveyed so it can be reassessed.

Social skill support can also be a useful intervention for the school to provide to the student. Encouraging informal dialogue with other students can be a way for the student with the disorder to begin to reestablish peer support. In addition, more formalized groups and interventions through the guidance office can allow the student to have additional supports.

Students with psychotic disorders other than schizophrenia may need similar supports. However, the intensity of the psychotic symptoms is often less than with schizophrenia.

PSYCHOTIC DISORDERS: SUMMARY

Psychotic disorders can present at any time in childhood. The most serious of these disorders is schizophrenia, and its onset, particularly in males, is commonly seen in the late teen years. This group of disorders is associated with significant loss of functioning and can be considered lifelong illnesses. Early recognition of symptoms and prompt multidisciplinary support can be very helpful.

Nine

Eating Disorders

EATING DISORDERS: BACKGROUND

The two primary eating disorders described in the *DSM-IV-TR* (American Psychiatric Association [APA], 2000) are anorexia nervosa (AN) and bulimia nervosa (BN). There are distinct differences between these two disorders, but there are shared characteristics that help to identify eating disorders. The core characteristics of eating disorders include both a severe disturbance in eating behavior and a disturbance in the perception of body shape and weight. A person with an eating disorder may first begin to appropriately lose weight, but to be classified as an eating disorder, this behavior intensifies at some point, and there is a sense of loss of control over food and body image.

Like other mental illnesses, these disorders have biological, psychological, and social influences. Having a parent with an eating disorder increases the likelihood of development in a teen. Psychologically the food or eating disorder can be used as a way to compensate for or hide from unnamable feelings. The Western social culture with an emphasis on thinness as attractiveness further intensifies this problem. However, there can be significant medical problems that occur as a result of this distorted relationship with food. Despite the appearance that these disorders are about food, it is important to remember that the distorted relationship with food has psychological meaning, and simply addressing the nutritional aspect is not helpful.

AN was first described as a clinical entity in the late 1800s, whereas BN was recognized as a distinct clinical entity almost a century later. At the present time, obesity is not considered an eating disorder. If there are believed to be strong underlying psychological factors that are contributing to the medical condition of obesity, there can be a diagnosis of eating disorder,

not otherwise specified. In addition, there is research under-
way to help define a new eating disorder called binge eating disorder.

ANOREXIA NERVOSA

Characteristics

The essential characteristic of AN involves the person's refusal
to maintain normal body weight (APA, 2000, p. 583). By definition the individual maintains a body weight that is below
normal for age and height, which is given the standard of 85%
below the expected weight. For a younger child, this can also
include failure to make expected weight gains while height
growth continues. Typically, the weight loss is achieved by
severely restricting caloric intake at times to the point that
only a few specific foods are consumed daily. In addition,
excessive exercise or purging by vomiting can contribute to
the weight loss.

The second characteristic of AN is an intense fear of gaining
weight or becoming fat. Interestingly, this fear often worsens
with additional weight loss. There can be a very strong preoccupation to the exclusion of other thoughts about the desire to
be thinner. Moreover, there is a significant distortion in body
weight perception and shape. This can include an overall
perception of being fat or can be focused on one or two body
parts being fat. For females who have begun to menstruate,
another criterion is the cessation of menstrual periods, termed
amenorrhea. Amenorrhea occurs as a result of a reduction in
levels of hormones critical in the regulation of estrogen. When
estrogen levels decrease, menstruation stops.

AN has two subtypes. The first is restricting type where the
weight loss is achieved through dieting, fasting, or excessive
exercising. The second type is binge eating/purging type. This
type can include those people who binge and purge during the
episode of weight loss. This is typically associated with significant times of caloric restriction as well. This subtype can
also include those who do not binge but regularly engage in
purging even after small amounts of food (APA, 2000, p. 589).

Individuals with AN commonly have other distortions
in their thinking. They can become inflexible with their
thoughts and lose social spontaneity. This is often seen as a
change from the person's baseline personality. Perfectionism
is a common feature that may have been present before the

illness but often becomes exacerbated during the course. The individual can lose or limit emotional expression in part due to the intense preoccupation with weight and body image. The cognitive distortions can be seen in the individual's perceived ineffectiveness at tasks, but in reality the individual's perfectionism often forces him or her to excel (American Academy of Child and Adolescent Psychiatry [AACAP], 2008).

Along with having cognitive distortions, the person often attempts to control the external environment. The person can become excessively controlling about the way in which food is prepared or consumed. Rituals about how the food is cut and chewed can also become prominent. There can be fears of eating in public or eating in front of other people. Typically, individuals with AN become unnecessarily focused on food. The individual can demonstrate this by excessively baking, collecting recipes, or even hoarding food. The desire for external control can also extend beyond food to rituals of hygiene or order.

Denial of this disorder is common. The person frequently denies that he or she is underweight. Presenting evidence is often not successful in changing this perception. There is limited ability for the person to recognize that a body distortion exists. In addition, it is common that the individual denies existing medical complications as a result of the illness.

A very common premorbid characteristic is perfectionism. For example, the teen is often a high achiever in school. However, this person who appears highly competent is actually suffering from low self-esteem. Many aspects of the person's life are not felt to be in his or her own control (AACAP, 2008).

Interestingly, some of these associated characteristics can be a manifestation of the starvation that the person is self-inducing. There was a study conducted at the end of World War II to understand the effects of starvation. Thirty-six conscientious objectors of the war agreed to complete a 1-year study of starvation and refeeding. During the phase of starvation, the men exhibited signs of increased preoccupation with food, depression, irritability, social withdrawal, and isolation. The preoccupation with food continued during the refeeding stages. The work is referenced in a two-volume textbook titled *The Biology of Human Starvation* (Keys, Brožek, Henschel, Mickelsen, & Taylor, 1950).

AN can have severe medical complications. Nearly all systems of the body are negatively affected by restricted caloric intake. The skin can become dry. Fine hair called lanugo can grow over the body. Nails and hair become brittle. Bones will begin to lose mass, which is called osteopenia. Muscle weakness or muscle loss can occur. Often the internal body temperature decreases, which causes the youth to feel cold all the time. Lethargy and cognitive slowing can occur. Anemia is common. Constipation occurs as the body generally slows down to prevent death. The cardiac system is particularly vulnerable to starvation. Blood pressure and pulse rates decrease. Cardiac arrhythmia can occur and can be a source of mortality. Dehydration is common. The thyroid becomes less active which results in a lower level of circulating thyroid hormones. Other hormonal changes are common and result in amenorrhea (see accompanying CD: 9.1). Brain imaging shows an increase in the ventricular-brain ratios secondary to starvation, and neurological problems can occur (Steiner & Lock, 1998).

Epidemiology and Comorbidity

AN rarely begins before puberty, but individuals with AN can have early memories of perceiving they were overweight. The lifetime prevalence of AN among females is 0.5% (APA, 2000, p. 587), and males experience this difficulty one tenth as frequently. Studies have suggested that AN is more common in industrialized societies. In the United States, approximately 95% of those affected are Caucasian, and 75% are adolescents. It is most commonly observed in middle and upper socioeconomic classes, although it can occur in any social class (National Institute of Mental Health [NIMH], n.d.). In addition, it is noted that there is a 7% increased incidence in first-degree relatives (Grice et al., 2002).

Adolescents who are involved in certain activities can have a higher likelihood of developing AN. Dancers, gymnasts, skaters, models, actors, wrestlers, and long-distance runners have been described as being at risk. This is thought to be related to the societal and performance pressure that thinness is desirable (Mehler, Gray, & Schulte, 1997).

Course

AN tends to begin in girls between the ages of 14 and 18 years. A stressful life event or illness can be a recognized precipitant. However, there are often times when no precipitant is identified. The course of the illness is variable. Some individuals have a rapid and complete recovery, whereas others have a more refractory course with fluctuating patterns of weight gain followed by relapse. A small percentage of girls experience a chronically deteriorating course of the illness over many years. Alternatively, the course of AN can change to BN. A younger teen who presents with the restricting type of AN can develop increased symptoms of bingeing and purging, and as she begins to gain weight in treatment, there can be a change of diagnosis to BN.

According to the NIMH, an individual with AN is 10 times more likely to die compared to a similar-aged youth without the disorder. Causes of death include cardiac arrest, electrolyte disturbances, or suicide (NIMH, n.d.).

From the family's point of view, before the onset of the eating disorder, the youth with AN had been a "model child." She was perceived as fitting in well with her family and met her parents' high expectations. Prior to the development of the disorder, the family is often unaware of any difficulties the teen is experiencing or any problems in the family's patterns of interactions. There are descriptions that families with poor boundaries between members are more likely to have a daughter with an eating disorder. This family pattern is often one of enmeshment, and classically the mother "gave up" a career to be a mother and begins to put her own expectations for success on her daughter. There is increased consideration that having an underinvolved father can further contribute to the illness. These family patterns are subtle, and the families often appear to others to be "perfect."

Despite this perception of perfection, the teen with AN classically feels distressed about her life and in particular experiences distress about growing older. She perceives that her life is not in her control. At some point before the illness emerges, she begins to want to assert herself and regain control of her life, but this is met with challenges. Most commonly, to be able to reassert some control of her life, she becomes focused and preoccupied about her eating and exercise habits. It has also been theorized that along with wanting to exert control on her life, another psychological trigger is her desire to avoid maturation and the transition into adulthood.

Evaluation

The evaluation of a youth with AN should include a thorough physical assessment completed by a pediatrician. This should include a comprehensive physical examination with close detail paid to the cardiovascular system. Laboratory data are needed to assess and ultimately monitor the fluid balance and electrolytes. Other laboratory data can include CBC, calcium, magnesium, phosphorus, and thyroid hormones. An EKG can be indicated. Depending on the duration of illness, the pediatrician might conduct a bone scan to determine the severity of osteoporosis.

A psychiatric evaluation is valuable. The psychiatrist will obtain a thorough history for both the individual and the family. It is important to review if any significant stressors were associated with the weight loss. As with other evaluations, the psychiatrist should also closely assess for other comorbid mental health problems that may need to be addressed.

Another important role that a psychiatric evaluation has is to help determine what treatment interventions are likely to be most helpful. For example, if the family patterns are found during the evaluation to be particularly strong, then it should be recommended that more in-depth family treatment occur. If there is a strong component of poor self-concept, then more directive individual therapy can be helpful. The body image distortions need to be carefully pursued during the evaluation as well.

The need for a higher level of treatment intervention is guided by physical parameters. Severe dehydration and lab abnormalities that cannot be effectively corrected through fluid replacement can be an indication for medical admission. A weight below 70% of ideal body weight is a guideline point for inpatient admission to an eating disorder unit or acute psychiatric unit. In addition, any identified medical problems such as orthostatic hypotension or severe dehydration can support a need for inpatient care.

The pediatrician and psychiatrist should have communication at least through the transfer of records. It is helpful for there to be strong collaboration between the providers both at the time of assessment and throughout treatment.

Therapeutic Principles

The early identification of symptoms is very helpful at promoting successful interventions. Friends and school personnel can often be instrumental in bringing the difficulty to the parents' attention. Prompt assessment and treatment should be sought. Treatment in the early stages can be as simple as nutritional support to correct misperceptions about caloric needs and psychotherapy to address the distorted body image.

If the early stages of the illness are missed or if the early interventions are not successful, there can be ongoing deterioration of the physical and emotional state of the youth. This combination often makes treatment interventions more difficult.

Depending on the severity of weight loss, the treatment is multimodal, including medical support, nutritional support, psychotherapy, and psychiatric consultation. For very low weight teens, inpatient hospitalization may be needed. More intensive therapeutic interventions can include treatment in a day treatment program or intensive outpatient treatment program.

Inpatient hospitalizations are pursued for teens who are below 70% of their ideal body weight. The more intensive structure and support that can be provided helps to support refeeding and other therapeutic interventions. A study was completed in 2006 that looked at the patterns of hospitalization for AN in 1970s compared to the 1990s. In the earlier hospitalizations, the adolescents stayed in the hospital longer and gained weight more slowly. They left the hospital at a lower weight but were less likely to require rehospitalization (Willer, Thuras, & Crow, 2005).

One of the most critical first steps of treatment of AN includes refeeding. If the teen is refusing to increase caloric intake, there should be consideration of using tube feeding. For a person who has a period of prolonged starvation, the refeeding needs to be done under close medical supervision to prevent electrolyte disturbances, which can be lethal. The majority of therapeutic interventions are unsuccessful if the teen is significantly underweight.

Psychotherapy Treatment

Psychotherapy can be an important treatment component for individuals with AN. The most common therapeutic approaches for AN include family therapy or individual therapy. The therapeutic approaches of cognitive behavioral therapy (CBT), cognitive analytic therapy (CAT), and nonspecific supportive therapy are useful. Specific psychotherapy is not successful until there has been a degree of weight restoration. However, early in weight restoration, supportive therapy can be useful to help build rapport and provide a degree of support.

Family therapy has been known to be a useful approach to the treatment of AN. The family's style of relating is believed to be an important component in both the start and the continuation of the illness. Working to change these roles and interactions is believed to be paramount to promoting long-term recovery.

Recently, the Maudsley model of family-based treatment for anorexia has been developed and supported by research as a successful family intervention. This model is now manualized (Lock, Le Grange, Agras, & Dare, 2001). In this intervention parents take an authoritative stand toward AN that is separated from the person as an individual. Parents are taught and supported to refeed the child and increase both the quantity and the nutritional value of food until a normal weight is achieved. The parents are also supported to not accept any of the anorexic behaviors regarding control and food rituals. Siblings can also be used to provide support to the patient. Once normal weight is achieved, the responsibility for eating is gradually returned to the patient. The Maudsley model is unique in the history of family therapy and AN, because it has been supported in randomized control trials. These trials have found that the Maudsley model compares favorably to individual therapy (Russell, Szmulker, Dare, & Eisler, 1987) and that outcomes are maintained at 5-year follow-up (Eisler et al., 2000). One of the limitations of the model, however, is that it does not work for all patients.

The CAT model of therapy tries to understand the reasons why change has been difficult. Like CBT the treatment is time limited and occurs during approximately 16 sessions. However, there is little focus on behavior; the focus is instead placed on understanding the unconscious factors that can be impairing growth and change. The treatment also focuses on promoting self-awareness. CAT has been investigated in trials and is considered an evidenced-based treatment intervention. Reformulation, recognition, and revision are used to guide the intervention (Denman, 2001).

CBT can also be useful when a more normal weight has been achieved. This approach can address body distortions or anxiety that occurs with weight gain. CBT has also been shown to be useful at maintaining weight gains that have occurred in adults.

Group therapy can also be used as a part of the treatment. This modality is particularly useful in treatment programs. Understanding that other people struggle with similar concerns can be supportive. Group interventions must include close monitoring to ensure that a negative group does not develop where increased competition to lose weight occurs. Group modalities incorporate cognitive behavioral strategies.

Less traditional therapies can be used in conjunction with the above-described treatments. These therapies more commonly occur in a hospital, and examples include yoga, psychodrama, and art therapy.

Medication

The primary medication strategy to treat AN is the treatment of comorbid conditions. There is no medication that is approved by the FDA to treat AN. It is consistently believed that no known medication works by solely promoting weight gain.

Antidepressants can be useful to treat comorbid depressive or obsessive symptoms. For this symptoms cluster, the SSRI antidepressants can be helpful (see accompanying CD: 6.2 and 6.3). At times the antidepressant mirtazapine (Remeron) is chosen because one of its known side effects is appetite stimulation. Mirtazapine works by prompting the release of serotonin and norepinephrine. This medication is also relatively sedating at low dosages, so it is to be taken at night. This sedative property can be helpful in promoting more restful sleep. It is believed that the antidepressants are less efficacious when a person is significantly below her target weight.

The atypical antipsychotics are at times used in this population because of their anxiety-reducing properties and their appetite-stimulation side effects. A study that was published (Bissada, Tasca, Barber, & Bradwejn, 2008) supported a benefit in weight gain and a reduction in obsessive symptoms in women with severe AN who were treated with olanzapine (Zyprexa) (see accompanying CD: 8.3 and 8.4). One of the difficult steps in pursuing this medication is consent. Individuals with AN are very concerned about gaining weight, and when the side effect of weight gain is explained, they can become very resistant to this pharmacologic intervention.

The psychopharmacological treatment of AN is very limited and should never be considered the only intervention for treatment. When medications are used, they are best used as part of a multidisciplinary treatment approach. They can help reduce anxiety, obsessive or ruminative thoughts, and feelings of sadness. Some medications can have a beneficial side effect of increasing appetite, but no medication successfully relieves the illness without other interventions.

Clinical Case

Karen was a 15-year-old Caucasian female who presented with a history of a 25-pound weight loss in the past 6 weeks. She was 5 feet, 5 inches tall with a baseline weight of 125 pounds. Her current weight was 100 pounds. Her pulse was 61 beats per minute, and her blood pressure was 110/70. She expressed significant reluctance to participate in the evaluation and repetitively insisted that there was nothing wrong with her. She stated that she wanted to lose an additional 10 pounds and was primarily focused on what she perceived as her large stomach.

Her family reported that she developed a gastrointestinal virus 2 months ago that resulted in her losing a small amount of weight. She began to enjoy comments that other people made regarding her weight loss and quickly began to interpret others' comments about becoming thin to mean that she had previously been overweight. She gradually began to restrict her intake of food, and by the time her parents became aware of her restriction, she was eating an orange for breakfast, plain baby spinach for lunch, and several bites of what was put on her plate for dinner. Her family also stated that she was sleeping only 5 hours a night, setting her alarm clock for 4:00 a.m. to complete homework and 500 sit-ups before her day started.

A pediatrician had assessed her and educated her about the health problems of low weight. However, he did not believe that she was presently suffering any health problems. Karen presented for a psychiatric evaluation at the request of the pediatrician. It became quickly clear that numerous treatment interventions would be critical for her recovery. One of the early challenges to this treatment approach was her denial of illness. However, fortunately, her weight loss was noted early during illness, and treatment began before her weight became critically low. With her parents' support and encouragement, she agreed to meet with a nutritionist who was familiar with the treatment of eating disorders.

The family received nutritional support and was able to set appropriate expectations. The parents began to prepare Karen's meals according to the nutritional guidelines that were given. Although initially Karen resented eating under supervision because of her parents' consistency, she was able to do so successfully.

As her weight began to increase, she became more willing to consider treatment interventions. She and her family began to address family interactions with a family therapist, and she was able to assert her needs and control in a more appropriate fashion. In addition, it became clear that she had very low self-confidence. She described a long-standing history of feeling sad and not feeling as though she fit in with friends. An SSRI antidepressant was added, which successfully reduced this feeling.

Karen had always been a high-achieving student. Even during her weight loss, she maintained very high grades, although this took additional effort because her concentration was poor. School personnel, particularly the guidance counselor, were useful to help provide a calm environment in which Karen could eat her morning snack and lunch. Her course of recovery was marked with a few setbacks where she began to restrict again. However, with gentle confrontation from her support team consisting of her parents, her nutritionist, her pediatrician, and her guidance counselor, over 3 months she was able to reach a weight of 120 pounds. She maintained this weight, and after working successfully with CBT, her body distortions continued to also improve.

BULIMIA NERVOSA

Characteristics

BN is characterized by periods of binge eating followed by inappropriate compensation to prevent weight gain (APA, 2000, p. 594). A binge is defined by eating an amount of food in a discreet time that is larger than what most people would eat. The typical length of a binge is 2 hours or less. The individual consumes the food in a way that is perceived as out of control. Satiety cues are often ignored, and the person may continue to eat to the point of physical discomfort. A single binge episode can change settings. For example, a person may begin to binge at a public place such as a restaurant and continue to binge upon returning home. Binge foods can vary but are usually sweet and calorie-dense foods. In addition, a person can identify certain foods that are likely to trigger a binge when consumed in regular quantities.

To reach the diagnostic threshold for BN, a person must, along with bingeing, take additional measures to prevent weight gain. These efforts can include purging, where the individual attempts to remove the binge by vomiting or misusing laxative, diuretics, or enemas (APA, 2000, p. 591). Most commonly, a person will induce vomiting either by creating a gag reflex with a finger or by taking syrup of ipecac. If self-induced vomiting is used routinely, eventually the vomiting can occur without a physical induction because the sphincter between the stomach and esophagus become weak. Diuretics, laxatives, and enemas can be used in large quantities following a binge as compensation. Alternatively, a person can avoid weight gain by using other inappropriate behaviors. This can occur through excessive exercise or extreme caloric restriction.

To reach the threshold criteria for BN, a person must binge twice a week and purge twice a week for 3 months. As with AN a person with BN must be inappropriately influenced by his or her body shape and weight. Finally, these episodes must not occur exclusively in the context of AN (APA, 2000, p. 594).

Individuals with BN are usually of normal weight but may have been overweight before the eating disorder began. Restricting caloric intake and identifying food as "good" or "bad" can help set the stage for this eating disorder. Purging can lead to some weight loss, but it is typically not a successful way to lose a significant amount of weight because calories are absorbed before inducing the purge. In some cases, a person with BN can be above or below normal weight.

The development of BN, however, is more complex than the person's relationship with food. Binges can be triggered by uncomfortable emotions or stress. A binge can be thought to be a way to reduce the uncomfortable feelings. Following the binge the uncomfortable feelings return and are magnified because of the fear of weight gain. If the individual purges, the purge event can also further reduce the negative emotions. It is not uncommon that an individual with BN has difficulty tolerating negative emotions. Both the binge and the purge episodes may be a way to help deflect the difficult emotions.

Another characteristic of BN is the secretiveness of the illness. The person will often take excessive steps to ensure that his or her secret is not discovered. There can be a series of rituals or rules with food to ensure that no one finds out that this behavior is occurring. Although a binge can start in a public place, the majority of the event occurs in private. The person experiences significant shame because of the recognition that this is not an appropriate relationship with food.

Medical complications are abundant in this disorder and occur in the absence of weight loss. Vomiting commonly causes tooth decay and enlarged parotid glands. Repetitive vomiting can lead to esophageal tears, gastric bleeding, and slowing of the gastrointestinal track. The gastrointestinal track struggles to stay regular because of inconsistencies in food intake and the movement of food normally throughout the intestinal system. In addition, dehydration and electrolyte disturbances can cause dizziness and lethargy and can result from all mechanisms of purging. The most severe complication of electrolyte disturbance can include cardiac arrest. Individuals who abuse syrup of ipecac to induce vomiting can develop a serious medical problem where the heart becomes enlarged and loses its effectiveness. For those who abuse laxatives, there can also be electrolyte disturbances or chronic diarrhea, and depending on the extent of this problem, this can be a lifelong problem. Menstrual irregularities can be another medical complication of the binge and purge cycle regardless of weight status (see accompanying CD: 9.2).

Epidemiology and Comorbidity

BN has a prevalence among women of approximately 1% to 3% (APA, 2000, p. 593). This statistic makes it more common that AN. Similar to AN, males can also be affected with BN at a frequency of 1 male to 10 females. This eating disorder is common in the United States across all races and socioeconomic classes but also remains most common among Caucasians.

Depressive disorders commonly co-occur with BN. The depressive disorder can predate the eating disorder or occur at the same time. Even if full-blown depressive disorders such as dysthymia or major depression are not present, low self-esteem is very frequent. Besides depressive symptoms there is also an increased likelihood of anxious symptoms. The symptoms of BN can be used as a way to tolerate these negative emotions.

Substance abuse is another common comorbidity. It is estimated that the lifetime prevalence of substance abuse or dependence is at least 30% among individuals with BN (APA, 2000, p. 591). The two most common substances of abuse are alcohol and stimulants. Interestingly, the stimulant use can first occur for the effect of appetite suppressant.

In addition, there appears to be an increased likelihood that personality disorders are more common in individuals with BN. When the eating disorder occurs with a personality disorder, the treatment is more difficult, and the outcome tends to be more guarded.

Course

Families with children who develop AN were described above as being potentially rigid, controlling, and lacking emotional warmth. The family characteristics that are more common for teens suffering from BN are chaos and discord.

The disorder begins in individuals in their mid-teen years, but there are cases where the disorder can first present well into adulthood. Individuals with BN report a long history of preoccupation with weight and a pattern of dieting behavior that predates the onset. BN can present as the individual's first eating disorder. Alternatively, it can occur after successful weight gain following an episode of AN.

The course of BN tends to be chronic. There are commonly episodes of relapse, and it can remain intermittent for years. As described above, the presence of a personality disorder with BN makes treatment more refractory. If a person sustains a remission for 1 year, there is a higher chance of full recovery.

Evaluation

Just as with AN, a thorough medical assessment is critical during the initial presentation for treatment if the adolescent is first brought to a psychiatrist's attention. Primary care physicians may be the first to question the illness, as there are distinct physical problems that can be used to identify the problem. Those who self-induce vomiting can display Russell's sign, which is dry, chapped skin on the first two knuckles caused by the teeth while the individual sticks those fingers down his or her throat. Enlarged parotid glands, which are located near the base of the jaw and neck, can also be another visible sign of vomiting. Dentists are another group of medical providers who first recognize and question symptoms of the illness because of the characteristic thinning of the dental enamel that occurs on the back of the teeth due to gastric acid.

A psychiatric evaluation is useful to determine both the symptoms of the eating disorder and the presence of other psychiatric illnesses. The information should be gathered from a number of sources, but a teen with symptoms of BN will often be more forthcoming about his or her eating disorder symptoms and patterns when seen individually. The teen often takes drastic steps to keep the purging hidden from family members, and there is extreme reluctance for the family to learn of the secrets. The psychiatric evaluation helps to identify patterns of thinking that contributed to the eating disorder and family patterns that can be perpetuating the illness.

The psychiatrist should also inquire about substance use and determine if an additional substance abuse assessment is needed. Depending on the responses to this inquiry, it can also be helpful to have a urine drug analysis completed.

Therapeutic Principles

The treatment for BN is best approached from a multimodal approach. If the severity of the illness is judged to be mild, outpatient treatment, which can include psychiatric care, psychotherapy, medical monitoring, and possibly nutritional support, is needed. For more moderate and severe symptoms, there may need to be a comprehensive treatment program using different levels.

The medical assessment can include weekly or monthly weight checks, a routine physical examination particularly if the person is repetitively dehydrated, and regular blood work monitoring. If the illness is recognized more quickly or if early medical assessments have not identified problem areas, this frequency of monitoring can be reduced.

Nutritional support is needed to ensure that the person begins to feel comfortable eating from a variety of food groups. A person may try to stop bingeing and purging by not allowing himself or herself to eat foods that historically trigger a binge. However, the primary nutritional standpoint is that full recovery from the eating disorder will allow the person to eat all food groups. Nutritional support involves generating a specific meal plan to be followed that is balanced and uses all of the food groups.

Very abnormal laboratory values in the context of a high number of binges and purges each day is needed for an individual to receive more intensive levels of treatment intervention such as inpatient or partial day treatment. Treatment programs often combine girls with AN and BN, which can be helpful but can increase the desire of an individual with BN to restrict.

Psychotherapy Treatment

The primary accepted psychotherapy treatment for BN is CBT. This modality is commonly used for both individual treatment and group treatment. Some sources believe that individual or group treatment is the best intervention, but most clinicians agree that a combination of both modalities with CBT premises is the best therapy intervention.

CBT focuses on the underlying thoughts and emotions that trigger a binge and looks for alternative strategies to manage these. CBT can also be useful to begin to address the body image distortion that is common. Teaching alternative problem-solving skills can be helpful, as can exploring other mechanisms for self-regulation. Interventions that also include informal nutritional support tend to be helpful.

Medication

When used in conjunction with other treatment interventions, medication can be an important component in the treatment of BN. The FDA has approved the use of fluoxetine (Prozac) for the treatment of BN. It has long been seen that there is a high comorbidity between the depressive disorders and BN. This has led to numerous studies (Fluoxetine Bulimia Nervosa Collaborative Study Group, 1992; Goldstein, Wilson, Thompson, Potvin, & Rampey, 1995) to assess the response of bingeing and purging to antidepressants. The placebo response rates in these studies varied widely, which suggests that factors other than the medication can have a role in improvement. Many of the studies supported the idea that the frequency of bingeing and purging was reduced by antidepressants, but these gains were not maintained throughout the studies.

There were two multicentered studies completed to assess the response to fluoxetine. These studies involved a larger study size and were of longer treatment duration. This has led to the support for the use of this medication to reduce the frequency of eating disordered behaviors. Interestingly, it was suggested in the studies that a higher dose of this medication is more effective. Most individuals with depression respond to dosages of 20 mg or 40 mg, but only the dose of 60 mg was superior to placebo (Fluoxetine Bulimia Nervosa Collaborative Study Group, 1992). This raises an interesting question regarding an adolescent's tolerability of this high dose. As discussed previously, adolescents can be particularly sensitive to the mood-activating side effects or can experience irritability and akathisia on higher dosages of SSRIs. If a low dose of this medication is not effective, a higher dose can be tried as long as there is adequate monitoring.

Other trials have looked at the use of lithium carbonate or naltrexone, which is an opiate antagonist. However, there were no consistent findings to support the efficacy of these medications.

Another medication that is receiving some recent interest is the anticonvulsant topiramate (Topamax). Bingeing and purging are reported to improve with this medication. In addition, there was noted improvement in self-esteem, body image, and anxiety (Hedges et al., 2003).

One antidepressant should be avoided in the context of an active episode of BN. Bupropion (Wellbutrin) was withdrawn from the market after its initial release 20 years ago when it was seen to be associated with a higher than expected rate of seizures. A review of the data found that the seizures were occurring in those who had BN. The underlying electrolyte disturbance likely increases the likelihood of an individual developing a seizure while on this medication. Subsequently, there have been two new preparations of bupropion that are longer lasting. Because of their pharmacologic profile, these two preparations may not be as likely to cause seizures in this population, but most clinicians remain very cautious about using this antidepressant in a person with BN.

Clinical Case

Maria was a 16-year-old Caucasian female who presented for a psychiatric evaluation and continuing therapeutic interventions. The reason for the referral was significant depressive symptoms. Maria had been complaining to her parents that she was sad and lacking energy. Her parents agreed that she was more withdrawn than normal and spent much of the evening sleeping in her room. There was a family history of significant depression, including death by suicide in two extended family members. Because of this history, when Maria began to complain of depression, her parents rapidly sought treatment.

During evaluation, Maria's parents described that until 1 year ago, Maria was a pleasant and happy child. She interacted well with adults and peers. She was doing well at school and worked part-time. They noted she began to be more sad and withdrawn over the months before presentation, but there were also times of improvement.

Maria quickly identified symptoms of depression. During the process of obtaining information from her individually, she seemed to change her demeanor when questioned about how the sadness was affecting her appetite and eating patterns. This was a rapid change, so more detailed questions about her eating were explored. Initially, Maria denied any body image distortion and denied food restriction, bingeing, or purging. However, on the second visit, Maria began the session by divulging that she was actively engaging in bingeing and purging. She admitted that this was really the reason she was interested in treatment, but she was very opposed to her parents' knowing of this struggle. She had been bingeing by buying food with money she made at her job and hiding the food and the trash in her car. She was purging by inducing vomiting, and because of her fears that she would be discovered, she would often purge into glass jars, which she kept closed and hidden in her closet. She was bingeing 6 days a week and purging by vomiting following each episode. Maria explained that since elementary school, she had felt overweight and that she did not fit in with peers.

Several visits were spent individually with Maria to establish a therapeutic alliance. As she began to feel more comfortable, it was gently introduced that her family needed to be informed of this problem to help her treatment and to help ensure that appropriate medical interventions were used. Reluctantly she agreed, and a family session occurred where the eating disorder was explained to her parents.

The parents accepted this information well and became important in her recovery. A medical assessment was conducted. She was of normal weight, and there were no laboratory abnormalities. She continued to see her pediatrician monthly. A nutritionist met with Maria and her family for two visits to explain appropriate nutritional information. Educationally she was doing well. She admitted that often she would begin a binge immediately after school when she would pass the candy machine. A plan was created to have her check in with the guidance counselor at the end of each day, which was helpful because it changed her route out of the school and offered additional support.

Psychotherapeutic treatment involved CBT to identify her automatic negative thoughts and poor tolerance for negative emotions. CBT was also used to address her body distortion. Fluoxetine was used to reduce both the binge–purge cycle and depression.

Maria responded very well to all of these interventions. Within a few months the frequency of her binges decreased, and she had stopped purging. Her depressive symptoms also improved. After a few months of stability, she was discharged from treatment.

However, 2 years later Maria returned for treatment after she returned to bingeing and purging when she started college. The challenges of college and independence likely retriggered the eating disorder symptoms. She decided to continue with CBT at college, and because of her early identifications of relapse, this episode was fortunately rather quickly and successfully treated.

BINGE EATING DISORDER

The *DSM-IV-TR* has a series of disorders that are believed to be in need of further study. Binge eating disorder is included in this category. Although it is not a clinically diagnosable entity at the present time, there are preliminary criteria that have been proposed and are being investigated. If this disorder is robustly supported through research as being a distinct clinical entity, it could be included in the next publication of the *DSM* (*DSM-5*).

EATING DISORDER, NOT OTHERWISE SPECIFIED: OVERVIEW

The diagnosis eating disorder, not otherwise specified is used for those individuals who do not meet full diagnostic criteria for AN or BN. It implies an ongoing significant struggle with body image and the inappropriate use of food. Currently, this is used as an accepted diagnosis for an individual who meets the criteria for binge eating disorder. Another example of this disorder includes a girl who meets all criteria for AN except that her menstruation is continuing. Another example includes the regular use of inappropriate compensatory behavior by an individual of normal body weight after eating small amounts of food (APA, 2000, p. 594).

EATING DISORDERS: EDUCATIONAL IMPLICATIONS

Adolescents with AN are commonly highly driven and perfectionistic students. They have high expectations and familial expectations and often have very high grades and a demanding academic workload. During early illness stages and in cases of mild symptoms, there are no overt educational struggles. However, prolonged caloric restriction can negatively affect concentration, memory, and energy. Along with experiencing changes within the brain, the teen can have reduced concentration caused by his or her ongoing obsessive thoughts of body distress and food. Depending on the balance between the high expectations and cognitive impairment, a decline in academic performance can be seen. Even if grades are not affected, the adolescent may complain of difficulty concentrating, and the perceived effort needed is greater. School teams can provide support by understanding the mental difficulties that the student may be experiencing when trying to concentrate.

Schools should not be involved in "policing" foods that are eaten. However, there can be support offered so the student can eat in a place free from distractions. The student may need to consume one or two snacks a day in addition to meals, and efforts may need to be made to ensure that this dietary need can be supported. In addition, the school nurse can be asked to periodically monitor the student's weight. If this option is requested, it is likely that the weight should be obtained in a way so the student cannot see the scale.

Students with BN can also have educational difficulties. If BN is the only diagnosis, there may be very little educational impairment except for a decline in concentration due to thoughts of planning the next binge or feelings of internal distress related to a prior binge. However, BN often occurs in students with other mental illnesses such as substance abuse, mood disorders, and personality disorders. When these diagnoses are present, there can be increased educational difficulties. This population of students frequently seeks attention from adults in the school system and creates chaos in a number of different environments.

Educators can be very helpful as members of the treatment team. Students with eating disorders spend a significant amount of time of the day in school. Supportive services during early treatment can include allowing the student to eat in a small setting with a supportive adult present and using teachers or a guidance counselor to "check in" with during the day if uncomfortable emotions are occurring.

EATING DISORDERS: SUMMARY

Eating disorders are common in adolescent females. The individual struggling with this disorder will often take great steps to avoid recognition of the struggle. In addition, the individual often has a significant amount of denial about the illness.

Early identification and treatment using a multimodal treatment team consisting of a psychiatrist, therapist, pediatrician, and nutritionist are needed for more severe degrees of illness.

There is often little educational impact for adolescents with an eating disorder. Individuals with AN have poor concentration but often have the ability to not let this interfere with schoolwork because of their desire to please others. At times school nurses can be asked to assist in monitoring weight. When this occurs it is important to know if the adolescent wants to know the weight or if the weight monitoring should be done blindly.

Ten

Pervasive Developmental Disorders

AUTISM SPECTRUM DISORDERS: BACKGROUND

The autism spectrum disorders are neuropsychiatric conditions that are characterized by patterns of difficulties in social interactions, communication, and repetitive behaviors. These disorders have an onset within the first few years of life. The *DSM* system calls these disorders pervasive developmental disorders, and five distinct clinical entities are recognized: autistic disorder, Asperger's disorder, Rett's disorder, childhood disintegrative disorder, and pervasive developmental disorder, not otherwise specified (NOS) (American Psychiatric Association [APA], 2000, p. 69). Each of these disorders is characterized by distinct developmental challenges in socialization, communication, and perseverating behaviors. Mental retardation can also be associated with these disorders. The diagnosis can be made at any point in life, but typically more severe illnesses are recognized in preschool children. These disorders are also conceptualized as existing on a spectrum, the autism spectrum disorders, with more blurring of boundaries between the different entities. Although this can be helpful thinking, the diagnosis should be made for an individual disorder.

Rett's disorder and childhood disintegrative disorder are significantly less common and for the purposes of this book will be summarized only briefly. Rett's disorder is characterized by a normal prenatal and perinatal life. There is also normal psychomotor development through the first 5 months of life. However, between the ages of 5 and 48 months, there is a slowing of the rate of head circumference growth. There is also a drastic notable loss of purposeful hand movements. Subsequently, there is a development of stereotyped hand movements that look like hand-wringing or hand washing. In addition, there is a loss of social engagement and severely impaired expressive and receptive language development. There is also an appearance of poorly coordinated gait or trunk movements. This disorder is associated with severe or profound mental retardation (APA, 2000, p. 77). It exists in females only, and a specific genetic mutation is involved in 95% of identified cases. The prevalence is very low, with 1 in 10,000 females affected (APA, 2000, p. 76).

Childhood disintegrative disorder is characterized by normal development for the first 2 years of life, with a loss of previously acquired skills in the areas of language, social skills, bowel or bladder control, and play or motor skills. The regression can be gradual or abrupt (APA, 2000, p. 79). The developmental losses continue to a certain point and then plateau, likely remaining constant at this level through life. This condition is associated with severe mental retardation. If there is prolonged normal development with a loss in skills, there should be a consideration for a neurologic assessment. It is also very rare and can be more likely to occur in males (APA, 2000, p. 78).

These two disorders are believed to be significantly more rare than the other pervasive developmental disorders, although childhood disintegrative disorder may be underdiagnosed (APA, 2000, p. 79). These disorders are associated with severe or profound mental retardation, and educational interventions are often based on the degree of cognitive impairment. However, both disorders also are characterized by deficits in communication, social interactions, and repetitive behaviors, which is why they are characterized on the autistic spectrum. Most commonly, neurologists manage individuals with these disorders.

Autistic disorder was first described over 60 years ago. In recent decades there has been a broadening of the thinking of this disorder. Asperger's disorder was also recognized around the same time, but the diagnostic clarification was reached only 20 years ago. Asperger's disorder shares some features with autistic disorder. Individuals with this disorder have less impairment in speech and language but have socialization difficulties and repetitive behaviors. Pervasive developmental disorder, NOS is diagnosed for individuals with some features of autism but not to the degree in which the person meets criteria for autistic disorder or Asperger's disorder.

AUTISTIC DISORDER

Types and Characteristics

Autism is characterized by a disturbance in each of the following areas: social relatedness, communication and play, and restricted repertoire of activity and interests. The onset must be apparent by the age of 3 years in at least one of the above areas. The difficulties in social relatedness are noted by impairment in nonverbal behaviors, failure to develop peer relationships as expected based on the developmental level, a lack of seeking to share interest with others, and a lack of social or emotional reciprocity. The impairments in communication can be a lack of spoken language or a marked difficulty in the ability to initiate or sustain conversations or repetitive language. The restricted repetitive stereotyped behaviors include preoccupation with restricted topics, adherence to nonfunctional routines, preoccupation with parts of objects, and specific motor mannerisms like hand flapping or body rocking (APA, 2000, p. 75) (see accompanying CD: 10.1).

Autistic disorder was first described in the 1940s by Dr. Leo Kanner. For many years there was diagnostic confusion between autism and childhood schizophrenia. It was not until the 1970s that it was firmly recognized that these two disorders were distinct and not on a spectrum of continuity. Autism was first included in the *DSM-III*, but with each successive *DSM*, there is increased diagnostic specificity and clarity.

There are clear genetic components related to the development of autism. Older fathers are more likely to give life to children with autism, which speaks to chromosomal abnormalities that can occur in the sperm with age (Reichenberg et al., 2006). There is a strong neuropathological component, and it is hypothesized that there are distinct brain circuits associated with the three core symptom deficits. Individuals with autism initially have a large brain volume, but then there is a regression in brain volume (Hazlett et al., 2005).

At times a child can be identified with "high-functioning autism." At the present time, no such diagnosis exists within the *DSM* system. This term is thought to be distinct from Asperger's disorder and for diagnostic purposes most clearly falls into the category of pervasive developmental disorder, NOS.

Epidemiology and Comorbidity

Studies of autism that were completed in the 1990s revealed an estimated prevalence of 4.8 per 10,000 people (Fombonne,

1998), but other studies suggested that the prevalence might be 1 in 1,000 (Bryson, 1997). However, recently these rates appear to be increasing, and there has been controversy about whether there is an epidemic of autism. It is estimated that 1 in 150 children is now diagnosed with an autism spectrum disorder (Centers for Disease Control and Prevention [CDC], 2007). This increase is related to a number of different factors. The term *autism spectrum disorder* is broader and encompasses children with Asperger's disorder and pervasive developmental disorder, NOS. There is increased screening for these illnesses, particularly by pediatricians, as it is believed that early intervention promotes an improved outcome. A child who was formerly considered to be mentally retarded may now receive this diagnosis because of its more common acceptance.

It remains debatable if there are environmental factors that can also be related to this noted increase, but to date there has been no single identified factor. There has been much publicity about the potential causative effects of vaccinations, but to date there has been no support linking thimerosal to autism.

Males are affected three to four times more often than females. However, when the diagnosis is present in females, there is a higher likelihood of severe retardation accompanying the diagnosis (APA, 2000, p. 73).

In Kanner's early study of the diagnosis, he noted that in almost all of his cases, the families were highly accomplished and highly educated. However, it is now believed that autism is present in families of all levels of educational and occupational achievement. It is also believed that there was a selection bias in his early studies (Wing, 1980). There is no known race difference noted.

Samples of individuals with autistic disorder support that 50% of the cases have severe or profound mental retardation, whereas 30% have mild to moderate mental retardation, and 20% have IQs in the normal range (Fombonne, 1998).

Along with having a high likelihood of mental retardation, children with autistic disorder have a high likelihood of other mental health diagnoses. There is a high level of hyperactivity and attentional problems. It used to be stated that attention-deficit/hyperactivity disorder (ADHD) as a diagnosis could not be given in the presence of autistic disorder. However, the *DSM-IV* changed this thinking, and both can exist, but ADHD is diagnosed only if the severity of the inattention is higher than what would be expected in a child with autism (APA, 2000, p. 74).

Mood and anxiety disorders can occur, but these are more prominent as distinct clinical entities in individuals who have less impairment from autism. However, there can be some clinical overlap between obsessive-compulsive disorder (OCD) and autism. It is common that children and teens with autism have obsessive compulsive–like symptoms, as they are excessively focused on certain topics.

Tic disorders are also common. However, these must be differentiated from any stereotypic behaviors that can be associated with the autistic disorder.

Schizophrenia is a distinct clinical entity that can co-occur with autistic disorder. However, it does not do so at a rate higher than would be expected based on statistical comparisons (Volkmar & Cohen, 1991).

Course

Infants with autism have been described as very content and happy babies who made few demands on the parents. The described difficulties in socialization and speech difficulties are the characteristics that are noted to develop first. Complaints can first be brought to the attention of the pediatrician around the age of 2 years because of the child's lack of language skills and poor communication. Socialization deficits are recognized as the child may become attached to objects rather than people. The perceived connection with the parent is lacking. The restricted areas of interest and stereotyped movements are more likely apparent after the age of 3 years.

By school age, most individuals with autism have some improvements in social responsiveness and communication skills. However, at this age problems managing change and transitions become more apparent. Small changes in the child's routine can cause significant distress. A variety of self-stimulatory behaviors also become apparent at this age, such as rocking and hand flapping. Disruptive behaviors including aggression can be a reason to seek psychiatric intervention.

In adolescence the outcome is variable. Some individuals begin to make marked developmental gains in all areas. However, there are also individuals who will deteriorate in their ability to manage their aggressiveness, impulsivity, and compulsivity.

Evaluation

Although severe autism is typically identified and diagnosed by a pediatrician, there are times that a psychiatric evaluation is sought. The psychiatric evaluation when autistic disorder is being considered should focus on acquiring information about development. There should be information gathered about pregnancy, labor, and delivery. A developmental history should inquire about the acquisition of developmental milestones with particular attention paid to language and motor milestones. It is helpful to learn when and why the parents first became concerned. This history can help to distinguish autistic disorder from other pervasive developmental disorders and other problems in the area of language and social development. During the social history, there should be a review of the response to any early intervention services or educational programs.

There should also be time spent with the parents to understand the child's current developmental level. The parents should describe what typical social interactions occur and how they appear. It is important to understand how the child interacts with family members, peers, adults who are known, and adults who are not known. The psychiatrist should explore what areas of restricted or unusual interest the child has. Finally, there should be an understanding of the specific problem behaviors that are interfering with functioning in different domains.

The clinical interview with the child is also very important. There should be an assessment of the child's reciprocal patterns of interaction. The type of rapport that is established can contribute to diagnostic clarity. Children with autistic disorder have difficulty establishing rapport and have difficulty sustaining conversation if they have some language abilities. The speech patterns and lack of emotional repertoire can also contribute to the picture seen during the mental status assessment (see accompanying CD: 10.2).

When the diagnosis appears more complicated, it can be helpful for the psychiatrist to observe the child in a setting other than the office. At times seeing the child in one or two natural environments can lend diagnostic clarity. This observation can clarify how the child responds in an environment that is known.

Besides a psychiatric evaluation, there are also other important assessments that should be done to help make the diagnosis and to rule out other concerns. These assessments include at minimum a comprehensive physical examination and a speech and language assessment. There can also be other assessments indicated depending on an individual's need.

A thorough medical history and physical examination should be obtained. Some medical conditions such as Fragile X and tuberous sclerosis are associated with autism (APA, 2000, p. 72). These disorders can be associated with physical characteristics to help determine if these medical problems are also present. There is a higher than normal rate of seizures in children with autism, so if this is suspected, an EEG can be indicated.

There is no definitive laboratory test to rule in or rule out autism. Laboratory testing can be considered during the medical assessment based on clinical areas of concern. One of these areas is if a young child with autism is engaging in pica, which is the ingestion of nonnutritive substances, a lead screen can be indicated. Hearing and vision tests may be indicated particularly in young children, as a lack of sensory input can appear similar to a young child with an autism spectrum disorder.

In addition, a speech and language assessment should be done to assess vocabulary, receptive and expressive language abilities, articulation, and pragmatic skills, which is a measure of the child's ability to use language in social context. Psychological assessment including intelligence testing may be needed to establish an overall level of functioning. An assessment of adaptive skills is needed to provide a diagnosis of mental retardation. Finally, occupational or physical therapy assessments may be indicated. An occupational therapy evaluation can be particularly helpful if there are sensory concerns as well.

Therapeutic Principles

It is believed that early identification and early intervention services are extremely effective at promoting further growth and development. Beginning to target the communication, behavioral, and social difficulties at an early age promotes significant improvement. Intensive and continual support is likely more effective than sporadic services that are less intense (Marcus, Kunce, & Schopler, 1997).

When providing treatment for an individual with autistic disorder, a multidisciplinary team is necessary. The components that need to be addressed include providing educational interventions, treating target symptoms, and monitoring the areas of functioning. Speech and language services are critical to promote the development of language. An occupational therapist can be useful to provide sensory integration. There must be consideration for which of the services will best meet the needs of the identified child.

The educational services that can be appropriate include specialized education and behavioral support. Ancillary services such as speech and language therapy, occupational therapy, and physical therapy can also be deemed appropriate to occur within the educational system. A psychiatrist who is treating a child with autism should be willing to communicate with school personnel.

Speech and language therapy is a critical service to help promote improvement. For individuals with severe autistic disorder, speech therapy can help to facilitate communication. For individuals with less severe cases of autism, speech therapists can begin to work on the pragmatics of language in a way to also help improve social skills.

There is interest in dietary changes that may be helpful at reducing the severity of autistic disorder. There are proponents who support the elimination of wheat and gluten or the consumption of a high-fat diet. Some individuals may have some benefit from these interventions, but there is currently no solid medical research that supports these interventions.

Psychotherapy Treatment

Behavioral support and intervention are among the cornerstones of treatment for a person with an autistic disorder. The focus of this intervention is to strengthen desired behaviors while decreasing maladaptive behaviors. Promoting rapid rewards for positive behavioral choices will strengthen desired behaviors. Providing consequences for aggressive behaviors in a calm and direct manner will help to extinguish negative behaviors. Behavioral interventions can also improve the acquisition of language and social skills. Social skills training is helpful not only to improve social skills in clinical areas but also to generalize these skills to real-life settings.

Family interventions are often very helpful to support the parents and siblings of children with autism. All family members should be encouraged to participate in both the assessment and treatment. It is important that the parents be included particularly early in the process. Parents should be offered time to discuss their concerns and how the diagnosis can have an impact on them. Parents also need support to learn to use behavioral reinforcement schedules.

When available, providing structured behavioral support with an aide can be beneficial. When the positive behaviors can be immediately reinforced, there can be learning. In addition, a behavior aide may be able to facilitate improving social skills by modeling appropriate social interactions and rein-forcing positive choices.

Traditional psychodynamic psychotherapy used to be con-sidered the primary treatment with intervention. However, particularly with comorbid mental retardation, there is little benefit to this treatment.

Medication

There is no specific medication cure for autism. There can be some benefit to pharmacotherapy if particular target symp-toms are present. There must be careful consideration of the balance between appropriate improvement that can occur compared to potential side effects.

The atypical antipsychotic risperidone, is approved for the treatment of autism. This approval came in 2006 after several well-designed studies showed it was effective at reducing irritability and aggression in children with autism (Hardan, Johnson, Johnson, & Hrecznyj, 1996). The treatment is initi-ated at a single low dose and can be increased every 2 weeks. The typical dosages that have been found helpful in this dis-order are 0.5 mg a day to 3.0 mg a day.

Although not approved by the FDA, other atypical antipsy-chotics can be useful in some situations. These can be tried if there is a hope to reduce irritability and aggression, and risperi-done was ineffective or not tolerated. Quetiapine (Seroquel) can be tried in this case. It can be helpful particularly if there is a sleep disturbance, as it can be mildly sedating when taken in the evening (see accompanying CD: 8.3 and 8.4).

There can also be a role for traditional neuroleptics in the treatment. Before the arrival of the atypical antipsychotics, haloperidol (Haldol) was used to reduce stereotyped behav-iors. However, there was a likelihood of the development of tardive dyskinesia, which made many families reluctant to use this class of medication (see accompanying CD: 6.2).

The SSRI antidepressants (see accompanying CD: 6.3) were initially of interest in autism. This interest came from the observation that individuals with autism have a high periph-eral serotonin level. However, peripheral levels of serotonin do not seem to be related to clinical response. This class of medication can be helpful to reduce the ritualistic behaviors and obsessive compulsive–like features. In addition, there can be affective symptoms such as irritability or depression that can be helped with the use of an SSRI. However, these medi-cations can be less effective than the atypical antipsychotics.

Mood stabilizers have little role in the treatment of an individual with an autistic disorder. However, if there is a strong family history of bipolar disorder, there can be some consideration for the use of one of these medications.

Clinical Case

Ned was a 15-year-old male who was referred for a psychiatric evaluation by his school district because of his increased behavioral problems. Ned was diagnosed with autism at the age of 3 years when he had developed no language skills. He preferred to interact by himself and would often sit on the hard wood floor and spin in circles. He began receiving intensive early intervention supports, and during the following years, he developed some language skills. The diagnosis was not in question. Ned had been receiving educational services in an autistic support classroom. This class of six students was very structured. Academic information was presented at his individual level, and as Ned showed more aptitude for mathematics, he participated in a regular education math class with behavioral support. He received speech therapy at school and participated in social skills activities. Ned had done well in the classroom for 1½ years before he began to demonstrate significant physical aggression. He would run out of the classroom and down the hall, yelling very loudly. He would throw items in the classroom, and on one occasion he almost turned over the teacher's desk.

Careful history did not identify any known changes in Ned's home or class environment. His parents reported that in early elementary school, he had demonstrated aggressive characteristics, but these were minimized with behavioral interventions. His parents also noted that he was appearing more frustrated at home. Although he had not been physically aggressive, he was generally louder in all interactions. They also noted that he was more sensitive to loud noises and at home preferred to wear headphones to block out noise. They also noted that his patterns of speech were more repetitive.

Ned's mental status examination showed a large adolescent male who appeared friendly. He readily smiled and attempted to interact. His speech consisted of two- or three-word sentences, and he referred to himself by his first name. He understood that he knew he couldn't leave the classroom at school and could not throw things at school, but he offered little insight into these actions.

It was decided to begin treatment with risperidone. A dose of 0.5 mg at night was initiated. Within a month there was slight improvement. He appeared less frustrated, and he was sleeping better. The dose was increased to 1 mg, and further improvement occurred. The aggressive outbursts began to decrease, and the episodes of perseveration were less frequent.

At the same time, Ned's classroom introduced additional strategies to help him. He began to do his regular math class work within the autistic support setting, and a personal behavioral aide was provided. In addition, Ned was encouraged to wear his earphones at school to help reduce his sensitivity to noise. These changes also were thought to be instrumental in reducing his aggressive outbursts in school.

Two years later, Ned continues on risperidone with general improvement in his frustration level.

ASPERGER'S DISORDER

Types and Characteristics

Individuals with Asperger's disorder have severe and sustained impairment in social interactions and demonstrate a pattern of restricted and repetitive patterns of behavior, interests, and activities (APA, 2000, p. 80). However, individuals with Asperger's disorder do not have significant delays in language acquisition, which is the primary distinction between autism and Asperger's disorder. Individuals with Asperger's disorder can have subtle social communication deficits, such as failure to use language in a reciprocal way (see accompanying CD: 10.3).

The social interaction difficulties are sustained and seen in all areas of life. It is common that there be marked impairment in the use of nonverbal communication. This can be seen as a failure to make sustained eye contact, unusual body postures, or the use of gestures rather than words to regulate social interaction. There can be a marked failure to develop peer relationships to an appropriate developmental level. Younger children have little or no interest in establishing friendships, whereas older individuals can desire friends but lack an understanding of social norms. There can be a lack of sharing enjoyment, interests, or achievements with others. Finally, there can be a lack of social or emotional reciprocity. To meet the diagnostic criteria, the person must manifest at least two of the above four difficulties (APA, 2000, p. 80).

The restricted, repetitive, and stereotyped patterns of behaviors, interests, and activities can be seen as at least one of the following: persistent preoccupation with parts of objects, repetitive motor mannerisms such as hand or finger flapping or complex whole-body movements, inflexible adherence to specific nonfunctional routines, or an encompassing preoccupation with one or more areas of interest that is abnormal in either intensity or focus, such as gathering excessive information about one topic and talking or thinking about this topic to the exclusion of other topics (APA, 2000, p. 80).

Hans Asperger, an Australian pediatrician, first described this illness in 1944, but it was only recently more definitively described. The hallmarks that Dr. Asperger used to distinguish individuals with this disorder compared to the individuals Leo Kanner was describing (autistic children) were its later onset and more normal language development.

Other clinical variations can be seen in individuals with Asperger's disorder and those with autistic disorder. Typically, individuals with Asperger's disorder are of normal intelligence or even gifted intelligence. Parents often report that children with Asperger's disorder had motor clumsiness early in life, and occasionally speech and language development occurred earlier than would be expected. In contrast, individuals with autistic disorder typically reach motor milestones without difficulty, but language milestones are significantly delayed (see accompanying CD: 10.3).

Epidemiology and Comorbidity

The epidemiological data regarding the prevalence of Asperger's disorder are varied. This has to do with the stringency with which the diagnostic criteria are applied. More recent studies have assessed for the prevalence of autism spectrum disorders, which is broader than Asperger's disorder.

There is no increased rate of mental retardation in students with Asperger's disorder. These individuals may have variability of cognitive functioning, with strengths in areas of verbal ability and weaknesses in nonverbal areas (APA, 2000, p. 81).

There can be increased rates of ADHD, and many individuals with Asperger's disorder are first identified with ADHD before the additional diagnosis of Asperger's disorder is recognized. Affective disorders, with a particular increased likelihood of depressive disorders, are also commonly associated with Asperger's disorder. Individuals with a higher degree of intelligence can be more prone to depression, as they can recognize differences between themselves and others. Finally, there can be overlap between Asperger's disorder and OCD. Differentiating these two disorders can be challenging, but one hallmark that can be used for this is individuals with OCD have a fear or worry connected with the pattern of behavior.

Course

Asperger's disorder is a lifelong disorder. However, individuals with Asperger's disorder have a more positive outcome than someone with autism. Asperger's disorder is typically recognized and diagnosed at an older age than autistic disorder. Because there is less cognitive impairment associated with Asperger's disorder, the degree of functional impairment is less. This is an explanation for both the later recognition of illness and the improved outcome.

The developmental history can suggest early speech and language development while motor delays and clumsiness were noted. In preschool years these children can show early interests in numbers and letters. There is attachment to parents and family members, but there can be idiosyncrasies in these children's approaches to new adults and peers.

The social difficulties become more evident in school-age children. The approach that these students take demonstrates an intense preoccupation with their area of interest, and this can cause excessive frustration if other students don't share this interest. Young school-age children often do not identify a desire to have friends and can spend long periods of time occupying themselves. By adolescence a person with Asperger's disorder can begin to express a desire to have friends but may continue to excessively struggle with interpersonal relationships. Adolescence can be a particularly tumultuous time, as teens can feel bullied and teased because of their idiosyncrasies.

These social difficulties can continue throughout life, but after the completion of adolescence, this area can cause less personal distress. Many individuals with Asperger's disorder marry and have a family.

Evaluation

The evaluation of a person with suspected Asperger's disorder appears similar to an assessment for autistic disorder. The family should be prepared to provide details about early development. Areas of particular interests during the preschool years should be obtained. Social development should also be closely reviewed.

When seen individually, a person with Asperger's disorder can appear excessively comfortable in a new environment. Often if the person begins to talk about his or her area of interest, this conversation can be sustained for prolonged periods of time without any input from the examiner. There are difficulties sustaining eye contact, which can be observed. The speech is stilted in its rhythm. The vocabulary is often large.

A medical examination should also be conducted, but this disorder is less likely to be associated with seizures and other medical illnesses. Psychological testing can be helpful to determine areas of cognitive strengths and weaknesses.

There are some helpful screening tools that can be utilized; however, these are only a piece of the assessment. The use of one of these tools can help to provide additional information about behavioral and social interactions. Some screening tools are the Autism Spectrum Screening Questionnaire, Childhood Asperger's Syndrome Test, Gilliam Autism Rating Scale, and Asperger Syndrome Diagnostic Scale.

Therapeutic Principles

Individuals with Asperger's disorder benefit from a multidisciplinary approach. Behavioral supports, social supports, speech and language supports, educational intervention, psychotherapy, and psychopharmacology can all have a role in treatment at various points in time (Marcus et al., 1997). Typically, less intense supports are needed when compared to autistic disorder, but again because the course is lifelong, interventions may be needed at differing points in time.

Adolescence can be particularly difficult for these children. At this age the social pressures can be high, and there can be increased personal identification of difficulties. Offering a variety of social supports can be helpful. The treatment plan should reflect increased social skills training and social skills support at different levels of development.

Psychotherapy Treatment

Individuals with Asperger's disorder can benefit from psychotherapy supports. Particularly, highly intelligent children can benefit from structured therapeutic intervention. Group therapy can be particularly helpful to address social skills deficits. This must be carefully conducted to help ensure that proper social communication is occurring.

Individual therapy can address social deficits, and particularly with younger children, social stories can be told and used to promote success in this area. Youth with potentially strong verbal skills can benefit from a therapeutic approach where direct verbal strategies are taught and practiced.

Families may need additional support to understand the strengths and weaknesses of their child. Psychoeducation can be critical as the family may begin to function better when they understand some of the reasons behind the child's preoccupations. This will often allow the child to fit better with the family. In addition, family therapy can take the form of supportive family therapy or can implement cognitive behavioral strategies to help improve the parents' response.

There are less commonly aggressive behaviors associated with Asperger's disorder compared to autistic disorder. However, there can be negative behavior responses due to high levels of frustration. Therefore, behavioral interventions may be needed to help promote more effective problem-solving strategies and improved behavioral choices (Rogers, 1996).

Medication

Medication has less of a role in Asperger's disorder than in autistic disorder. If comorbid conditions such as ADHD or depression are present, these problems should be identified and treated if necessary and desired with medication. Stimulants can be useful for the treatment of inattention and distractibility. Caution should be taken, however, because occasionally the stimulants can increase the intensity of some of the repetitive behaviors.

One target symptom that is sometimes present in individuals with Asperger's disorder is the narrow range of interests and intense preoccupations. This characteristic can at times be lessened in intensity by the SSRI antidepressants (see CD: 6.3). In addition, the SSRI antidepressants can be helpful to treat any comorbid depressive disorders.

Clinical Case

Matt was a 10-year-old boy who was referred for a psychiatric evaluation by his school district. There were concerns that Matt was inattentive and not completing work within the classroom. In addition, there were concerns that Matt was not making friends and seemed sad. His parents expressed frustration that Matt would not engage in family activities such as hikes and trips to the playground because he preferred to remain in his room. His mother had found lists that he had repetitively written of popular songs.

His parents reported no problems with pregnancy, delivery, or early neonatal life. It was recalled that he talked early and was slightly delayed in his acquisition of motor milestones. He was easy to care for and made few demands. He also easily entertained himself and "taught himself to read" by age 3½ years. The primary concern was that Matt was uninterested in playing outside or interacting with peers. The family had made arguments trying to encourage Matt to engage in these activities and expressed frustration that "he usually wins the battle."

Matt spoke in a rhythm of speech that can best be described as "a little professor." His grammar was precise, and each word was spoken in a staccato-like manner. He made no eye contact, preferring to peer slightly over my shoulder throughout the interview. He answered questions willing but with direct questions provided only minimal information. Matt clearly preferred to talk about songs. He would have listed the 100 top songs of the year, but I stopped this after the first 20. Along with having the list memorized, he knew the year and primary artist. He reported he did not have "much in common" with his peers or his family, but he denied distress over this feature. He also reported that school was "boring," and if the teacher was talking about a topic he was uninterested in, he would begin to write his list.

Matt met criteria for Asperger's disorder. There was explanation of this diagnosis to his parents and his school. His parents benefitted from additional education regarding this disorder, and gradually the family interactions improved as they allowed Matt more time to himself and began to take an interest in music. As this happened, Matt was able to interact in some physical activities with them.

The school pursued psychoeducational testing, and it was realized that Matt has superior intelligence in reading. He began to participate in some gifted support services, which improved his interest and focus in school. Intermittently, Matt participated in social skills groups provided through the guidance office, but throughout his adolescence Matt remained rather uninterested in establishing friendships.

PERVASIVE DEVELOPMENTAL DISORDER, NOS

Types and Characteristics

The *DSM-IV-TR* does little to specify criteria for pervasive developmental disorder, NOS (PDD, NOS). This category is to "be used when there is a severe and pervasive impairment in the development of reciprocal social interactions associated with impairment in either verbal or nonverbal communication skills or with the presence of stereotyped behavior, interests and activities" (APA, 2000, p. 84). It can be used if the full threshold for autism and Asperger's disorder are not met. It is also the diagnostic term for individuals with "high-functioning autistic disorder." These individuals can have features similar to the features of individuals with Asperger's disorder based on higher levels of intelligence and less severe impairment, but their language skills are more impaired.

Despite this lack of specificity, this term is gaining clinical popularity and is frequently used where children with an autism spectrum disorder are diagnostically placed. There must be caution, however, for clinicians to not overuse this diagnosis. When there are less specific criteria needed to define a given diagnosis, there is a chance that it can be overused. Individuals with a diagnosis of PDD, NOS must have some degree of impairment in their ability to socialize with others and must have some degree of repetitive behaviors. There must be certainty that the pattern of repetitive behaviors is of abnormal interest or intensity. Caution should be used if the primary behavioral fixation is something like video games, because depending on the age of the child, this can be developmentally normal. This term is not to be applied to children who are primarily rigid and inflexible. These two characteristics are certainly apparent in individuals with PDD, NOS, but there must be additional difficulties other than these two traits to make this diagnosis.

There was consideration that Kayla had features consistent with PDD, NOS (see Chapter 1). This diagnostic entity was first considered during one of her initial psychiatric evaluations. When she was an inpatient at a psychiatric unit, there was increased consideration for this problem. However, as she was seen in the therapeutic emotional support classroom, there has been increased opportunity to observe her pattern of interactions with peers and adults. It has become apparent that she does not have struggles in this domain. Her perfectionism is related to anxiety, not the rigidity that is expected for an adolescent with a PDD.

Epidemiology and Comorbidity

Definitive data are difficult to obtain for PDD, NOS, as more often the studies are assessing the prevalence of autism spectrum disorders. These studies support an increased prevalence of autism spectrum disorders in boys compared to girls at a ratio of 4 boys to 1 girl. Prevalence for autism spectrum disorders has ranged from 3.3 to 10.6 per 1,000 children (CDC, 2002).

It is likely that individuals with PDD, NOS come to clinical attention later than children with Asperger's disorder, as there may be fewer evident difficulties in preschool years.

Similar comorbidities exist with PDD, NOS as do with the other two PDDs. These include attentional problems, affective disorders, and obsessive compulsive–like symptoms. In addition, there can be a higher likelihood of anxiety disorders in individuals with PDD, NOS.

Course

Individuals with PDD, NOS likely continue to have mild long-term impairment in functioning. However, when the core symptoms of the disorder are more subtle, there can be less obvious lifelong impairment. The social deficits that are apparent as primary problems tend to cause the most difficulty during adolescence. Teens with PDD, NOS can have a strong desire to interact with peers and can be particularly sensitive to not fitting in. If this is noted, there should be careful assessment regarding the development of depressive or anxiety symptoms.

Evaluation

There is no difference for the evaluation of a child suspected of having PDD, NOS compared to the assessment for the other PDDs. There should be a comprehensive social and developmental history obtained. In addition, there should be careful inquiry into social skills and repetitive behaviors. This diagnosis is one that is made by exclusion of full criteria for Asperger's disorder or autistic disorder.

Careful screening for the presence of other psychiatric disorders such as ADHD, depressive disorders, or other behavior disorders is needed. At times this diagnosis is used while additional information is gathered. If this is initially the reason for the diagnosis, it should be clarified in the visit what additional information is needed before diagnosing a definitive type of PDD.

Therapeutic Principles

The therapeutic principles of treatment for PDD, NOS closely resembles the treatment interventions for Asperger's disorder.

The options to be considered include medication, different types of psychotherapy, educational supports, social skills supports, and speech or occupational therapy. The treatment recommendations should be based on the individual's cognitive strengths and behavioral or emotional needs. As with the other PDDs, this condition is likely a long-term one that will require long-term support, so the treatment plan should be designed with this in mind.

Psychotherapy Treatment

Individual, family, and group therapies can all have a role at varying times during illness. More directed types of intervention can be more beneficial. Behavioral supports should be considered, and social skills support should be included in some form. Families often require support and education.

Medication

Medication intervention for PDD, NOS is also based on the treatment of comorbid conditions or target symptoms. For impairment based on irritability or behavioral disturbances, a trial of an atypical antipsychotic can be considered. There is increased use of this class of medications for children with PDD, NOS. However, there should be a very careful assessment completed that compares the potential benefits from treatment to the potential side effects. For depressive, anxious, or obsessive-like behaviors, a trial of an SSRI medication can be helpful.

Clinical Case

Ryan was a 7-year-old boy when he first presented for a psychiatric evaluation at the request of his outpatient therapist. His therapist was looking for diagnostic clarification. Ryan was described as being inattentive, impulsive, and intrusive and was having difficulty adjusting to second grade.

His parents reported that pregnancy was complicated by a second-trimester intrauterine bleed that resolved after 2 weeks of bed rest. Pregnancy after that event was uncomplicated. Ryan was born without any complications. Early development was marked by significant motor delays, and physical therapy was used as an early intervention service. Ryan was noted from a young age to be easily distracted and inattentive. These symptoms did not cause difficulty until first grade. During the same year, it was noted that Ryan was interested in playing by himself and did not initiate social contact with others. In fact, he preferred solitary play, which consisted of lining up trains. He would become upset if there was any disruption to his order, and on several occasions he became physically aggressive to students who moved his trains.

During the clinical interview, Ryan chose to line up blocks in a straight line and talked about how he wished these blocks were trains. He would not answer any questions unless the inquiry was about trains. He maintained fair eye contact when he was talking about his topic of interest; otherwise he continued to rearrange his line of blocks.

Ryan had a fair ability to interact with one child at a time, but in group settings he would withdraw. He expressed a desire to have friends but struggled to understand why everyone was not as interested in trains as he was.

From a diagnostic perspective, he had an excessive interest in trains, which were his preferred method of play and communication. His social skills were delayed based on his struggles interacting with groups of peers but did not meet diagnostic threshold for excessively developmentally lagging.

A diagnosis of PDD, NOS was given. His therapist began to address his social skills and social communication through group therapy. His parents began to work informally on him interacting with peers at a playground. He began to participate in friendship groups at school. Initially, no medication treatment was used, but with Ryan's advancing age, his inattention was thought to be related to deterioration in his grades. When Ryan was 9-years-old, a low dose of Adderall was added, and his inattention improved.

Follow-up continued throughout several years, and although Ryan at times struggled with appropriate social interactions, he negotiated his early teen years without significant difficulty. He remains on Adderall and needs ongoing support to be able to talk about topics that are of interest to other people.

AUTISM SPECTRUM DISORDERS: EDUCATIONAL IMPLICATIONS

Educational programming for students with autism spectrum disorders can be difficult. Individuals with moderate to severe autism and mental retardation are typically placed in life skills classrooms, but an understanding of their unique needs is required for their success in this placement. This is successful as long as intensive structure and behavioral supports are available. Steps must be taken to ensure that the transitions and changes in the classroom are kept to a minimum. When appropriate, allowances for the fixations can be helpful. For example, if the student is excessively interested in trains, allowing him to write a paper about trains can be helpful. However, there should also be opportunities taken to increase areas of interest. For very aggressive students in this category, having a single identified aide or behavioral support person can be helpful, as the redirection becomes more predictable. Speech therapy and occupational therapy should also be considered.

When autistic disorder is less severe and not accompanied by mental retardation, the educational placement often includes a blend of regular education with autistic support services. There must be attention paid to ensure that the balance of services is meeting the student's needs. If the academic or social demands are too high, there can be an observable deterioration in behavior. Providing direct behavioral intervention through a behavioral support plan can be helpful when consistently applied.

Children and teens with Asperger's disorder typically do well academically, and there must be certainty that there is enough academic challenge to keep them engaged. Speech and language supports can be effective to work on nonverbal social cues and socialization techniques. Participating in structured friendship groups can also meet the person's needs for improved social skills.

Perhaps one area where placement becomes more challenging is a student with both a PDD, NOS diagnosis and a comorbid emotional disturbance identification. These students tend to struggle in an emotional support classroom, as their perseverations are more likely to be seen as a feature of their emotional disturbance, and attempting to discontinue this is met with significant reluctance. However, this student's emotional reactivity can make placement in an autistic support classroom difficult. There is some local interest in working to provide one classroom for students with both difficulties, but currently these students often receive a combination of intervention services until there seems to be some stabilization.

Regardless of the diagnosis, if there are clear aggressive behavior and a change in irritability, it would be important to communicate this information to the involved psychiatrist. In addition, if there is an increase in repetitive behaviors and fixations, this information can be conveyed to the psychiatrist.

These two areas seem to be target symptoms of the PDD, which may respond to a medication.

AUTISM SPECTRUM DISORDERS: SUMMARY

Autism spectrum disorders are a lifelong condition that can cause mild to severe functional impairment. There must be difficulties in communication (verbal or nonverbal), socialization, and behavior for an individual to be considered on this spectrum. Educational challenges are also further intensified by mental retardation. Cognitive and language abilities are often a guide to the type of treatment and placement that can be offered.

Multidisciplinary treatment approaches are most successful at promoting an improvement in the different domains. The treatment must meet the student's needs at the given time, and because of the chronicity of the illness, long-term interventions must be considered.

Eleven

Treating Target Symptoms

BACKGROUND INFORMATION

There are times during the course of intervention with a child or teen that it is not possible to determine a definitive diagnosis in a timely way. Often it is perceived that additional information is needed or that following the person over a period of several months will provide more diagnostic clarity. If possible, medication intervention should wait until there is a clear diagnosis. However, in this situation there may be a clinical decision that the individual is having serious impairment in functioning and development because of easily identified symptoms.

The psychiatrist can also make the decision to treat identified target symptoms if these symptoms are present in the context of a likely personality disorder. Personality disorders are placed on Axis II in the *DSM* diagnostic system. This placement refers to the fact that these disorders are based on personal characteristics that are less likely to be due to biological features. However, personality disorders can cause significant distress to the individual or those around the individual. Treating identified target symptoms can help to make the person's life easier to manage, although the medications are not curative.

Finally, a decision can be made to treat target symptoms if there is no Axis I diagnosis present. Not everyone who presents for a psychiatric evaluation meets criteria for a diagnosis. However, there can be symptoms without an obvious source that are causing impairment. Once again, the psychiatrist, youth, and family can make the decision to treat the distressing symptoms.

Once a medication has been evaluated by the manufacturer and studied in humans, the FDA reviews the data to determine if it is safe to use and if it is effective for what it was designed to treat. The FDA will then approve the medication to be used for a specific indication. However, once the FDA has approved the medication, physicians can make a reasonable decision to use the medication for a different reason. This is termed prescribing a medication in an "off-label" way. Typically, university hospitals and research institutes will conduct studies of medications for different indications. These studies are published in research journals, and if the results are positive, support begins to build for clinicians to use the medication.

Drug companies are less likely to study psychotropic medications for use in children and adolescents. However, research is ongoing for the use by youth of medications that are approved for use in adults. As described in Chapters 6 and 8 there are only a few antidepressants, a few atypical antipsychotics, and lithium approved to treat mood disorders, anxiety disorders, and psychotic disorders. Each time a psychiatrist chooses to treat a child with a medication that is not approved by the FDA, it is considered an off-label use of the medication. If the psychiatrist has made a decision that the risks of the medication are low enough compared to the impairment that the symptoms are causing, the idea of using a medication in an off-label way can be presented to the family for consideration.

When medications are being used to treat target symptoms, the prescription is considered off-label because medications are approved to treat a known diagnosis. As with the prescribing of medication for a diagnosis, the psychiatrist must clearly discuss the medication and indications for its use. It must be clearly stated that the use is off-label, and informed consent must be given. There must also be similar monitoring of the medication as occurs when the medicine is being used to treat a known diagnosis. If the medication is being used when diagnostic uncertainty exists, the follow-up visits should also be used to finalize the diagnosis.

The prescribed medication can be very effective at reducing the identified target symptom. However, the improvement that is noted based on a medication should not be used in any way to clarify the diagnosis. For example, it is not a clinical standard to prescribe a mood stabilizer to treat impulsivity and later report that because the mood stabilizer reduced the impulsivity that the individual has bipolar disorder. In addition, the positive response to a stimulant should not be used to make the diagnosis of attention-deficit/hyperactivity disorder (ADHD).

The following sections of this chapter describe common target symptoms and possible psychopharmacological interventions. These can be considered pharmacologic Band-Aids and can be used for varying lengths of time depending on clinical need. It is important to note that medications should never be the only intervention to treat these symptoms. Psychotherapy should also be used as an additional treatment intervention. However, for this chapter, the focus will be on describing potential target symptoms and medications.

AGGRESSIVE BEHAVIOR

Characteristics

Aggressive behavior is typically easy to recognize. It can best be defined by any action that causes injury to one's self, to others, or to objects. However, it can take many different forms, which have different treatment implications. Physical aggression is a common reason for referral for a psychiatric evaluation. Both acute and chronic aggressive episodes can result in such referral. When making a clinical decision to treat aggressive behavior with medication, the clinician must perform a thorough history to have an accurate sense of the characteristics of the aggression. There should be full inquiry of both the family and the youth to understand any recognizable patterns and the degree of impairment that results from the behavior.

It is sometimes helpful for the clinician to understand if the action is acute or chronic. The type of aggression is also important. Physical aggression can have more impact on functioning than verbal aggression. It is also important to differentiate if the aggressive act was overt or hidden. In some situations aggression can be adaptive or protective, whereas in other settings the same action is maladaptive. Finally, the amount of planning or the predatory nature to the aggression can have clinical implications.

Acute aggression is most often seen in drug-induced states or in the midst of a florid psychotic episode. When this type of aggression occurs, it can be considered a clinical emergency, and acute treatment should be provided to sedate the patient for his or her own safety and the safety of others. This pattern is less seen in children or adolescents.

Chronic aggression in children and adolescents can be associated with oppositional defiant disorder, conduct disorder, ADHD, bipolar disorder, or intermittent explosive disorder. In addition, mood disorders can cause irritability, which can also contribute to a pattern of chronic aggression. These disorders can cause significant physical aggression, which can be impulsive or planned. Significant harm can occur to others or self when the aggression is severe. Because of the number of diagnoses that can be associated with aggression, the differential diagnosis of a youth presenting with aggression can be difficult. When the aggression puts people at risk or significantly impairs functioning, a decision can be made to pursue medication. In addition, if the aggression is appropriately reduced with medication, the psychiatrist can be better able to assess the diagnostic picture and make an informed decision regarding diagnosis.

Pharmacologic Treatment

Acute physical aggression is considered a psychiatric emergency. If it is not possible in a short period of time to use behavioral interventions to calm the person down, then emergency care should be sought. In most extreme examples, the person will require an intramuscular injection of one medication or a combination of medications for safety. This should never be done without a medical examination, and if possible there should be an understanding of what if any substances were ingested that are contributing to this mental status change.

Benzodiazepine medications such as lorazepam (Ativan) are commonly used. These medications affect the GABA system within the brain and work by primarily causing sedation. In times of extreme agitation and aggression, a combination of intramuscular lorazepam (Ativan), haloperidol (Haldol), and diphenhydramine (Benadryl) are used for even faster sedation.

More commonly, the desire to treat physical aggression can be made after a more comprehensive assessment. Chronic aggression is certainly concerning but less often results in an emergency assessment. An episode of aggression can result in a youth being assessed in an emergency room or crisis center, but typically by the time the assessment is completed, the youth is no longer acutely aggressive. Therefore, youth rarely receive immediate medication for safety.

When a decision is reached to pursue medication treatment of aggression, there are several pharmacologic options. The psychiatrist can choose one of the options based on information that was obtained about the pattern of aggression and any other associated mental health symptoms that were recognized in the evaluation.

The atypical antipsychotic medications at low dosages have been helpful at reducing physical aggression in individuals with autistic disorders. Risperdal is approved for this indication. This finding has led some clinicians to utilize low dosages of medications such as risperidone (Risperdal) and quetiapine (Seroquel) for chronic physical aggression. The dosages that are used are typically less than those used to treat psychotic disorders or mood disorders. These medications can be effective at reducing impulsivity, improving frustration tolerance, and being mildly sedative (see accompanying CD: 11.1).

At times chronic physical aggression can occur in the context of mood variability. This pattern of mood swings might not meet clinical threshold for bipolar disorder because of the intensity, frequency, or time of mood change. However, if mood variability is identified, using a mood stabilizer, specifically lithium, can reduce aggression (W. Green, 1995, p. 11).

There can be consideration for a trial of an antidepressant. This class of medications can be helpful at reducing aggression if there is a quality of irritability in the youth's mood. However, antidepressants should be used cautiously, particularly if there is any concern that there is a possibility of bipolar disorder. If the aggression is related to bipolar disorder, an antidepressant can have the effect of triggering a mania, therefore increasing aggression.

A final pharmacologic treatment intervention can be the beta-blockers. This class of medications was initially used to control hypertension and other cardiac abnormalities. This class of medications reduces peripheral autonomic tone, which can lead to a perception of reduced anxiety. There have been some studies conducted in adults that support that these medications reduce anxiety. There have also been several studies using a particular beta-blocker, propranolol (Inderal), in the treatment of physical aggression. Many of the studies conducted consisted of children and adolescents with "minimal brain dysfunction," implying mental retardation and other neurological problems. However, there was support that this medication was well tolerated and reduced the frequency of "rage outbursts" (W. Green, 1995, p. 236).

Clinical Case

Bill was a 9-year-old boy who was referred for a psychiatric evaluation for physical aggression after he had had repeated visits to the emergency room over a 1-year period of time. He would become angry and agitated over small insults and was unable to contain or control this emotion. Bill described that when he became angry, he had little warning of this feeling and quickly lost the ability to "think." He had broken windows within the house. He had punched his mother in the face, causing a nosebleed. He scratched his 13-year-old sister, leaving large welts and scars on her arms and legs. He had pushed over his desk at school and had been involved in three fights on the playground.

Numerous interventions had been tried, including outpatient therapy with both an individual and a family approach. Bill had been psychiatrically hospitalized one time for 3 days. Community mental health treatment in the form of a therapeutic support staff was provided. He was receiving education in a small self-contained emotional support classroom. The police had talked to him on numerous occasions, but formal charges could not be pursued because of Bill's age.

His parents said, "We are at our wit's end. We have no idea what to do to help him." Bill reported that he wanted to stop being "bad and mad." He described that following one of these events, he would begin to feel guilty and sad for his actions. He was able to describe that he knew the behaviors were wrong, and he was afraid that he was going to lose more friends. There was no identified change in mood or anxiety. There were no psychotic symptoms. Triggers were Bill's not receiving his own way or believing that others did not want to interact with him.

After reviewing the rationale and side effects of several different medication options, Bill's parents chose to begin treatment with risperidone (Risperdal). Initially, he was given 0.25 mg at night. This dose was well tolerated but did not result in any noticeable change. After 1 month, the dose was increased to 0.5 mg, and there began to be a gradual reduction in the episodes. Although Bill still became highly frustrated and explosive, he was able to shift the aggression from physical explosiveness to verbal explosiveness. There continued to be episodes of physical aggression, but these were less frequent. After an additional month, the dose was increased to 0.25 mg in the morning and 0.5 mg in the evening. On this dose there continued to be ongoing improvement, and the physical aggressive episodes decreased to one time per week. In addition, there began to be improved control of the verbal aggression. There were no further emergency visits. In addition, Bill and his family worked with a new family therapist and became able to more accurately help Bill verbalize his feeling of frustration, which further improved his self-control.

One study conducted by Reyes, Buitelaar, Toren, Augustyns, & Eerdekens (2006) looked at the use of risperidone to treat individuals with oppositional defiant disorder or conduct disorder. The study was large and involved several sites. The medication was continued for 6 months. There was a reduction in negative behavior, including aggression, in those who received risperidone.

SELF-INJURIOUS BEHAVIOR

Characteristics

Self-injurious behavior (SIB) can occur in adolescents, and there is an increased prevalence among females. SIB can be a distressing symptom, particularly when adults learn of its presence. In many instances it is school personnel who first become aware of this pattern. They can learn of the behavior through observation of the injury, or more commonly, a concerned friend will report this action to a teacher or guidance counselor.

Most commonly, the form of SIB is cutting. The cuts are typically superficial on the arms or legs. However, there are times when the cuts are more hidden, in such places as the abdomen or inner thighs. Instruments used to inflict the cuts can vary from a razor to a knife or to the blunt end of a paper clip. In addition to cutting, burning with a curling iron or hair straightener or pouring scalding water over the skin can be used to induce self-injury.

The common reason that an adolescent engages in SIB is to relieve psychic discomfort. The teen can describe that the physical pain feels better than the emotional pain. Alternatively, the teen can report that the action does not induce pain but rather provides relief. Finally, some teens view this is a form of self-deserved punishment. Most adolescents are able to clearly differentiate that the behavior is not intended to cause death. Although it is difficult for others to understand the action of self-injury, this behavior is very effective at relieving inner emotional turmoil. Individuals who are not familiar with this symptom struggle to react in helpful ways. It is most helpful to recognize the pain the person must be feeling. Placing too much emphasis on punishment can indirectly increase the incidence. A calm approach to discussing this is best.

SIB is a self-rewarding behavior. First, the action provides quick and immediate relief of distress. This alone makes it more likely to continue. It is also believed that endorphins are released during the act of self-injury, and this brain neurotransmitter provides relief and reward.

SIB can occur in the context of a mood or anxiety disorder. In this case the purpose is to relieve sadness or anxiety. SIB can also occur in individuals struggling with eating disorders, particularly bulimia nervosa. The reasoning behind this action can be related to negative self-image or body loathing. Individuals with emerging personality disorders will often engage in cutting to provide a relief from anger or feelings of abandonment. Finally, if abuse, particularly sexual abuse, has occurred in the past, the teen will manage the negative feelings of this with SIB. The reasons can be varied and complex, and SIB is not clearly linked with one diagnosis.

Pharmacologic Treatment

Antidepressants, particularly the SSRIs, can be useful medications to reduce the negative feelings that lead to self-injury. These medications can reduce sadness or anxiety that fuel the discomfort. If there is less subjective discomfort, the need to engage in SIB can be reduced.

When there is a history of abuse, the SSRIs can reduce the posttraumatic sequelae by reducing flashbacks, nightmares, and hyperarousal. In some situations the SSRIs can also reduce impulsivity, which can allow the teen to reconsider the act of cutting and find a healthier alternative for managing the distress.

Another alternative class of medications to consider is the atypical antipsychotics. Although these medications have a higher likelihood of side effects compared to the SSRIs, they can be helpful at reducing anxiety and stabilizing mood symptoms. Another potential benefit of these medications is that they can be sedating. The ability to fall asleep more quickly can be helpful if the cutting is occurring at night (see accompanying CD: 11.2).

Clinical Case

Elizabeth was a 15-year-old female who was referred for a psychiatric evaluation by her school after it was learned that she was engaging in cutting. In this situation it came to the attention of the school that there was a group of six girls who met in a specified restroom three to four times a day to "cut together." The guidance counselor had met with the girls as a group and as individuals, and it was determined that two of the girls were considered the "primary" cutters who talked the other four girls into this behavior. The two girls who engaged in this behavior in places other than in school and for reasons that appeared to be more psychologically based were referred to treatment.

Elizabeth reluctantly agreed to participate in the evaluation. She had taken the perspective that "it is my own body, and I can do to it what I want." However, her parents were calmly insistent that she receive treatment. There was no history of previous mental health interventions, and until 1 year prior, her parents had no concerns about her. However, 1 year ago her grades began to decline, and she began to dress in a gothic style. Her peer group changed, and she was more isolated from her family.

Elizabeth admitted that she did not feel as if she fit in with peers at her school. She stated, "Because I don't fit in, I want to stand out as very different." She admitted to some sadness, but it was not a pervasive quality. She denied anxiety. She reported having "mood swings" and becoming very angry over what she later perceived as small insults. She described that the cutting that she did was to relieve internal pain. Seeing the blood from her superficial cuts was needed to appreciate the relief.

After she, the family, and clinician spent several weeks gathering information and discussing strategies to delay this action, Elizabeth had not been able to reduce the frequency of this behavior. Her motivation improved in part because summer was approaching, and she wanted to wear sleeveless tops. She and her family both wanted to pursue medication.

A low dose of fluoxetine (Prozac) was tried. After 2 weeks, Elizabeth began to have some success at delaying her urges to cut. She also reported that her anger was beginning to decrease, and she was better able to manage frustration. Her affect appeared brighter, and her family was pleased that she was beginning to participate in activities with them. She was able to put forth more effort into schoolwork, and her grades improved.

In this case over the course of time it was determined that Elizabeth had dysthymia. Psychotherapy was used to address her low self-confidence and perception of not fitting in. She was better able to manage frustration and sadness. After Elizabeth was on fluoxetine for 1 year, the medication was discontinued, and her mood symptoms remained stable, and there was no return to SIB.

IMPULSIVITY

Characteristics

Impulsivity is described as an inability to stop and think before acting. This characteristic can be seen with both verbal and physical responses. It can occur in the context of other psychiatric illnesses or as an independent symptom or disorder. This characteristic can cause significant distress to the person affected and to those around the person. Statements that are made impulsively can hurt another person's feelings. Impulsivity can be dangerous if the person continues to engage in reckless behaviors without thinking through the consequences. When there is a likelihood for accidental self-harm, it is often wise to consider pharmacologic treatment.

Impulsivity is a symptom in several different psychiatric illnesses. The majority of individuals with ADHD have impulsivity as a core symptom. Impulsivity is frequently seen in those with bipolar disorder, and engaging in reckless behaviors without forethought is a diagnostic description of mania.

Impulsivity can also occur as an independent illness. In fact there is a listing within the *DSM-IV-TR* of different types of impulse control disorders. These include intermittent explosive disorder, kleptomania, pyromania, pathologic gambling, trichotillomania, and impulse control disorder, not otherwise specified. The essential feature of these illnesses is a "failure to resist an impulse, desire or temptation to perform an act that is harmful to the person or others" (American Psychiatric Association [APA], 2000, p. 663). Trichotillomania involves the repeated pulling of body hair. Kleptomania is stealing objects that are not needed from stores. Pyromania is a repeated urge to set fires. Some clinicians consider many of these impulse control disorders as peripherally related to anxiety disorders or specifically obsessive-compulsive disorders. The term *obsessive-compulsive–related disorder* can be used to describe trichotillomania, pathologic gambling, and kleptomania. Although these actions are impulsive, there is an underlying need to engage in the behavior for anxiety relief. The person recognizes an urge to engage in the behavior, which causes distress, and relief and pleasure occur after the act is completed.

Intermittent explosive disorder is characterized as a "discreet episode of failure to resist aggressive impulses that result in serious assaultive acts" (APA, 2000, p. 663). The aggressive act is thought to be out of proportion to the precipitant. These acts can be associated with rage, increased energy, or racing thoughts. This diagnosis should be made cautiously and only after it is clear that the explosive episodes are not occurring in the context of a mood disorder.

There is a belief that the neurotransmitter serotonin is important in regulating impulsivity. A study of individuals with significant impulsivity showed these individuals had reduced amounts of serotonin in the central nervous system (Coccaro, 1989, 1990).

Pharmacologic Treatment

The pharmacologic treatment of impulsivity is dependent on the context in which it is occurring. If there are other symptoms of inattention and hyperactivity present along with impulsivity, it is appropriate to begin medication with a stimulant. If this is effective, it is again important to highlight that a positive treatment response to a stimulant should not be used to make the diagnosis of ADHD. That diagnosis is made only when sufficient symptom criteria are met in two different settings.

If there are clinical suspicions that the impulsivity is occurring in the context of a mood disorder such as bipolar disorder or major depression, pharmacologic treatment can be initiated with either an antidepressant or a mood stabilizer. Valproic acid is a mood stabilizer that can have positive benefit for reducing impulsivity. SSRI antidepressants can also be helpful if there is pronounced irritability along with impulsivity.

For pharmacologic treatment of the impulse control disorders that are considered obsessive-compulsive–related symptoms, a trial of an SSRI is warranted. This medication can reduce the subjective urge to engage in the inappropriate behavior. In addition, the SSRIs can reduce the anxiety that might be underlying the behavior. Depending on the individual's tolerability, at times higher dosages of SSRIs can be beneficial, but this must be done with caution to prevent disinhibition. In more severe situations, using a combination of an SSRI and a mood stabilizer can be more effective at improving the control of these behaviors.

It should be noted that pyromania is a serious impulse control problem. There is essentially no literature supporting pharmacologic treatment of this condition.

Intermittent explosive disorder can be a significant problem. Pharmacologic intervention can be helpful to reduce the intensity and frequency of the outbursts. Anticonvulsant mood stabilizers, atypical antipsychotics, lithium, and SSRI antidepressants can be helpful. These medications do not reduce the anger itself but can improve the lack of impulse control that causes the destructive acts (see accompanying CD: 11.3).

Clinical Case

Carl was a 16-year-old male who was referred for a psychiatric evaluation at the request of his school district. He was more withdrawn in school, and his grades were declining. In addition, it had become very obvious that he was missing large sections of hair on the back of his scalp.

Carl and his mother reported that over the past 10 years, he had had four episodes of pulling out his hair. The previous episodes had each lasted several weeks, and he was able to use cognitive distraction to prevent continuing this behavior. This episode had been present for 2 months, and Carl was unable to use cognitive distraction or thought stopping techniques.

Carl described a building urge to pull his hair or scratch his skin. At times he recognized that this urge occurred if he was experiencing internal anxiety or distress. At other times he recognized the urge but could not understand what event or emotion was connected with it. Finally, at other times he found that he had pulled out several hairs without recognizing distress or even that he was engaging in the behavior until it was too late.

Carl had participated in individual cognitive behavioral therapy during a prior episode, but returning to the same treatment was not effective for this occurrence. Carl was motivated to change and was distressed by how much hair he had pulled. There was no significant family psychiatric history. Carl had some symptoms of anxiety, but the majority of his distress was related to his frustration with his inability to stop pulling his hair and the way he perceived himself.

A low dose of fluoxetine (Prozac) was started. There was minimal improvement after 1 month, so the dose was increased to 20 mg. At this dose there began to be a subjective improvement in Carl's ability to delay the action. However, he continued to rather frequently engage in this behavior, complaining that the new hair that was growing in was itchy. By scratching his head, he was continuing to break off hair. There was a further dose escalation to 30 mg, and at this amount there was marked improvement in his distress and control. Treatment was continued for 1 year beyond the improvement, and the medication was gradually tapered over 3 additional months. At the present time, when Carl experiences worry or tension, he is able to use a "stress ball" appropriately and has not returned to trichotillomania.

INSOMNIA

Characteristics

Insomnia can exacerbate symptoms of depression and anxiety. It can also worsen behavioral control. In addition, insomnia can be a symptom of both depressive disorders and anxiety disorders. Insomnia is also believed to be a risk factor for suicide in adults who are depressed (Cassels, 2009). There is increased investigation into adolescent sleep disorders, as this can also be a risk factor in adolescent suicide. Aggressively treating sleep disturbances can often improve a person's outlook and self-perception. If the sleep disorder is occurring in the context of a depressive or anxiety disorder, this problem should be treated, but a decision can be made to also treat the sleep problem.

If a person is having difficulty falling asleep, this is called initial insomnia. Waking up throughout the night with subsequent difficulty returning to sleep is called middle insomnia. Early morning awakening is called late insomnia. It is important to understand which pattern is present or if two or more patterns are present which is causing the most distress.

If significant sleep disturbance occurs and is not responsive to both behavioral interventions and pharmacologic interventions, there can be consideration to refer the youth to a sleep clinic for a more thorough sleep study to identify problems such as obstructive sleep apnea, restless leg syndrome, or narcolepsy.

Although the primary emphasis of this chapter is on pharmacologic interventions, when medicating sleep disturbances it is crucial to also review basic sleep hygiene strategies. Some helpful strategies include consuming no caffeinated products within 6 to 8 hours of sleep, regularly exercising but not doing intensive cardiovascular exercise within several hours of bedtime, going to sleep and awakening at approximately the same time each day, limiting naps to 20 minutes a day, and not remaining in the bed trying to sleep if it is clear after 15 minutes that sleep is not occurring.

Sleep disturbances in teens can occur from a shift in the sleep–wake cycle. A teen can stay up very late to communicate with friends online and then sleep through the morning into the afternoon. It is then difficult to return to bed until very late at night again. This pattern is best addressed by waking up at the expected time for several days.

Pharmacologic Treatment

Medications can be useful for initial insomnia and sometimes for middle insomnia. The majority of medications that promote sleep are designed to leave the body in about 4 to 6 hours to ensure that the individual can awaken in the morning without feeling excessively sedated. Therefore, early morning wakening is difficult to treat with pharmacologic interventions.

Children and adolescents are very rarely prescribed sleeping pills such as temazepam (Restoril), zolpidem (Ambien), eszopiclone (Lunesta), or zaleplon (Sonata). These medications are likely too sedating for youngsters even when very low dosages are used. In addition, some of these sleeping pills can have addicting properties, so they should be avoided in youth. Finally, particularly young children can have reverse effects to these medications, and wakefulness can occur.

For short-term sleep problems, taking diphenhydramine (Benadryl) can be useful. One of this antihistamine's side effects is sedation, and if it is used occasionally, it can be effective at promoting and sustaining sleep.

A natural substance that is gaining popularity in promoting sleep is melatonin. Melatonin is made in our brain and is involved in the regulation of the sleep–wake cycle. It can be taken in a pill form, which is available over the counter and sold with vitamin pills. Melatonin is not a sleeping pill but can promote ease of falling asleep and a perceived improved quality of sleep. Some people notice some mild sedative properties within the first day or two of treatment. Others notice a more gradual improvement in sleep over several weeks.

An old antidepressant, desyrell (Trazadone), is also used to help promote sleep more commonly in teens. At high dosages this medication is an antidepressant, but very few people can tolerate the dosages that are needed because of its sedative properties. Therefore, it is commonly used as a sleeping aid. It must be used cautiously, as it can also cause some behavioral disinhibition, but this occurs rarely because of its relative low dose. Another potential downside of this medication is that over time it loses its efficacy as the body accommodates to the sedation (see accompanying CD: 11.4).

Clinical Case

Samantha was a 17-year-old female who was referred for a psychiatric evaluation by her pediatrician. Her pediatrician had appropriately diagnosed her with a single episode of major depression 6 months earlier. Fluoxetine (Prozac) was used to treat this episode. There was an initial positive response, but after several months the dose was increased when Samantha perceived the symptoms were beginning to return. This pattern of dose escalation occurred several times, and ultimately she was on 40 mg of fluoxetine. At this dose she began to experience irritability, impulsivity, and suicidal thoughts. The pediatrician discontinued the medication and referred her for an evaluation.

At the time of the evaluation, Samantha had been medication free for 6 weeks. She reported that over the past 3 weeks, her energy had begun to improve. She no longer had suicidal thoughts. She continued to feel sad and irritable. She was having significant difficulty falling asleep and was sleeping only 3 to 4 hours a night, as she had to awaken early each morning for school. Both Samantha and her family were reluctant to immediately pursue another antidepressant because of her negative response to fluoxetine.

It was therefore decided that treatment should first be targeted to her insomnia. Samantha believed if she felt better rested, she would be able to better control her frustration and irritability. She chose to begin to take melatonin 3 mg each night.

When seen for follow-up 2 weeks later, she reported that she was now able to sleep 6 to 7 hours a night. After 1 week of melatonin, she noted that the length of her sleep was improving. She was seen again 4 weeks after starting melatonin, and at that time she was consistently sleeping 7 hours a night. Samantha reported that her irritability was significantly reduced. As her relationship with those around her began to improve, she was more interactive and felt less sad.

After 3 months of taking melatonin nightly, Samantha stopped taking it. Her positive sleep patterns remained, and over the past year there has been no return of depression.

AFFECTIVE INSTABILITY

Characteristics

Affective instability is a term that describes an unstable pattern of mood and affect regulation. The person with affective instability has mood shifts that occur frequently throughout the day. Most commonly, these changes are in response to external events, but there can also be internal thoughts that contribute to the change in mood. The mood can go from happy and pleasant one moment to excessively sad or angry the next. This pattern to a mild degree is present in most early adolescents as they struggle to negotiate development. However, it is the more severe presentations for which this clinical term can be used.

This characteristic is differentiated from bipolar disorder in part based on the length of mood shifts. By mid to late adolescence, the pattern of bipolar disorder is more similar to an adult presentation with prolonged mood changes to depression or mania. The term *ultra-rapid cycling bipolar disorder* is sometimes used to denote rapid shifts in mood similar to affective instability. However, the associated symptoms of mania, such as grandiosity, rapid speech, and racing thoughts, are lacking in affective disorder.

Most commonly, affective instability is seen in the context of a personality disorder. If a personality trait is inflexible and maladaptive and causes impairment or distress, a personality disorder can be considered (APA, 2000, p. 686). This diagnosis requires a long-term assessment of the person's patterns of functioning. This diagnosis should not be made abruptly but rather be made after there has been an established pattern of stable maladaptive personality traits.

Borderline personality disorder (BPD) is a particular personality disorder that has a high likelihood of patterns of affective instability. This diagnosis can be given to an adolescent if the maladaptive traits have been present for at least 1 year, are persistent, and are not related to a developmental stage of an episode of another clinical problem. However, because the personality of adolescents is still developing, the diagnosis of BPD should be reserved until it is certain.

The core characteristic of BPD is a pervasive pattern of instability of relationships, self-image, and affects. It is associated with marked impulsivity. Five of the following symptoms must be present: frantic efforts to avoid abandonment, a pattern of unstable and intense interpersonal relationships, identity disturbance, impulsivity in at least two areas that are potentially self-damaging, recurrent suicidal behavior, affective instability due to a marked reactivity of mood, chronic feelings of emptiness, inappropriate and intense anger, and transient stress-related paranoia (APA, 2000, p. 710).

BPD is rarely diagnosed in children because of their ever-changing characteristics. However, some clinicians use the term *borderline pathology* to refer to a pattern of disruptive behavioral problems, mood and anxiety symptoms, and cognitive symptoms. Follow-up studies of these children show that they have a tendency to develop a wide range of personality disorders, not just BPD (Finley-Belgrad & Davies, 2005).

Affective instability as a symptom can cause significant distress. The person's ever-changing internal mood state can cause impairment in relationships, education, and decision making. Individuals with this pattern can be clinically challenging and can demand excessive attention from those around them. Affective instability can be related to self-injury and suicidal ideas. These events can be impulsive, as when the individual is in a different mood state, there can be an extreme sense of hopelessness.

Whether affective instability occurs in the context of a personality disorder or is present without other such characteristics, psychotherapy should never be the first treatment intervention offered. Personality disorders by nature are more resistant to psychopharmacological interventions, as the disorder is due to the individual's core perception of the world. However, there can be some benefit from medication to help alleviate the intensity of the mood shifts.

Pharmacologic Treatment

The first medication intervention that should be considered is an SSRI antidepressant. This class of medication can help to reduce the intensity of the anger and dysphoria that the person experiences. Just as impulsivity can be related to low serotonin activity in the brain, affective instability can also be partially related to this feature. Typically, the SSRIs are associated with fewer side effects than other medications, but again they should be monitored closely for the emergence of suicidal thinking. There must also be careful assessment for the presence of a mania being triggered by the antidepressant.

The second line of medications to consider is the mood stabilizers. There is potential benefit, as these medications can both decrease the intensity of any elevated moods and reduce the low and angry moods. These medications can stabilize the mood, but some individuals perceive that the place of mood stabilization is on the lower end of the normal range. In other words, the individual feels more depressed.

There is increasing support for the use of atypical antipsychotics to treat this population. They can reduce the affective shifts by acting as mood stabilizers. However, this class should be carefully considered in adolescents because of the potential appetite stimulation effect (see accompanying CD: 11.5).

Clinical Case

Susan is a 16-year-old female who was referred for a psychiatric evaluation by her school district. She had disclosed to a guidance counselor that 2 weeks prior she had ingested 10 aspirins in the restroom of the school. This information was shared with her mother, who contacted the pediatrician. It was appropriately determined that because of the low quantity of medication and the length of time from the ingestion that a medical assessment was unnecessary.

The psychiatric evaluation determined that Susan had significant affective instability. She described that her moods changed suddenly and in a way that she perceived was not in her control. There was no report of sustained sadness, irritability, or grandiosity. Sleep, appetite, interest, and concentration were generally appropriate, although at times of emotional distress, her concentration was noted to be worse. At the time of the assessment, there were no suicidal ideas. Susan did report occasional self-injury by cutting her wrists with a razor blade.

Her past history was significant for sexual abuse by her mother's boyfriend. This abuse took place when Susan was 7 to 9 years old. Susan was able to disclose this abuse at the age of 10, and an investigation supported its occurrence. The man was charged and sentenced to a prison term. At the time of the disclosure and for 2 years afterward, Susan participated in outpatient therapy. Currently, she reported some intrusive memories of the abuse, but other criteria for post-traumatic stress disorder were not met.

Susan had a pattern of dramatic interactions with others. School personnel described that Susan's presence in the school was generally known because of her volatile and explosive arguments with friends and teachers. She excessively sought support of teachers and guidance counselors to help address her unstable peer interactions.

Susan had many features consistent with BPD. However, during this first-time assessment, this diagnosis was not made. She was given a diagnosis of mood disorder, not otherwise specified. Extensive treatment recommendations were made, but the medication treatment recommendations included a trial of sertraline (Zoloft). This agent was chosen because of a positive familial response.

Sertraline therapy was initiated gradually and increased over several months to 100 mg a day. There was no response or stabilization of her symptoms with this dose or as a result of other treatment interventions. A decision was made after Susan took sertraline 100 mg a day for 2 months to try a different medication. The sertraline was decreased over 1 month, and after Susan went 1 week without medication, the atypical antipsychotic risperidone (Risperdal) was initiated. This medication was titrated very slowly because of Susan's complaint of sedation. However, at a dose of 0.25 mg in the morning and 0.5 mg at night, Susan began to experience a subjective improvement in her affective instability. School personnel and her mother also began to notice that her moods were more even and that she was generally less dramatic. This improvement was modest but reflected the first minor reduction in this characteristic. Higher dosages were not tolerated, and a decision was made to continue this dosage strategy.

TREATING TARGET SYMPTOMS: EDUCATIONAL IMPLICATIONS

The target symptoms of physical aggression, impulsivity, and affective instability can cause significant difficulties within an educational setting. When these are identified, there can be consideration for a psychiatric evaluation to ensure that these symptoms are not related to a definitive diagnosis.

There can be potential reduction in the intensity of these symptoms with medications. However, no medication will successfully eliminate the problem. In addition, there can be significant side effects that are more concerning than the identified problem.

School personnel can assist in the monitoring of side effects and can assist in providing clear communication to family members about any positive effects. It is important to remember that for the majority of these medications, it takes several weeks for the patient to note benefit.

In addition to medication, there needs to be additional behavioral support for these symptoms. Small-group instruction can be helpful. Also providing appropriate consequences for disruptive behavior should occur.

SIB and insomnia cause less disruption in the school setting than the other described problems. However, providing support for these difficulties can be helpful for the overall improvement of the student.

TREATING TARGET SYMPTOMS: SUMMARY

It is sometimes helpful to use pharmacologic interventions to reduce identified target symptoms. This treatment involves more trial and error with both type of medication and dose compared to treating known disorders. Caution should be used to make certain that the medication that is being used is not causing an inadvertent increase in the symptoms or triggering the emergence of other target symptoms.

It is important to stress again that successful medication response should not be used to provide diagnostic clarity. Also it is very important to reiterate that medication should never be the solo intervention to treat target symptoms, as treatment is much more complex.

Twelve

Medicating Children

C hild and adolescent psychiatry has emerged as a sub-specialty of general psychiatry because of distinct differences in treating young people. Children do not have the same ability to articulate their feelings as adults. This is because children do not have the cognitive ability to understand and verbalize feelings. This feature can compound an evaluation and makes it important to rely on numerous sources of information when gathering information.

This same language, cognitive, and emotional difficulty can make monitoring the medication difficult as well. An adult can describe if he or she is experiencing a side effect to medication more clearly than a child can. Children also have a difficulty with time conceptualization, and if questions about problems or side effects occur, it is important to help children place them in a correct time. Adolescents can be reluctant to pursue medication because they believe the medication will cause them to "change." More details about what the medication can do and what it will not do need to be explained in developmentally appropriate ways to a teen. This often takes more time than explaining the same information to an adult.

Along with having cognitive and emotional differences, children metabolize medications differently than adults do. Children, particularly those under the age of 15 years, tend to require higher dosages of medication per body weight than an adult (W. Green, 1995, p. 11). The overall dosage of medication may be lower, but the ratio of dose to body weight is higher for younger children. This may be due to the faster metabolism by the liver or faster clearance of the medication by the kidneys. In addition, children and adolescents are more prone to certain side effects, so the medication must be titrated more cautiously for children than for adults.

PSYCHIATRIC CARE

Evaluation

Throughout earlier sections of this book, the importance of a thorough psychiatric evaluation was stressed. One of the primary reasons a given treatment intervention or medication is ineffective is that the diagnosis that guides the treatment is incomplete or incorrect. Although the evaluation is viewed as a onetime snapshot view of the youth, all efforts should be made to have this assessment be comprehensive. The more information the clinician can review during the evaluation, the more complete it is. Having more participants provide information also increases the comprehensiveness of the assessment.

However, there are times when all efforts are made to provide a clear diagnostic picture in one visit, but sometimes there are more questions than answers. In this situation it can be helpful to prolong the assessment period to provide clarity. Although there is certainly pressure on the psychiatrist to quickly make decisions, a prolonged evaluation can ultimately be more helpful. Ideally, at the end of the evaluation, a diagnosis is determined. However, should the diagnosis remain unclear, treatment can be initiated based on the presence of target symptoms.

At times, a youth and family can present for a psychiatric evaluation with the goal of obtaining medication. Caution should be used in this situation to make certain that all information is being accurately portrayed. With increased diagnostic and treatment information readily available (the Internet and medication advertisements), the family may have a predetermined idea about what medication is appropriate. They can inadvertently present information incorrectly to obtain their desired diagnosis or treatment. Care should be taken by the psychiatrist to ensure that the information given is accurately portrayed. If a child or adolescent begins to use technical terms to describe symptoms, there should further exploration to make sure that the youth is not repeating terms about which he or she may have read.

Other times, a youth and family will present with no desire for medication. Either the youth or the family will minimize the symptoms in a way to ensure that no medication is recommended. However, the psychiatrist should gently confront the minimization and ensure the family that the decision to use medication must be agreed upon by everyone. In this situation the psychiatrist should provide information about the medication in a nonconfrontational manner. Sometimes having additional information will ultimately lead the family to a pursue medication at a later time.

When patients and physicians are considering medications, the choice of agent is ideally guided by diagnosis. However, there are times when it is appropriate to have treatment options be guided by target symptoms. A medication can be used as an FDA-approved treatment for a specific disorder, such as use of lithium to treat an adolescent with mania. However, the same medication can also be used to treat a target symptom, as lithium can be helpful in reducing aggression as a target symptom. It is called off-label usage when a physician uses an approved medication in a way that is not approved by the FDA. Physicians have the liberty to prescribe medications in this way if the patient consents.

Medication can be a portion of the treatment plan. Medication is never indicated as the sole treatment intervention to treat a mental illness. The psychiatrist might not always conduct the other components of the plan, but there should be certainty that other interventions are also being implemented. These interventions can include specific types of psychotherapy, educational interventions, family support, case management services, or community treatment programs. The psychiatrist does have responsibility to ensure that the other portions of the plan are being pursued.

Initiation of Medication

Informed consent must be given before starting medication. The treatment options should be clearly reviewed with the parents and youth. When this discussion occurs, the psychiatrist should describe the diagnosis and the risks and benefits of the proposed treatment. Alternative treatment possibilities should also be discussed. For example, the psychiatrist should describe what can happen without any treatment, what can be expected to happen if no medication is chosen, and what can happen if an alternative medication is selected. The parent or legal guardian must be able to make an informed decision and must not feel coerced. The likelihood of success of the treatment should be reviewed along with risks of the medication. It is important to review if the medication is being used in a way that is approved by the FDA or if the medication is being used in an off-label way (W. Green, 1995, pp. 21–22).

Adolescents are also important in providing informed consent. Medication should be clearly explained to children of all ages, but developmentally an adolescent has the cognitive ability to participate in treatment decisions by as early as age 12 years. States differ in their rules regarding the age of when an adolescent has the primary role in decision making. Pennsylvania, for example, has allowed adolescents by the age of 14 years to make the decision to pursue specific mental health treatment, including medication.

It is necessary to have the consent of both parents. If agreement between both parents cannot be reached, then it is not possible to begin treatment with medication. If the parents are separated or divorced with shared medical rights, both parents must agree to the treatment, and ideally both should sign an informed consent disclosure.

The risks of the medications must be clearly expressed and documented. Potential side effects and management of these must be reviewed. It is important that the youth and family be aware of how to assess both response and side effects. The clarity with which this information is presented is important for subsequent follow-up. It is also important to describe some side effects in a developmentally appropriate way so the individual can help to monitor these as well.

When medication is discussed with young children, it should be clarified that the medication is not being used to help control behavior. It is not helpful for young children to believe that the medication is needed to make them "good." Medications can reduce impulsivity or irritability, but they are not to help the child behave. Adolescents should be warned about the known interactions between the medication and alcohol or other illicit substances. Many psychotropic medications will intensify the effects of the illicit substances. Adolescent females should be aware of the potential negative effects the medication can have on a developing fetus so they should take significant precautions to prevent pregnancy. If sedation is possible, there should be a caution for the adolescent not to drive until this effect is clearly not occurring.

Compliance with medications is very important. Except for stimulant medications to treat attention-deficit/hyperactivity disorder (ADHD), psychotropic medications take several weeks before efficacy can be determined. In addition, there can be withdraw effects if the medications are stopped abruptly or if dosages are missed. The withdraw effects can look like a worsening of symptoms, which can cause significant clinical confusion. Compliance should be emphasized before initiating medication and again at follow-up visits.

Medications must be safely maintained in the home. A consideration includes keeping the medications out of the reach of small children to prevent accidental ingestion. If there is an adult or teen living in the home who has a substance abuse problem, controlled substances (stimulants) should be kept in a place where that individual does not have direct access. Certain medications can be highly lethal in overdose. All efforts should be made to monitor these medications closely, particularly if the youth has expressed suicidal ideas.

Once it is clear that medication is needed and consent is given, it is important to gather baseline assessment data before initiating treatment. This information includes behavioral assessments, physical assessments, and laboratory studies. These measures are used to help measure the response to treatment and to help monitor potential side effects.

Behavioral assessments should include observations of the child's behavior. They can be a formal assessment such as a functional behavioral assessment or an informal description of behavioral patterns based on the observation of the clinician and others. It is also important to obtain an accurate description of sleep and appetite patterns, as these can change with medication. Informal measures of the person's mood can be obtained by having the youth rate his or her mood or anxiety on a scale from 1 to 10. School personnel can also be helpful in gathering and reviewing behavioral data. Teachers can have an understanding about what can trigger a recognized behavior. In addition, there can be data available about what interventions have been successful at reducing behaviors. When there is consent to exchange information between the school and the psychiatrist, the data can be concisely presented verbally or in writing.

Formal rating scales can also be useful when gathering baseline data. There are rating scales, such as the Conners' Teacher Rating Scales and Conners' Parent Rating Scales, which teachers and parents can complete. These scales measure inattention, hyperactivity, and oppositionality. These same scales can be repeated after medication treatment as a way to demonstrate concretely any changes that occurred during the treatment. Another baseline behavioral assessment includes the Children's Depression Inventory, completed by the child, when the diagnosis is major depression.

It is important that before the psychiatrist initiates medication, the patient has received a comprehensive physical evaluation. Typically, a primary care physician will have conducted a physical examination within the past year. In addition, the treating psychiatrist should record current pulse, blood pressure, respiration rate, height, and weight data. These vital signs are an important component of the follow-up medication visits.

Laboratory studies should be considered but are not always necessary. Blood tests that can be indicated include a complete blood count, liver function tests, electrolytes, thyroid function tests, and kidney function tests. These studies can suggest underlying medical problems, but what is more important is they are needed as a baseline comparison. For medications such as lithium, which is known to have long-term effects on the thyroid, the kidney, and white blood cells, it is important to be certain before initiating medication that each of these are within normal limits. In addition, teenage girls should have a pregnancy test before initiating some psychotropic medications because of their known chance of contributing to birth defects.

If a medication that can cause cardiac problems is to be used, there should be a baseline EKG. Some examples of medications where an EKG should be considered include stimulants, clonidine, and tricyclic antidepressants. Recent information further supports that EKG monitoring is important to consider in youth who are going to be placed on a stimulant medication (Gould et al., 2009) (see accompanying CD: 12.1).

CHOICE OF INITIAL MEDICATION

Once there has been a comprehensive evaluation, informed consent, and acquisition of baseline assessments, the psychiatrist must select the starting medication. When possible the medication should be approved by the FDA to treat the identified diagnosis. Because there are only a few medications that are approved to treat a small group of psychiatric illnesses, this goal is not always possible. The clinician should next consider a medication that has been involved in several randomized controlled trials, as these medications have the next most support for use. The volume of randomized controlled clinical trials for children and adolescents severely lags behind that of studies for adults. So if this level of research is not known, then a medication should be considered that has had some research support as open trials.

Another factor that can guide medication selection is family response. If a genetically close family member has had a robustly positive response to a particular medication for a particular diagnosis that is shared by the patient, then that medication can be equally effective. Alternatively, if a family member had a negative reaction to a medication, then that medication might not be chosen for an initial medication if other options are available.

At times the potential side effect profile can guide a medication selection. For example, if major depression is diagnosed and the individual is having difficulty sleeping, then a more sedating antidepressant can be chosen. If this medication is taken in the evening, it can quickly improve sleep.

Once the medication has been selected, it is important to describe the timing of when it should be taken. Most medications should be taken at approximately the same time each day, and for some medications this is more critical. Medications that can be activating should be taken in the morning, whereas medications that can be sedating should be taken in the evening. Most medications are better tolerated if taken with food. If possible, waiting to begin a medication on a weekend can allow parents more comfort because they can be available to monitor the emergence of any early side effects.

Most psychotropic medications used for children and adolescents are started at the lowest possible dose and titrated slowly based on response. One dose should be used for several weeks before it is increased. In an outpatient setting, it is often wise to initiate only one medication at a time or to change the dose of one medication at a time. This allows there to be more clarity if there is a positive or negative reaction to the change.

PSYCHIATRIC CARE: FOLLOW-UP VISITS FOR MEDICATION

Once a medication has been prescribed, the physician who wrote the prescription is responsible for monitoring its effects. Most psychiatrists conduct follow-up in visits called "medication checks." These visits last from 15 to 25 minutes. During the process of this visit, the response to medication and side effects are assessed. The psychiatrist makes a determination about whether the dose is appropriate or needs to be adjusted to improve tolerance or benefit. Medication checks are also a time to check in with the youth and family regarding the benefit of other treatment interventions. Vital signs are often checked.

Early medication visits should include gathering information from the parent and the youth. Ideally, this should be done with them providing information independently. Even younger children should be given the opportunity to explain their view of the medication without the parents present. The family could also prefer to give information independently. For example, the parents might question if a particular behavior is a side effect, but they do not want to discuss this in front of the child, as the child could be suggestible. It is also very important to gather information from other sources including teachers, day care providers, and extended family members.

Assessing side effects and treatment response is clearly one goal of frequent medication assessment. However, early in treatment more frequent visits can help to improve the therapeutic alliance between the provider and the family. It also helps to send an important message to the youth, as compliance and consistency with the medication are critical. Compliance should be addressed at each visit because this is a critical piece of information regarding both side effects and treatment response.

Medication visits should also include screening questions to determine if other symptoms or illnesses are developing. Psychiatric diagnoses can change with time. What is normal development for a person at one age can become a disorder for that person at a different age. Illnesses themselves can evolve. The most frequent example of this is a teen with a single episode of major depression can present with mania several years later, changing the diagnosis to bipolar disorder. At other times when one diagnosis is successfully treated, it becomes apparent that there is a secondary diagnosis present. For example, a teen can present with a single episode of major depression, but after that fully resolves, it becomes apparent that there is also ADHD, primarily inattentive type.

Different medications have different treatment response curves. Except for antidepressants there are no definitive guidelines to suggest the frequency of follow-up visits. However, psychiatrists will sometimes make the determination of visit frequency particularly early in the treatment course based on the type of medication that has been prescribed.

Antidepressants

When antidepressants are prescribed, the FDA has recommended that there be weekly visits during the first month of treatment, two visits during the second month of treatment, and one visit during the third month of treatment (U.S. Food and Drug Administration, 2004). This has been part of the concern that emerged earlier this decade regarding youth suicidal thoughts during treatment with antidepressants. It was found that more frequent monitoring allowed for the emergence of these thoughts to be recognized earlier. Some psychiatrists have weekly medication checks when an antidepressant is prescribed. Others meet slightly less frequently but have phone contact on a weekly basis. In other scenarios if a therapist is involved in providing treatment for the child, there can be coordination of schedules to have the child seen weekly by alternate providers. It should be made very clear that there is no expectation of response in this early monitoring stage, but these visits are occurring to ensure safety and tolerability.

The practicality of this intensity of follow-up is difficult. In addition, there has been some concern that these recommendations were made without any evidence-based research to show the necessity. Psychiatrists tend to follow these guidelines more closely than pediatricians. The FDA guidelines have emphasized the need for close monitoring (Morrato et al., 2008).

Antidepressants take several weeks to begin to show efficacy. Dosage adjustments should not occur until there has been sufficient time to determine that there has not been a response at the lower dose. Raising the dose of these medications too quickly can complicate the treatment decisions, particularly if side effects occur.

Mood Stabilizers

Mood stabilizers also take several weeks to show efficacy. Again in early treatment close monitoring is important, although it is not uncommon for the family to return several weeks after the start of medication.

A unique feature of the medication check for some of these medications includes blood work monitoring (see accompanying CD: 12.2). Lithium and valproic acid have described therapeutic blood levels. After several weeks of treatment, the blood level can be checked, and the dose can be more precisely adjusted based not only on treatment response but also on the blood level.

These types of medications can also cause an increased appetite, which leads to weight gain. Having medication checks every few weeks allows weight to be checked more frequently. If weight gain is occurring, there can be a discussion with the family that can perhaps support better nutritional choices to moderate this effect.

Stimulants and Nonstimulants for ADHD Treatment

Stimulant and nonstimulant medications show a more rapid treatment response than other psychotropic medications. Stimulant response can be seen after the first dose or at least within the first week. Atomoxetine is titrated with a lower dose prescribed for the first 4 to 6 days, followed by a scheduled increase. This schedule is derived based on the person's weight. Atomoxetine shows a response within 7 to 10 days.

Because of the more rapid response of these medications, the dosages can be adjusted as frequently as once a week. Stimulants and nonstimulants are dosed based on the individual's weight. However, if the youth has never been on a medication before, most psychiatrists will begin treatment at a lower dose. This helps to minimize side effects and helps to ensure that if a lower dose for weight is beneficial that this benefit is not overlooked.

The medication assessment at these visits will focus on both side effects and response. Early in the course of treatment, it is beneficial to obtain information from numerous sources to help monitor efficacy at different times of the day. A stimulant at a low dose can be more effective in the morning than in the afternoon, so understanding from a teacher if there is a recognized difference at points throughout the day can be helpful. In this case raising the morning daily dose slightly can have the effect of longer lasting coverage. After-school providers can also be helpful sources of information regarding rebound phenomena as the medication leaves the system. These providers can be acutely aware of the time at which the medication loses all efficacy. Numerous sources can complete checklist assessments or can provide written summaries to the physician.

Stimulant medications are controlled substances. This is because of their potential for misuse. Because these medications are considered controlled substances, a new prescription must be written each time the medication is needed. Refills without a new prescription are not allowed. The medications cannot be called into a pharmacy, and the prescriptions cannot be faxed. There must be clear communication between the prescriber and the family to ensure that medications are written in a timely manner.

Antipsychotics

The antipsychotic medications also take several weeks or in some cases months to reach full efficacy. However, there can be early improvement in target symptoms such as sleep, anxiety, or agitation that can occur within the first few weeks of treatment. As with the traditional mood stabilizers, these medications frequently cause a dramatic increase in appetite, which can lead to weight gain and other metabolic problems. Monitoring weight at frequent intervals can result in observing the weight trend so that adjustments in nutrition, dose, or medication can be more promptly made.

MEDICATION TREATMENT

Adjusting the Dose

With most medications the visit that occurs 4 to 6 weeks after the initiation of medication is the one where additional time is spent monitoring the response to medication. This information is obtained from as many sources as possible, but by this time the youth's perception of response is important. It is not uncommon for the parents to notice response earlier in treatment than the youth, but by the 6-week mark, most youth should be aware of any improvement. It is uncommon that maximum benefit is reached at this point, but there should be some clear evidence that there is benefit. A decision regarding dosage often occurs at this visit. If there is significant or even modest improvement, the decision can be made to continue the medication at the same dose. However, if there is minimal improvement, a decision can be made by both the physician and the family to increase the dose.

If the dose is increased, there should again be regular and frequent monitoring of potential side effects. Any side effects that occurred on medication initiation have a chance of recurring on a higher dose. In addition, new side effects can occur with dosage increase. Some side effects such as sexual side effects or neurologic side effects are more likely to happen at higher dosages.

If the dose of the medication remains the same, there can be a reduction in the frequency of visits. However, this frequency of visits should be gradually reduced. Most psychiatrists prefer to see children at least every 3 months once the medications and symptoms have been stable for some time. This frequency of visits allows for vital signs to be checked to ensure that there have not been any gradual weight, pulse, or blood pressure changes. In addition, individuals on some medications may need blood work to monitor their blood levels or to ensure there is no negative effect on different body systems.

Changing the Medication

There are times when after there has been a trial of one medication it is determined that there is not sufficient efficacy to continue treatment. Before changing to a different medication, it is important to make sure that an adequate dose of medication has been used for an adequate length of time. This is another important time to review compliance, as medications do not work effectively if not taken every day. Another time to consider a change of medication is if there is a positive response but there are also significant side effects that are impairing.

Before making a decision to change the medication, the psychiatrist should also review whether the diagnosis that is being targeted with medications is the correct diagnosis. Along with noncompliance, another common reason for failure of response to a medication is an inaccurate diagnosis.

Ideally, the medication that is going to be discontinued should be tapered rather than abruptly stopped. Most medications should have the dose reduced by 25 to 50% every week. Depending on the type and dose of medication, this could take several weeks. The faster most medications are tapered, the more likely withdraw effects are to occur. Antidepressants in particular can be associated with significant withdraw effects, which are reviewed later in this chapter.

The person should then remain medication free for several days to a week. This ensures that all the medication's active metabolites are given time to clear the body. In addition, it gives a brief period of time for the baseline symptoms to be reassessed.

The new medication can be initiated after this washout occurs. This agent should be started at a low dose and gradually increased based on treatment response. The benefit of this stop-and-start type of medication change is that it allows a clear explanation between withdraw effects during the taper and side effects during the start of the new medication.

Depending on the severity of symptoms, the psychiatrist can determine that a different schedule for medication change is needed. The schedule to stop one medication, allow a few days off medication to ensure washout of metabolites, and start a new medication can take 1 to 2 months. Depending on the severity of the youth's withdraw symptoms, the psychiatrist can determine that it would be more beneficial to change the medications more rapidly. The faster change in medication can complicate the clinical picture if problems emerge, but if there is significant impairment in functioning or development, it may be necessary to take this chance. In this situation there are two different medication change schedules that could be applied.

One of these schedules includes continuing the person on the former medication at the same dose and initiating treatment with a different medication. The new medication can be slowly increased to efficacy. Once symptom improvement has been achieved, the first medication can gradually be discontinued. Using this schedule also allows clarity of side effects that occur with the start of the new medication compared to withdraw effects that occur when the first medication is discontinued. The negative aspect of this schedule is that it can become difficult to tell if the treatment response is based on the new medication or is a result of the combination treatment. In addition, some individuals are reluctant to be on two medications for the same problem.

The second medication strategy that can be employed to change medication is referred to as a crossover model. In this situation the dose of one medication is lowered at the same time the new medication is started at a low dose. Every few days the old medication dose is reduced slightly while the new medication dose is increased. Over several days to weeks, the former medication is gradually discontinued at the same time the new medication reaches therapeutic efficacy.

Psychiatrists will often choose one of these treatment strategies based on the reason for the change in medication and the degree of functional impairment. Regardless of which model is used, the family should be aware of both the withdraw effects from one medication and the side effects of the other. As with initiating a medication, there should be careful review of the indications for the change, and new informed consent must be given.

Polypharmacy

Polypharmacy is the term that is used when more than one psychotropic medication is prescribed to the same person. This can occur because there have been two separate illnesses that require two different medications to treat. Another reason that polypharmacy occurs is that one medication at a therapeutic dose is not effective at reducing the severity or symptoms of illness. A final common reason that polypharmacy occurs is that a second medication may be needed to treat emergent side effects from an effective medication.

One example of an individual who is receiving two medications for two illnesses is an adolescent who has both ADHD and major depression. If the youth has never been on medication previously, a decision must be made as to which illness is causing the most distress or interference in functioning. Treatment with a medication should be pursued for this illness. Once the symptoms of the primary illness are treated, a second medication to treat the other illness can be added. If the youth's functioning is severely impaired by both illnesses, some psychiatrists will choose to begin treatment for both illnesses at the same time. Although not contraindicated the problem with this approach is that determining which medication is causing a side effect can be more difficult.

In some individuals treatment with one medication for the illnesses is not fully effective. The most common single illness that requires two medications to effectively treat is bipolar disorder. Often a traditional mood stabilizer such as valproic acid is combined with an antipsychotic for its additional mood stabilization properties. In addition, this type of polypharmacy can occur to minimize side effects from one medication at a higher dose. For example, a child with ADHD can show a very positive response to a stimulant medication, but at the dose that is most effective, weight loss occurs because of a reduced appetite. In this case continuing the same stimulant at a lower dose while adding a low dose of atomoxetine can produce the same benefit without the weight loss.

Finally, polypharmacy can occur by adding a second medication to treat emergent side effects of an effective medication. If the medication is not effective and generating side effects, it should simply be changed. However, there are many times when numerous medications have been tried that have produced partial efficacy and one is found that is more effective. If this effective medication is causing a side effect that can be treated with an alternative medication, this can be done. Some antidepressants such as bupropion are activating in nature and can begin to impair sleep. In this case adding a second antidepressant that is sedating at night can be useful.

When two or more psychotropic medications are prescribed, it should be done cautiously. It must be checked that the medications will not interact negatively with each other. In addition, some medications can have the effect of increasing another medication's blood level. Side effects can be cumulative, so there should be very close monitoring of known side effects such as sedation.

Coordination of Care

For many children and adolescents with serious mental illnesses, there need to be a number of providers involved in treatment. A psychiatrist is one piece of this team, but other members can include a therapist, community mental health services, school-based treatment team members, a pediatrician, a juvenile probation officer, children and youth caseworkers, and a case manager, to name a few. When a variety of individuals are involved, there must be close communication between the members (see accompanying CD: 12.5). This helps to ensure that there is consensus of diagnosis and that treatment services are being delivered effectively.

If the youth is receiving care from a number of service levels and a number of providers, a case manager is assigned to this job. A case manager can be instrumental in coordinating schedules and assisting the family in practical ways. The case manager can be the conduit of information between providers, taking reports or verbal information from one appointment and giving it directly to a different treatment team member.

A youth can have several treatment team members but no case manager. For example, the treatment team members can include only a psychiatrist and a therapist. In this situation someone needs to be responsible for ensuring that there is communication between the different providers. At minimum in this situation the diagnostic impressions and treatment plan that the therapist and psychiatrist each generate should be shared with the other. This ensures that each provider has reached the same diagnostic conclusion and that each is addressing the problem in complementary ways. It is also helpful for the therapist and psychiatrist to have periodic direct communication to share observations and treatment responses. In some situations family members or the patient can help to facilitate this communication. However, this should not be relied on as the only source of communication, as information can be misinterpreted or misrepresented.

It is also imperative that the psychiatrist have communication with the school. The youth spends a significant portion of the day in a setting where there is no family involvement or observation. Teachers, administrators, and guidance counselors have important observations regarding changes in behavior or mood state. In addition, school personnel have the opportunity to observe the youth in situations of peer interactions, which can be helpful in monitoring treatment response.

Unless the psychiatrist is providing care directly in the school system, the parents and youth must give permission for communication between the school and the provider. In most situations this is highly desired by everyone, and the consent form is signed. However, in some cases the parents or the youth does not want there to be communication. In these situations the family's request must be honored. However, it is also important as the psychiatrist continues to treat the youth that ongoing efforts be made to allow there to be communication with the school.

Parents are sometimes concerned that if a school receives mental health information that the child will be treated differently. Parents need to be educated by both the clinician and the school team that the sharing of information ensures that the youth is treated in an appropriate way. Most often when teachers are aware of a particular area of struggle for the child, there is an increased ability to work in a cooperative way. Most commonly, teachers can view that a student is being oppositional by not completing work while it may be fear of failure. When the motivation behind the work refusal is understood, the teacher can be more supportive.

When the school team members have received communication from the psychiatrist, they have received confidential information that must be used appropriately. Teachers in particular must be sensitive to how this information is used. At least yearly I hear complaints from a student that in a moment of frustration a teacher made a comment to the student in front of the class to the effect of "Didn't you take your medication today?" Although made in frustration or made as a joke, this often causes significant distress to the youth and can ultimately result in a discontinuation of medications.

Discontinuation of Medication

A psychiatrist can work with the family and pediatrician to transfer the continuation of medication to the pediatrician or other primary care provider when there has been sufficient stabilization of symptoms. At minimum this should occur with a transfer of records between the two providers. Ideally, a brief phone conversation to ensure treatment continuity should occur. The transfer of care should be done only when it is certain that stability of symptoms has been achieved and that the dose response of medication is well tolerated. At times the psychiatrist can also include guidelines for subsequent changes in the dose of medication, but the pediatrician ultimately assumes decision-making abilities. The benefit of this transfer is that it allows ease of access for the family and also allows the psychiatrist's time to be utilized by individuals with more acute problems.

The other way in which psychiatric care is appropriately ended is when there has been an ongoing period of symptom stability without medication changes. Children and adolescents with depressive disorders or anxiety disorders might not need long-term medications. As described in the chapters on mood and anxiety disorders, treatment for these illnesses consists of an acute phase and a maintenance phase. Most guidelines suggest that after a maintenance phase of 6 to 12 months, there should be a consideration for dosage reduction and ultimately discontinuation. Children and adolescents on other medications can also have periods of time without medication to reassess their treatment needs.

Throughout treatment and follow-up visits, compliance with medication has been assessed. The psychiatrist should ensure that the person has continued to take the medications as prescribed. During these conversations there can be times when the parent or the child wishes to discontinue medication. The understanding for this wish should be explored. If the family understands the potential risks of stopping the medication and continues to support its discontinuation, the psychiatrist should offer guidelines to safely discontinue the medication.

Below are listed some general principles for discontinuing psychotropic medications. These are guidelines, and there should be individual differences considered. In addition to ensuring that the medications are safely stopped, there should be discussion to review the warning signs about the returning illness. This will enable the family and youth to more closely monitor the illness and, ideally, return to treatment sooner if needed. The timing of medication discontinuation should be considered. It is never wise to taper or stop a medication during a particularly stressful time.

Antidepressants

Antidepressants as a class of medications are best gradually and slowly discontinued. The dose should be reduced by 25% or 50% and maintained at that level for at least a few weeks. This allows for a minimum amount of withdraw effects. Withdraw effects can mimic a return of symptom presentation, or these effects can have a somatic presentation. Nausea or a headache can develop. There can be tremors or shaking or in extreme cases a somatic perception of electric shocks. Two antidepressants, paroxetine and venlafaxine in particular, are more prone to the development of withdraw symptoms. If withdraw symptoms occur even with very incremental dosage reductions, they can be ameliorated by an alternating day strategy of a slightly higher dose one day followed by the dose reduction on the other day (see accompanying CD: 12.3).

Along with preventing withdraw effects, the other benefit for gradual dosage reduction is that it allows an opportunity to ensure that symptoms will not recur on lower dosages. If the symptoms do recur, it is easier to more quickly return to the therapeutic level.

Depending on the starting dose of medication, this dose reduction strategy can take several months to have the individual be medication free. If the person has been off medication for 1 to 2 months and no symptoms have returned, the likelihood of remaining off medication for an extended time is increased.

During the dosage reduction stage, there should be some time spent reviewing the history of the depressive illness. This type of education can be very helpful for the youth and family in more quickly spotting an illness return at a point in the future. For example, if the adolescent's first neurovegetative symptoms of depression included social isolation and frequent night awakenings, these symptoms will more likely be present if the illness returns at a point in the future.

Mood Stabilizers

Most commonly, children and teens who are diagnosed with bipolar disorder are believed to need longer term medication intervention. Although not definitive, this illness is more likely to be a lifelong one that requires continual treatment. However, mood stabilizers are also used to treat impulsivity and rage, and when they are used to treat those target symptoms, it is necessary to occasionally discontinue them to determine if they are still necessary.

These medications less often have withdraw effects, but the dose should be reduced in a step-down strategy similar to that of antidepressants, with dosage reductions of 25% to 50% every few weeks as tolerated. At times an individual may wish to pursue more rapid reduction, and this can be considered as long as it is clear that the person might experience some irritability or withdraw effects.

Stimulants

If a child has been maintained on a stimulant medication and has demonstrated a year of stability, there can be a consideration for a medication-free trial to determine if the medication remains necessary. It is very important to appropriately plan for this trial. The medication should not be discontinued during the first month of school, as this might not be a sufficient academic load to determine necessity of medication. In the same way, the last month of school is also not an appropriate time to discontinue medication, as the academic load increases, and there can be final examinations. Some families elect to discuss this trial with the teacher before it occurs, whereas others do not inform the school because of their belief that this will allow more objectivity. Fortunately, because of the pharmacokinetic properties of stimulants, there is not a need for a gradual dose reduction. The medications can be stopped and restarted quickly if needed.

Antipsychotics

Antipsychotic medications likely require longer term medication because of the underlying illness that is being treated. If an antipsychotic is being prescribed to treat a target symptom such as anger, there can also be a consideration to try a dose reduction or elimination after a year of stability. If low dosages have been used, these medications can be stopped. However, if more moderate dosages have been used, it can be more prudent for the clinician to gradually reduce the dose to prevent withdraw effects.

COORDINATION WITH SCHOOLS

Psychiatric follow-up can be improved with communication from schools. Teachers, guidance counselors, and other school personnel are in a unique position to observe students daily on a longitudinal basis. Subtle improvements in mood, anxiety, attention, and impulsive behaviors can be noted when students are observed over time. It is important for the family and psychiatrist to communicate to the school the reasons the student is on medication and what the medication is intended to do. This information can come directly from the provider but also can come from the family and student. If the school personnel have a question about the reasons for the medication or the indications for which it is being prescribed, one representative should contact the physician's office to ask the question.

Once it is clear what is expected from the medication, school personnel can provide helpful information to the psychiatrist. Side effects should certainly be communicated. In addition, it is helpful to report if any positive changes have been noticed. Different formats for this communication can occur. Some teachers will e-mail the parents with direct observations, and the parents will share the e-mail. Some teachers will fax a written note to the office before the appointment. Some psychiatrists prefer to have checklists such as the Conners' Teacher Rating Scale completed at regular intervals. This checklist can summarize changes in attention, impulsivity, and hyperactivity domains for a child with ADHD.

When communicating with the psychiatrist, school personnel will find it helpful to be clear and concise with observations. If there are variations noted throughout the day, this should be explained. If there are ongoing concerns that have not improved, this should be shared. A few specific examples of the positive changes can be offered. It is helpful to express this information without attempting to offer an opinion regarding efficacy. The psychiatrist should help to process the information and will ask questions as needed (see accompanying CD: 12.4).

MEDICATING CHILDREN: SUMMARY

When a psychiatrist is involved in a child's or adolescent's care, one of the main roles of this treatment is to initiate and monitor medication. This involves a therapeutic treatment alliance to ensure compliance with medication. Finding the appropriate medication and dosage of medication can take time and patience. There must be informed consent for this treatment, as well as ongoing monitoring of treatment response and side effects. The psychiatrist will often guide the patient and family as to when and how to discontinue the medication. Although the psychiatrist guides the treatment, input into these decisions must come from the child, family, and, ideally, school systems.

Thirteen

Mental Health Crises

MENTAL HEALTH CRISIS: BACKGROUND

A mental health crisis can occur at any time. A psychiatrist must be available in different settings to have an understanding of how to best manage these situations. Some examples of crises include suicidal statements, homicidal statements, self-injurious behaviors, and physical aggression. This chapter will focus on each of these situations. Information will be presented to explain the nature of the crisis. There will be a summary of how these situations can be managed acutely within the school system and a summary of how a psychiatrist can contribute to these situations outside the school.

When a crisis arises within the school, school personnel are assigned to begin an intervention. This intervention can be easily completed and contained within the school system. In more severe situations, a crisis worker or psychiatrist conducts a comprehensive mental health assessment. The ability of the student and school personnel to communicate the nature of the concerns to the individual doing the risk assessment is critical. The more information that is available to the evaluator, the more complete the risk assessment will be.

SUICIDE ASSESSMENT: BACKGROUND

Youth suicide is a significant concern. Although recently the trend has been a stabilization of the number of completed suicides, for several decades the incidence continued to rise. Suicide in children before puberty is very rare. The incidence of suicide attempts reaches a peak during mid-adolescence. Suicide remains the third leading cause of death in youth ages 10 to 24 years (Centers for Disease Control and Prevention [CDC], 2007b). Many individuals who committed suicide made a statement or comment that could have been a warning sign.

However, suicide can also be an impulsive act, and there may be no warning signs. In addition, many people who have thoughts of wanting to die will share those thoughts spontaneously or if asked about them directly. Suicide is associated with mood disorders, behavioral disorders, psychotic disorders, and substance abuse disorders. All suicidal statements need to be understood, and the individual's risk of acting on the thoughts must be assessed.

Suicidal ideation and *suicidal ideas* are clinical terms used to mean that a person is contemplating taking his or her own life. *Suicidal plan* is the term used to report what the person's ideas have been to make this happen. A *suicidal attempt* is the carrying out of the plan. A *suicidal gesture* is a term that is used when a person has made a suicide attempt but either the intention was not to die or the lethality of the plan was significantly low. A *completed suicide* implies death has occurred.

Factors that are associated with completed suicide include the presence of preexisting psychiatric disorders, stress events including a loss of romantic relationship, disciplinary troubles, legal problems, academic difficulties, and family difficulties. It is estimated that 90% of adolescents who commit suicide have a present psychiatric disorder, and perhaps as many as 50% have had mental health treatment in the 2 years before death (Brent, Baugher, Bridge, Chen, & Beery, 1999).

Risk factors that are associated with suicide completion include a prior attempt of suicide, male gender, the presence of a current mental disorder or disordered mental state, the presence of comorbid substance abuse, and the presence of irritability and agitation. Another risk factor is the degree to which the plan has been thought out and the potential lethality of the plan. Approximately 30% of those who complete suicide had a prior attempt (Brent et al., 1999; Shaffer et al., 1996) (see accompanying CD: 13.1).

Completed suicide is more common in adolescent males by a ratio of 3:1 (CDC, 2008a), but adolescent girls more commonly attempt suicide. The increased lethality of suicide in males is related to the fact that males often engage in methods that are more lethal, such as death by firearms. In addition, males have a higher rate of substance abuse, and this disorder is a common factor in completed suicides. Caucasians have a higher incidence of suicide than other races, but in recent years there has been an increase in suicide attempts and completions among African American males. Significantly more youth attempt suicide than die by suicide. A nationwide survey of high school youth found that 15% of students reported seriously considering suicide, 11% reported creating a plan, and 7% reported an attempt (CDC, 2008a).

It had previously been believed that inquiring about the presence of suicidal ideas could cause someone who did have these thoughts to begin to develop them. It was also believed that inquiring about suicidal thoughts would cause someone to act on these thoughts. However, it is now firmly believed that asking about suicidal ideas does not cause them to occur. Asking about suicidal ideas is protective because often when the person reveals the thinking, a safety plan can be put into place and relief occurs. It is also known that associating with people who have suicidal ideas such as occurs in a treatment facility does not increase the chance of one developing these thoughts. Interestingly, though, it has been seen that being exposed to a suicide can increase the likelihood of an adolescent attempting or completing suicide. It is not uncommon for youth suicides to occur in a cluster.

Some youth who have suicidal ideas will divulge these when asked during an evaluation. Alternatively, a youth may divulge suicidal ideas to a teacher, guidance counselor, or peer. Finally, a student may share this thought with a peer who subsequently shares it with an adult. Regardless of the way the information is learned, a risk assessment must be completed to further understand the safety steps that must be put into place for the student.

SUICIDAL STATEMENTS

Questions to Consider in Preliminary Assessment

The initial assessment of a student who has expressed suicidal ideas is where information regarding potential risk factors is determined. It is first important for the examiner to understand the meaning behind the suicidal statement. The questions should be asked calmly and with no judgment. It is first important to establish if there are suicidal ideas or plans or if there has been a suicidal attempt. If an attempt has occurred, the first step should be transportation to a hospital for a medical assessment. If there has not been an attempt, then a preliminary understanding of the suicidal statements can begin.

The first step in this assessment is to determine if a more detailed intervention is needed to either ensure safety or have

a mental health assessment. If the person divulges strong suicidal thoughts and has a plan that could potentially be carried
out, it is important to ensure that the person receive a mental
health assessment, and this may need to be facilitated directly
from the school. However, if there is no definitive plan, the
present examiner can continue to provide the assessment.

When determining the necessity of intervention, the examiner will often find it helpful to balance risk factors with protective factors. If in the balance there are more risk factors
than protective factors, then a crisis assessment completed on
an emergency basis may be needed. The risk factors to understand are a history of past attempts, the intrusiveness and
intensity of present suicidal thoughts, feelings of hopelessness,
identification of substance abuse, the presence of an active
mental health disorder, the presence of an acute identifiable
stressor, and a sense of isolation. Protective factors include
specific reasons not to engage in the behavior (religious, fear
of loss) and the ability to articulate that it is a thought or wish
but not intended to be done at this time. In addition, if a youth

is future oriented and talking about future plans, the risk can
be mitigated (see accompanying CD: 13.2).

This second level of assessment should be completed by a
crisis intervention service, psychologist, or psychiatrist. The
school personnel can be instrumental in ensuring that this
more detailed assessment occurs. It is helpful for the mental
health specialist conducting the second assessment to have
the accurate information about what may have been shared
in the screening. If the school assessor does not believe there
is a need to have an assessment completed immediately, the
person needs to share this information with the student's parents. The parents ultimately decide to pursue a more detailed
evaluation. Parents may need to be instructed as to how to
have the assessment occur. This can occur acutely through an
emergency room or mental health crisis center.

If it is determined that the risk of immediate action is low,
it can be more appropriate to connect the student with an outpatient therapist or psychiatrist. If safety is not an immediate
concern, this intervention can be more helpful, as treatment
can occur with the same provider.

Alternatively, if the student who makes a suicidal statement
is already involved in mental health treatment, this comment
should be shared with the treatment provider. Ideally, the
school personnel who discussed the comment with the student should talk directly with the outpatient provider. This

continuity of care not only ensures safety but also helps with the treatment.

Mental Health Assessment

Psychiatrists routinely assess for suicidal thoughts. Each individual who is seen should be assessed each time for potential suicidality. General questions can be asked to determine if a youth has had thoughts of death. Some examples of these questions are as follows: "Have you ever felt so sad or mad that you wished that you were dead?" or "Have you ever done something that you knew was dangerous and hoped that you would die from it?" or "Have you ever thought about killing yourself?" If theses questions are answered positively, more specific questions should be asked to elicit any potential current suicidal thoughts or plans.

The assessment of suicidal thoughts should also include an attempt to understand the motivating feelings behind the thoughts or attempt. This feature can help the clinician to understand the ongoing presence of the thoughts. For example, if a teen had suicidal thoughts to avoid a perceived intolerable situation and the situation remains, the suicidal thoughts may still remain.

If the suicide assessment is being conducted following a suicide attempt, the suicide assessment can be more difficult. The underlying motivation and intention should be reviewed. Risk factors that increase the risk of a second attempt following a first attempt include male gender, increased age, living alone (runaway or homeless), a pattern of past attempts, attempts with a method other than ingestion or superficial cutting, and having taken steps to avoid detection. A final high level of concern is if there is significant anger and frustration that the attempt was unsuccessful.

If the suicidal assessment is being completed after there have been known suicidal statements, the examiner must first work to establish a rapport to allow the adolescent to feel comfortable divulging internal thoughts. There should be a review of current psychiatric symptoms to determine if a mental health diagnosis is present. There should be a review of past suicidal thoughts, plans, and attempts. There must be careful investigation into social stressors that can be a factor. Coping strategies should be reviewed; if there are minimal coping strategies, the risk is higher. Family history should be reviewed, and the perception of family support is also helpful to understand. If the examiner perceives that there is a reasonably high likelihood of action, there must be steps taken to ensure safety.

At times during a mental health assessment or psychiatric evaluation, the concept of a "suicide contract" can be presented. In this informal agreement, the examiner writes a specific contract that specifies steps the student will take if the intensity of suicidal thoughts increases to the point of action. Both the student and the examiner sign this contract. These contracts do not offer any legal protection, but a contract can be useful clinically. It is also very significant if an individual refuses to sign a contract.

Levels of Intervention

If there is believed to be a moderate or high risk of completing the suicidal thoughts, there is a need to have intensive intervention. Ideally, this should take place in a hospital where safety can be ensured throughout the day. In addition, within the hospital, therapeutic supports can be more readily available. Recently, the length of inpatient hospitalization stays are decreasing, so when safety is more easily assured, the person can be stepped down to a less intense intervention like partial hospitalization. This option allows ongoing intensive therapeutic support and can safely be used if there is a degree of comfort that the family can provide safety monitoring in the evening and night.

Acute intervention, such as hospitalization, should be provided for all youth who have made a known suicide attempt. Hospitalization should also be considered for a youth who has specific suicidal plans and there is concern that the family will not be able to provide a high level of monitoring to ensure safety. Suicidal thoughts in the presence of an altered mental status, such as the presence of mania, substance intoxication, agitation, or psychosis, should also be acutely managed in a hospital setting.

If the risk is high but not judged to be acute, there can be outpatient interventions offered. However, there must first be assurance that the family or social supports are present to help provide monitoring for safety. The family should be prepared to make certain that no weapons are in the home. In addition, there should be no access to alcohol. A family member may need to be available to stay in the youth's room.

Treatment interventions to help with suicidal thinking include treatment or stabilization of the underlying mental illness. In addition, cognitive behavioral therapy strategies can be useful to help identify underlying cognitive distortions and improve coping skills in managing negative emotions.

Pharmacotherapy is needed to treat any underlying mental health disorders that can be contributing to the suicidal thoughts. In addition, one meta-analysis of adult studies found that lithium maintenance reduced the recurrence of suicide attempts eightfold in adults with affective disorders. In addition, when the lithium was discontinued, there was a sevenfold increase in the rate of suicide attempts (Tondo, Jamison, & Baldessarini, 1997). However, if this medication is prescribed to a suicidal youth, it must be very carefully monitored by an adult because of the potential lethality with overdose.

Follow-up in the Educational Setting

A suicidal youth can require frequent reassessment or at least the opportunity to discuss current feelings and stressors. Suicidal thoughts can become a recurrent problem, and particularly until the underlying mental health disorder is stabilized, there is a heightened risk of death. Ongoing mental health, educational, and social supports are needed.

Educationally the student can benefit from periodic check-ins with a guidance counselor or other supportive adult. Efforts should be made to minimize intense academic pressure, but there should not be avoidance of all work because of suicidal thoughts. A balance must be sought where the student feels less pressure but does not escape academic demands.

HOMICIDAL STATEMENTS

Background

Adolescents can commit horrific acts of violence, including homicide. Homicide is the second leading cause of death among youth aged 5 to 18 years (CDC, 2007b).

It has been estimated that less than 1% of youth homicide occur in the school setting. From July 1999 through June 2006, a total of 116 school-associated homicides occurred. Sixty-five percent of the deaths occurred by gunshot wounds. Twenty-seven percent were caused by stabbing or cutting, whereas beatings were the cause of the final 12%. Calculations using National Center for Health Statistics (NCHS) mortality data for July 1999 through June 2004 indicated that the proportion of homicides among school-age children that were school associated was 0.96% (i.e., 79 of 8,236 total homicides) (Modzeleski et al., 2008). This statistic supports that 1% of youth homicides occur within a school setting. Despite this low percentage, significant media attention is placed on each event. Within the school system, there is a need to identify students who may be at risk to complete one of these atrocious acts. Each threatening statement that is made by a student can be considered a mental health crisis.

Anytime a threatening statement is made by a student, numerous steps must take place to determine the particular risk that the student has of acting on this statement or thought. These statements come to the attention of school personnel through written notes, through threats made specifically to teachers or students, or from one student disclosing what another student has talked about.

The prediction of violence is difficult, and there is no definitive answer to this problem. Some clues can be found that increase or decrease a student's likelihood of acting on a homicidal statement. A threat assessment will often report on the potential of following through with a specific act and can make a statement about the overall prediction of future violence. The threat assessment can also describe acute risk, meaning the potential to act in a violent way in the very near future, or chronic risk, meaning long-term potential for violence. Finally, the assessment can provide steps to be taken to help reduce the act of violence.

Questions to Consider in Preliminary Assessment

Each threatening statement is taken seriously. However, there must be developmental context. A young elementary student who makes a comment about wanting to "blow up a school" has a different meaning than an adolescent making the same comment. Younger children do not have a fully developed idea of death. In addition, younger children may not have learned to distinguish between reality and fantasy, so this comment may not be an actual desire. The context in which the statement was made is also important to understand. A threatening statement that is made while a student is playing a game can have a different meaning than one made when a student is frustrated and angry.

School personnel are in a unique position to be able to obtain information about the actual threat. It is easy to learn the context in which the statement was made. In addition, there is access to people who have known the student over time, and there can be other prior statements or acts that in retrospect may have had a different meaning. In addition, school personnel, particularly a school-based therapist or guidance counselor, can talk to the student soon after the threat was made. This timing can allow for more honest answers to specific questions of intention. When there is a delay in questioning about the statement, the youth can have the opportunity to minimize the statement or to not correctly remember the details of the statement or emotions related to the statement.

When an initial risk assessment is conducted, a discussion of the threat with the student is needed to understand the thinking behind the statement and to hear from his or her perspective what frustrations may have been underlying the statement. An initial threat assessment can also investigate the student's ability to carry out the threatened statement. If there is a high likelihood of follow-through with the threatened statement, a more emergent mental health assessment in a crisis center or emergency room should be sought. If there is not a developed plan, it can be reasonable to wait to have an outpatient assessment completed.

Some risk factors that must be considered in the initial screening include having a past history of violent acts, being a victim of mistreatment, having a poor connection with adults and peers, having a well-thought-out plan of action, and having taken action to initiate the plan (see accompanying CD: 13.3).

Along with investigating the threat and interviewing the student, the clinician must inform the family. A parent's response to the statement can also provide useful clues to the final risk assessment. Many parents respond by minimizing the concern and perceiving that the comment was not intended or was taken out of context. However, there must still be follow-through on their part, and it is a higher level of concern if the parents continue to minimize the statement and do not follow-through with the steps that may be requested to ensure the safety of other students.

Mental Health Assessment

Psychiatrists are often asked to provide a risk assessment following a specific statement made by a student or following the identification of a potential weapon on school property. This assessment is best done in the context of a psychiatric evaluation because the statement or action is best understood when there is a broad understanding of development, strengths, weaknesses, and mental health treatment that may have been provided to date.

A psychiatrist attempts to understand the underlying thoughts that are related to the threat, as well as any steps that were taken to make the threat come true. The more advanced the planning is or the more steps that have been taken to complete the plan, the higher the risk. The emotional state that contributed to the student's making the threat is also important to understand. Statements made in a brief flare of anger can have a different level of risk than those made in a calm and planned way. The psychiatrist also tries to understand the degree of impulsivity that is present. Individuals who are highly impulsive can make threats to others when angry that are not meant when the anger is gone.

The psychiatrist will also make an assessment based on the way in which the student reports the incident. If there is little remorse and little understanding of the severity of the event, there is more concern. Individuals who are emotionally isolated or appear unfeeling can present with a higher level of concern. Those who have a history of being poorly connected to reality can also present with a higher degree of concern.

The threat assessment should include information from a number of sources, and it is important to see each participant individually. The parents should be able to provide background information regarding their child's patterns of interaction with others, ability to manage frustration, emotional reactivity, and past history of violent statements or actions. The degree of connection between the child and parents and the child and peers is also important to understand. A history of being mistreated whether it be having a history of physical abuse or being the victim of peer bullying is needed, as this history can increase the potential risk of violence.

School personnel should be present to provide not only information about the given incident but also background information regarding the student's history of interactions. The information that the school obtained during the preliminary investigation is important to share.

Factors that can be associated with a mediating risk include having positive family and community support, having guilt and remorse about the statement or action, being honest when describing the events, and not having a specific plan (see accompanying CD: 13.4). These protective factors must be weighed against the risk factors to determine the level of intervention that is needed.

Levels of Intervention

The primary reason for a threat assessment is to ascertain the risk that a student has to act in a violent way toward others. Psychiatrists are expected to take action to protect society from individuals who are a known risk. If the threat assessment indicates a high risk of action, then steps must be taken to ensure safety. Often this requires an inpatient hospitalization. If the threat is specific to one person, it can also be prudent to warn the person and there is a legal obligation for the psychiatrist to warn the police. If there is believed to be a high level of potential of violent behavior but no specific individual is named, there should still be a consideration for inpatient hospitalization. However, partial hospitalization or outpatient treatment can be decided to be an appropriate level of intervention.

The primary intervention strategy involves treating the underlying mental health conditions. In addition, using cognitive strategies to reduce frustration tolerance and improve impulsivity can be effective mental health treatment options. There is clearly no medication for the treatment of homicidal ideas, but medication may be needed to treat target symptoms such as anger, impulsivity, or mood swings.

Depending on the severity of the threat, the court system and juvenile probation department can also become involved with the student. This system can offer additional structure to the family, which can be helpful. In addition, this system can have access to programs that are designed to help individuals manage anger and improve compliance. For example, weekend wilderness programs and boot camps can be used.

Follow-up in the Educational Setting

Most times when a specific threat is made, the school provides a consequence such as out-of-school suspension. During this time it is often expected that a formal risk assessment take place. If it has been determined that there is no risk of near injury, the student will return to school. However, there can be a consideration to offer the student additional supports to help minimize frustration.

If the risk assessment predicts a higher likelihood of violence, the school can seek to have the student educated in a different setting. This can ensure that the student receives even more support and helps to ensure the safety of the school.

In this situation a placement in an alternative education program or emotional support program can be helpful.

SELF-INJURIOUS BEHAVIOR

Background

As described in Chapter 11, self-injurious behaviors can occur in adolescents. Individuals engage in self-injury as a way to escape emotional pain or to induce self-punishment. The intent is not to cause death, which is its distinguishing characteristic from suicidal behavior. School personnel can be the first to learn of this behavior, as a peer can divulge its presence. The initial response by an adult to this behavior can be very important for the treatment.

Questions to Consider in Preliminary Assessment

The first consideration is to ensure that the intention of the behavior is not to cause death. If it is learned that the individual did the cutting in a way that he or she hoped would lead to death, there should be an assessment of suicidality.

The next consideration is to request to see the areas of self-injury. Because the majority of self-injury occurs on the extremities, a trusted adult can make this request. If there has been cutting in more private regions of the body, the school nurse or the primary care physician can do the examination. The purpose of this examination is to make certain that the degree of self-injury does not require medical attention based on infection or very deep cuts. Ideally, this should be done in a way that does not reinforce the behavior. Some individuals, particularly those with borderline personality disorder traits, cut to obtain the attention of examination. In other words, a balance is needed to ensure that the cuts are healing without placing too much emphasis on this assessment.

The next consideration is to determine the best way to make the family aware of this behavior. It is sometimes preferable for the school personnel to make the first call explaining the behavior. Alternatively, there can be an arrangement where the student tells the parents, then following the discovery of information, the parents and school representative talk. Finally, there can be some consideration for the parents to come to the school and for the student and school representative to talk to the parents together. The purpose of parental involvement is to make certain that this behavior is known and that treatment interventions can begin. When discussing this with the parents, school personnel will find it important to balance the need to take this situation seriously but not to overreact in a way that causes the behavior to become more hidden.

The final consideration for the treatment of self-injury when it is learned within the school system is to refer the student for outpatient treatment. Self-injurious behavior is a concern and can signify underlying mental health difficulties, which must be assessed and treated within the mental health setting. The family may need support and guidance to ensure that this occurs (see accompanying CD: 13.5).

Mental Health Assessment

A mental health assessment will help the psychiatrist continue to understand the patterns of the behavior, including frequency and emotional triggers. The psychiatrist will also assess any other emotional difficulties or psychiatric disorders present that would be helpful to treat. This assessment can be done in a crisis assessment if there is a high level of concern. A psychiatric evaluation can be conducted if there are suspected underlying difficulties. If a psychiatric disorder is present, treatment for the identified disorder and the self-injury will be more effective.

A psychiatric evaluation should include a screening for all potential mental health disorders. There should be an individual interview with the student and an interview with the parents. Teens will be able to discuss the thinking and emotion associated with the behavior if they are made to feel comfortable and if they do not perceive that the psychiatrist believes they are "crazy." Often the examiner will give common reasons behind cutting as a way to show the student that this behavior is understood.

Levels of Intervention and Treatment

Only rarely does self-injury require psychiatric hospitalization. For severe self-injury, particularly in the presence of an Axis I disorder or borderline personality disorder, partial hospitalization can be used for more intensive support. However, the majority of individuals who engage in self-injury are treated on an outpatient basis. Because this behavior is generally effective at reducing intrapsychic distress, the treatment course is generally long, and there can be periods of remission and relapse before the behavior is fully extinguished.

Psychotherapeutic interventions often use models of individual cognitive behavioral therapy. The thoughts that contribute to distress and therefore increase the urge to cut need to be identified and changed. Beginning to address the individual's self-concept can also reduce the distress associated with cutting. Interpersonal therapy and dialectic behavior therapy also have been tried to address the core symptoms related to the urges to cut.

Strategies that can be useful to reduce and eliminate self-injury include delaying the response to cut. Teaching positive problem-solving skills such as relaxation and distraction during times of emotional turmoil is needed. The therapist can work with the youth to generate a list of alternative behaviors, such as drawing, walking, journaling, or calling a friend, to use to delay or avoid cutting. In cases of more severe self-injury, some clinicians consider first shifting the self-injury from cutting to something less dangerous such as applying ice, which can generate some similar nerve sensations.

Follow-up in the Educational Setting

The school team can be important in the student's recovery from self-injury. Typically, it is useful to have trusted school personnel, such as the guidance counselor, be available to the student during the day if there are intense urges to cut. Early in treatment the student's ability to verbalize feelings is difficult, and having an additional person for the student to talk to at the time of the urge is helpful. This attention must be watched, however, to make certain that the student is using it appropriately and that the attention is not inadvertently reinforcing the action. However, this mental health crisis without other symptoms or diagnoses rarely causes educational disturbance. The primary intervention should be in the mental health system with backup supports provided through the guidance office.

PHYSICAL AGGRESSION

Background

Numerous psychiatric disorders can be associated with physical aggression. This symptom can look different depending on the age of the individual. The aggression can be present at a low chronic level, or it can be more episodic and intense. Elementary-age children can engage in physical aggression by throwing items, shoving or hitting peers, or pushing large furniture items. Adolescents can engage in similar behaviors, but the intensity of the outburst can be greater. Because of their larger size, there can be more potential risk to other people. Aggression can be related to specific diagnoses such as bipolar disorder, intermittent explosive disorder, or acute psychotic disorders. It can also be present and more likely to occur in individuals with oppositional defiant disorder, conduct disorder, or attention-deficit/hyperactivity disorder. The episodes can be brief, lasting only minutes, or in some cases they can last several hours.

Within the school setting physical aggression can be a concern, as there is a necessity to keep children and staff safe. Children and adolescents with serious emotional disabilities can frequently demonstrate aggressive behaviors, and these behaviors may have been the reason for the initial identification with an emotional disturbance. Students with emotional disabilities tend to have difficulty managing frustration, and this feature in conjunction with academic demands can lead to significant outbursts.

Questions to Consider in Preliminary Assessment

When assessing an episode of physical aggression, the clinician will find it important to understand if this is a new behavior or if it is a chronic one. It is helpful to understand if the episode was triggered by a particular event or if it occurred without any known provocation. The duration of the episode can guide the level of intervention. If the student is able to deescalate rapidly, there can be less of a need to pursue an evaluation on an emergency basis.

Chronic types of physical aggression often require assessment over a longer course of time. A functional behavior assessment can be helpful for the clinician to understand the variety of triggers and settings in which the disruptive or aggressive behavior occurs. Close observation in different school settings can also help to identify triggers that are initially unrecognized (see accompanying CD: 13.6).

During or immediately after an episode of physical aggression, a decision must be made about whether the episode is one in which the police must be contacted or whether an emergency assessment at a crisis intervention must be used. If the student is engaging in a behavior that is potentially very unsafe to himself or herself, then there must be a more intensive intervention. Some examples of this can include placing items in an electrical socket, attempting to break glass, attempting to swallow tacks or harmful items, or placing a cord around the neck. If the student is engaging in behaviors that have the potential to cause significant harm to others, then an immediate assessment must occur. Some examples can include biting staff, threatening direct actions to students, or threatening direct physical actions that endanger adults. Depending on the acuity, police can be utilized to ensure safety and transportation to the hospital. Significant physical destruction of property can also be a reason to pursue an evaluation, but if there is no direct threat of danger to self or others, there can be a decision to not pursue an emergency mental health assessment.

Another time that a more intensive assessment can be indicated is if there is a pattern of constant aggression that is escalating either in frequency or in intensity. Although there might not be a high level of acuity, an escalating pattern of aggression needs to be assessed.

In summary, engaging in behaviors in which there is a high level of risk to self or others should result in an emergency mental health assessment. Disruptive and aggressive behaviors that are occurring but not in a way that places individuals in danger may require a mental health assessment, but this can be done in a more planned fashion. Psychiatrists are less commonly involved in the emergency mental health assessment, because the goal of that process is to determine which level of treatment is needed. However, a psychiatrist may become a critical piece of a mental health assessment that can occur during an inpatient setting.

Mental Health Assessment

The emergency assessment of physical aggression first provides an assessment of the youth's immediate safety needs. This assessment is determined based on obtaining the facts of the recent incident and learning more about the pattern of aggression. The assessment can be obvious based on the presenting mental state of the youth. If there is still a high degree of agitation and lack of self-control, the assessor may determine that inpatient hospitalization is necessary for safety and to provide a more detailed assessment at a future time.

More commonly, by the time a student who has been involved in a severe instance of physical aggression presents to the emergency room, the student has begun to deescalate. In this situation the assessment should include a review of other potential mental health disorders that can be related to the aggression. The evaluator must also determine if on the basis of the pattern obtained, the student is at high risk to become aggressive in the future.

This prediction is difficult, but one important consideration is the past history of physical aggression. The more serious this pattern is, the higher the likelihood of recurrence. In addition, family instability, social stressors, academic stressors, and other social stressors can also increase the likelihood of recurrent episodes.

When a psychiatrist becomes involved in the mental health assessment of physical aggression, this occurs during the context of a psychiatric evaluation. As with other levels of concerning behavior, the psychiatrist attempts to place the behaviors in the correct social, emotional, and developmental contexts. The pattern of behavior and the stressors that can precipitate the events are examined. Efforts are made to understand the underlying feelings and emotions. There is careful screening for any potential psychiatric diagnoses that be contributing to the pattern as well.

Levels of Intervention

A crisis assessment can result in a referral to an inpatient psychiatric unit. This decision is made if there is a high likelihood of underlying psychopathology, an inability of the student to deescalate during the crisis assessment, or a concern about the family's ability to provide safety.

Alternatively, lesser levels of care may be needed, including partial hospitalization, intensive outpatient treatment, or outpatient therapy. There can be a recommendation for a psychiatric evaluation to understand any underlying psychiatric diagnoses.

Treatment of the underlying disorder is the first level of intervention. Depending on the disorder, this can take the form of therapy or therapy and medication. If there is no clear diagnosis, there can be consideration to treat the target symptoms of aggression with a medication.

Intervention strategies that can be successful include improving coping strategies, improving frustration tolerance, and teaching relaxation strategies to use when the anger begins. Depending on the age of the youth, group therapy can also be an effective method to reduce physical aggression.

Medication can be considered to reduce aggression if the behavior is occurring in the context of an identified disorder. In addition, medication can be considered to treat the aggression if it is determined that the aggression is severe and impairing. Medication should be used only in conjunction with other forms of intervention.

Follow-up in the Educational Setting

When physical aggression happens in a repetitive fashion, the educational placement should be carefully assessed. The placement may need to be changed, or additional support within the present classroom may be needed. An objective observer to the classroom may be able to identify triggers that have been overlooked by the teacher.

DISCLOSURE OF ABUSE

Background

Child abuse and neglect have been defined as "any recent act or failure to act on the part of a parent or caretaker which results in death, serious physical or emotional harm, sexual abuse or exploitation, or an act or failure to act which presents an imminent risk of serious harm" (Child Abuse Prevention and Treatment Act [CAPTA], 1996, p. 2). Each year about 1 million children in the United States are identified as abused (Sedlak & Broadhurst, 1996). It is likely that this statistic is less than the actual occurrences of abuse.

Schools are most often perceived as a place of safety for students. This safety can allow children or adolescents to divulge to a trusted adult if they are being mistreated or feel unsafe. In addition, because of the daily contact, school personnel can become the first people to observe bruises or injury that can occur from physical mistreatment. School personnel and medical personnel are mandated to report any suspicion of abuse to the local child protective agency.

Questions to Consider in Preliminary Assessment

The first question to consider when there is a concern of safety is the sense of imminent danger. If a student presents with striking marks or injury that recently occurred and could have potentially been life threatening, it is imperative that a report of abuse be made to the local child protective agency immediately, and the urgency of the report be made known.

This can be a situation that requires immediate investigation to ensure that the person's safety needs are met.

More often, however, there is not the sense of immediate harm. In this situation it can be appropriate for the adults within the school system to quickly discuss information and gather data to include in the report. This should not be delayed, but it can be helpful for the investigating agency to have as much data as possible.

When a student discloses a situation of abuse, there must be reassurances that steps will be taken to ensure safety. The student must understand that this information cannot be kept confidential but this breach of confidentiality is taken to ensure his or her safety.

Depending on the situation, it may be appropriate to inform the parents once a report of abuse has been made. There can be times, however, that it is inappropriate to report this to the parents, as it can place the child at risk of greater harm.

Mental Health Assessment

During the early stages of known abuse, there may be little need for a mental health assessment. The best course of action may be for the children and youth agency to fully investigate the claim and ensure safety before mental health assessment is used. Younger children in particular can be prone to have variations in their "story," which occur the more often the abuse is talked about. This feature can potentially skew the investigation. If a mental health assessment is needed at the beginning of the abuse investigation, the examiner should avoid asking any direct question about the incident but should focus on understanding the child's response to the event.

A mental health assessment can be quite necessary after the abuse has been substantiated. This assessment is needed to guide treatment and to ensure that there is an assessment of the person's response to the abuse. Following the assessment, treatment is often needed. The focus of this is to provide support to ensure that the youth is appropriately processing the events and to manage any posttraumatic symptoms that can be a result. Supportive therapy and cognitive behavioral therapy are the preferred treatment interventions.

Levels of Intervention

The level of safety intervention is determined by the children and youth agency. There can be a decision to immediately remove the child from the home to ensure safety. Alternatively, a safety plan can be put into place to ensure that the home environment is safe. Unless there is a concern about immediate safety, the process of having a child removed from the home and placed in foster care can be lengthy. The hope is to provide necessary services to family members and use a safety plan as a way to keep the family together.

If the child's safety is determined not to be at significant risk, there can be additional interventions put into place to support the family. Family preservation services of family-based mental health treatment teams can begin to provide support to the child and family. In addition, the children and youth agency can recommend a mental health assessment of the parent or child with encouragement for the recommendations made by that provider to be followed.

Follow-up in the Educational Setting

There is little that a school needs to do following a disclosure of abuse. It is important, however, that regardless of the findings of the investigation, the student needs to feel supported. It also can be helpful to ensure that if treatment is recommended that the school communicate with the treatment provider.

During times of complicated cases, the school can be requested to provide information to the investigating agency or the court system. This information should be conveyed in the manner it was requested and in a professional way. School personnel can be very helpful advocates to students.

SUMMARY OF MANAGING CRISIS SITUATIONS

School teams need to be intimately involved in managing difficult situations and ensuring the safety of students. Often situations arise at school that need to be quickly addressed. If there is a high level of concern that a behavior could cause serious harm to a person, there should be prompt involvement of a mental health assessment through an emergency room or crisis intervention center. Depending on the nature of the crisis, the police or ambulance may need to help facilitate the transfer to the location.

When the potential for injury is lower, a period of ongoing monitoring can be helpful. A planned psychiatric evaluation can be a piece of the monitoring to ensure that all potential treatment interventions are being addressed. When a psychiatric evaluation is utilized, the school system can be helpful in arranging the assessment. In addition, the school system can provide detailed information regarding the presentation at time of crisis, a history of social or family stressors, and a history regarding the pattern of behaviors as it has occurred over time.

References

Ahmad, A., & Sundelin-Wahlsten, V. (2008). Applying EMDR on children with PTSD. *European Child and Adolescent Psychiatry, 17*(3), 127–132.

Akbarian, S., Bunney, J. W. E., Potkin, S. G., Wigal, S. B., Hagman, J. O., Sandman, C. A., et al. (1993). Altered distribution of nicotinamide-adenine dinucleotide phosphate-diaphorase cells in frontal lobe of schizophrenics implies disturbances of cortical development. *Archives of General Psychiatry, 50*, 169–177.

Albano, A. M., & Kendall, P. C. (2002). Cognitive behavioural therapy for children and adolescents with anxiety disorders: Clinical research advances. *International Review of Psychiatry, 14*, 129–134.

American Academy of Child and Adolescent Psychiatry [AACAP]. (1998a). *Practice parameter for the assessment and treatment of children and adolescents with obsessive-compulsive disorder.* Retrieved from http://www.aacap. org/galleries/PracticeParameters/Ocd.pdf

American Academy of Child and Adolescent Psychiatry. (1998b). *Practice parameter for the assessment and treatment of children and adolescents with posttraumatic stress disorder.* Retrieved from http://www.aacap.org/ galleries/PracticeParameters/PTSDT.pdf

American Academy of Child and Adolescent Psychiatry. (2001). Practice parameter for the assessment and treatment of children and adolescents with schizophrenia [Supplement]. *Journal of the American Academy of Child and Adolescent Psychiatry,*X*40*(7), 4S–23S. Retrieved from http://www.aacap.org/galleries/PracticeParameters/ JAACAP%20Schizophrenia%202001.pdf

American Academy of Child and Adolescent Psychiatry. (2007a). Practice parameter for the assessment and treatment of children and adolescents with anxiety disorders. *Journal of the American Academy of Child and Adolescent Psychiatry, 46*(2), 267–283. Retrieved from http://www.aacap.org/galleries/PracticeParameters/ JAACAP_Anxiety_2007.pdf

American Academy of Child and Adolescent Psychiatry. (2007b). Practice parameter for the assessment and treatment of children and adolescents with bipolar disorder. *Journal of the American Academy of Child and Adolescent Psychiatry*, *46*(1), 107–125. Retrieved from http://www.aacap.org/galleries/PracticeParameters/JAACAP_Bipolar_2007.pdf

American Academy of Child and Adolescent Psychiatry. (2007c). Practice parameter for the assessment and treatment of children and adolescents with depressive disorders. *Journal of the American Academy of Child and Adolescent Psychiatry*, *46*(11), 1503–1526. Retrieved from http://www.aacap.org/galleries/PracticeParameters/Vol%2046%20Nov%202007.pdf

American Academy of Child and Adolescent Psychiatry. (2008). *Facts for families*. Retrieved from http://www.aacap.org/page.ww?section=Facts%20for%20Families&name=Teenagers%20With%20Eating%20Disorders

American Psychiatric Association. (2000). *Diagnostic and statistical manual of mental disorders* (4th ed., text rev.). Washington, DC: Author.

Apter, A., Fallon, T. J., King, R. A., Ratzoni, G., Zohar, A. H., Binder, M., et al. (1996). Obsessive-compulsive characteristics: From symptoms to syndrome. *Journal of the American Academy of Child and Adolescent Psychiatry*, *35*, 907–912.

Arnold, L. E. (2000). Methylphenidate vs. amphetamine: Comparative review. *Journal of Attention Disorders*, *3*, 200–211.

Barkley, R. A. (1997). *ADHD and the nature of self-control*. New York: Guilford.

Barrett, P. M., Dadds, M. R., & Rapee, R. M. (1996). Family treatment of childhood anxiety: A controlled trial. *Journal of Consulting and Clinical Psychology*, *64*, 333–342.

Biederman, J., Faraone, S., Milberger, S., et al. (1996). A prospective 4-year follow-up study of attention-deficit hyperactivity and related disorders. *Archives of General Psychiatry*, *53*, 437–446.

Bird, H., Canino, G., Rubio-Stipec, M., Gould, M., Ribera, J., Sesman, M., et al. (1988). Estimates of the prevalence of childhood maladjustment in a community survey in Puerto Rico: The use of combined measures. *Archives of General Psychiatry*, *45*, 1120–1126.

Birmaher, B., Arbelaez, C., & Brent, D. (2002). Course and outcome of child and adolescent major depressive disorder. *Child and Adolescent Psychiatric Clinics of North America, 11*(3), 619–637.

Birmaher, B., Axelson, D. A., Monk, K., Kalas, C., Clark, D. B., Ehmann, M., et al. (2003). Fluoxetine for the treatment of childhood anxiety disorders. *Journal of the American Academy of Child and Adolescent Psychiatry, 42*(4), 415–423.

Birmaher, B., Ryan, N. D., Williamson, D. E., Brent, D. A., Kaufman, J., Dahl, R. E., et al. (1996). Childhood and adolescent depression: A review of the past ten years. Part I. *Journal of the American Academy of Child and Adolescent Psychiatry, 35*(11), 1427–1439.

Bissada, H., Tasca, G. A., Barber, A. M., & Bradwejn, J. (2008). Olanzapine in the treatment of low body weight and obsessive thinking in women with anorexia nervosa: A randomized, double-blind, placebo-controlled trial. *Am. J. Psychiatry*, (Oct); *165*(10):1281-1288. Epub. 2008 Jun 16.

Black, B., & Uhde, T. W. (1994). Treatment of elective mutism with fluoxetine: A double-blind, placebo-controlled study. *Journal of the American Academy of Child and Adolescent Psychiatry, 33*, 1000–1006.

Brent, D. A., Baugher, M., Bridge, J., Chen, J., & Beery, L. (1999). Age- and sex-related risk factors for adolescent suicide. *J. Am. Acad. Child Adolesc. Psychiatry*, 38:1497–1505.

Brent, D. A., & Birmaher, B. (2002). Adolescent depression. *New England Journal of Medicine, 347*, 667–668.

Brent, D. A., Holder, D., Kolko, D., Birmaher, B., Baugher, M., & Roth, C. (1997). A clinical psychotherapy trial for adolescent depression comparing cognitive, family, and supportive treatments. *Archives of General Psychiatry, 54*, 877–885.

Bridge, J. A., Iyengar, S., Salary, C. B., Barbe, R. P., Birmaher, B., Pincus, H. A., et al. (2007). Clinical response and risk for reported suicidal ideation and suicide attempts in pediatric antidepressant treatment: A meta-analysis of randomized controlled trials. *Journal of the American Medical Association, 297*, 1683–1696.

Bryson, S. (1997). Epidemiology of autism: Overview and issues outstanding. In D. J. Cohen & F. R. Volkmar (Eds.), *Handbook of autism and pervasive developmental disorders* (2nd ed., pp. 41–46). New York: Wiley.

Burke, J. D., Loeber, R., & Birmaher, B. (2002). Oppositional defiant and conduct disorder: A review of the past 10 years. Part II. *Journal of the American Academy of Child and Adolescent Psychiatry, 41*, 1275–1293.

Burns, B. J., Costello, E. J., Angold, A., Tweed, D., Stangl, D., Farmer, E. M., et al. (1995). Children's mental health service use across service sectors. *Health Affect (Millwood), 14*, 147–159.

Carlson, G. A., Loney, J., Salisbury, H., & Kramer, J. R. (2000). Stimulant treatment in young boys with symptoms suggesting childhood mania: A report from a longitudinal study. *Child and Adolescent Psychopharmacology, 10*, 175–184.

Cassels, C. (2009). Chronic sleep problems linked to increased risk for suicidal behavior. *Medscape.* Retrieved from http://www.medscape.com/viewarticle/591179

Centers for Disease Control and Prevention (CDC). (2002). Prevalence of autism spectrum-disorders: Autism and developmental disabilities monitoring network, 14 sites, United States. *MMWR Surveillance Summary, 56*, 12–28.

Centers for Disease Control and Prevention. (2007a). Prevalence data. Retrieved from http://www.cdc.gov/ncbddd/autism/faq_prevalence.htm

Centers for Disease Control and Prevention. (2007b). *Web-based Injury Statistics Query and Reporting System (WISQARS™).* Atlanta, GA: US Department of Health and Human Services, CDC. Available at http://www.cdc.gov/ncipc/wisqars/default.htm.

Child Abuse Prevention and Treatment Act (CAPTA), (42 U.S.C.A. §5106g). http://www.childwelfare.gov/pubs/factsheets/whatiscan.pdf. p. 2 (accessed November 3, 2011).

Coccaro, E. F., Siever, L. J., Klar, H. M., Maurer, G., Cochrane, K., Cooper, T. B. et al. (1989). Serotonergic studies in patients with affective and personality disorders: Correlates with suicidal and impulsive aggressive behavior. *Archives of General Psychiatry, 46*, 587–599. [Published erratum appears in *Arch Gen Psychiatry* 47:124, 1990.]

Code of Federal Regulations, Title 34, Section 300.7(b)(9) (2001, January). NICHEY Fact Sheet Number 5 (FS5). National Information Center for Children and Youth With Disabilities.

Compton, S. N., March, J. S., Brent, D., Albano, A. M., Weersing, V. R., & Curry, J. (2004). Cognitive-behavioral psychotherapy for anxiety and depressive disorders in children and adolescents: An evidence-based medicine review. *Journal of the American Academy of Child and Adolescent Psychiatry, 43*, 930–959.

Connor, D. F. (2002). *Aggression and antisocial behavior in children and adolescents: Research and treatment.* New York: Guilford.

Costello, E. J., Egger, H. L., & Angold, A. (2004). Developmental epidemiology of anxiety disorders. In T. H. Ollendick & J. S. March (Eds.), *Phobic and anxiety disorders in children and adolescents* (pp. 61–91). New York: Oxford University Press.

Cox, A., & Rutter, M. (1985). Diagnostic appraisal and interviewing. In M. Rutter & L. Hersov (Eds.), *Child and adolescent psychiatry: Modern approaches* (2nd ed., pp. 233–248). Oxford, UK: Blackwell Scientific Publications.

Deblinger, E., Lippman, J., & Steer, R. (1996). Sexually abused children suffering posttraumatic stress symptoms: Initial treatment outcome findings. *Child Maltreatment, 1*, 310–321.

Denman, C. (2001). Cognitive analytic therapy. *Advances in Psychiatric Treatment, 7*, 243–256.

Durston, S., Hulshoff Pol, H. E., Schnack, H. G., Buitelaar, J. K., Steenhuis, M. P., Minderaa, R. B., et al. (2004). Magnetic resonance imaging of boys with attention-deficit/hyperactivity disorder and their unaffected siblings. *Journal of the American Academy of Child and Adolescent Psychiatry, 43*, 332–340.

Eisler, I., Dare, C., Russell, G., Szmulker, G., Le Grange, D., & Dodge, E. (2000). Family and individual therapy in anorexia nervosa: A five-year follow-up. *Archives of General Psychiatry, 54*, 1025–1030.

Emslie, G. J., Rush, A. J., Weinberg, W. A., Kowatch, R. A., Hughes, C. W., Carmody, T. et al. (1997). A double-blind, randomized, placebo-controlled trial of fluoxetine in children and adolescents with depression. *Archives of General Psychiatry, 54*, 877–885.

Fergusson, D. M., Horwood, L. J., Ridder, E. M., & Beautrais, A. L. (2005). Subthreshold depression in adolescence and mental health outcomes in adulthood. *Archives of General Psychiatry, 62*, 66–72.

Findling, R., McNamara, N. K., Branicky, L. A., Schluchter, M. D., Lemon, E., & Blumer, J. L. (2000). A double-blind study of risperidone in the treatment of conduct disorder. *Journal of the American Academy of Child and Adolescent Psychiatry, 39*, 509–516.

Findling, R. L., McNamara, N. K., Stansbrey, R. J., Maxhimer, R., Periclou, A., Mann, A. et al. (2006). The relevance of pharmacokinetic studies in designing efficacy trials in juvenile major depression. *Journal of Child and Adolescent Psychopharmacology, 16,* 131–145.

Finley-Belgrad, E., & Davies, J. (2005). Personality disorders: Borderline. *Medscape.* Retrieved from http://www.emedicine.com/ped/topic270.htm

Fluoxetine Bulimia Nervosa Collaborative Study Group. (1992). Fluoxetine in the treatment of bulimia nervosa. *Archives of General Psychiatry, 49,* 139–147.

Fombonne, E. (1998). Epidemiology of autism and related conditions. In F. R. Volkmar (Ed.), *Autism and pervasive developmental disorders* (pp. 32–63). Cambridge: Cambridge University Press.

Foy, D. W., Madvig, B. T., Pynoos, R. S., & Camilleri, A. J. (1996). Etiologic factors in the development of posttraumatic stress disorder in children and adolescents. *Journal of School Psychology, 34,* 133–145.

Frederick, C. J. (1985). Children traumatized by catastrophic situations. In S. Eth & R. S. Pynoos (Eds.), *Posttraumatic stress disorder in children* (pp. 71–100). Washington, DC: American Psychiatric Press.

Friedman, R., Katz-Leavy, J., Manderscheid, R., & Sondheimer, D. (1996). Prevalence of serious emotional disturbance in children and adolescents. In R. W. Manderscheid & M. A. Sonnenschein (Eds.), *Mental health, United States, 1996* (pp. 71–89). Washington, DC: U.S. Government Printing Office.

Garrison, C. Z., Bryant, E. S., Addy, C. L., Spurrier, P. G., Freedy, J. R., & Kilpatrick, D. G. (1995). Posttraumatic stress disorder in adolescents after Hurricane Andrew. *Journal of the American Academy of Child and Adolescent Psychiatry, 34,* 1193–1201.

Geller, B., Fox, L. W., & Clark, K. A. (1994). Rate and predictors of prepubertal bipolarity during follow-up of 6- to 12-year-old depressed children. *Journal of the American Academy of Child and Adolescent Psychiatry, 33,* 461–468.

Geller, B., & Luby, J. (1997). Child and adolescent bipolar disorder: A review of the past 10 years. *Journal of the American Academy of Child and Adolescent Psychiatry, 36,* 1168–1176.

Glasbourg, R., & Aboud, F. (1982). Keeping one's distance from sadness. *Developmental Psychology, 18,* 287–293.

Goldstein, D. J., Wilson, M. G., Thompson, V. L., Potvin, J. H., & Rampey, A. H. Jr. (1995). Long-term fluoxetine treatment of bulimia nervosa. *Br. J. Psychiatry,* 166:660–666.

Gould, M. S., Walsh, B. T., Munfakh, J. L., Kleinman, M., Duan, N., Olfson, M., et al. (2009). Sudden death and use of stimulant medications in youths. *American Journal of Psychiatry, 166,* 992–1001. doi:10.1176/appi.ajp.2009.09040472

Green, A. H. (1985). Children traumatized by physical abuse. In S. Eth & R. S. Pynoos (Eds.), *Posttraumatic stress disorder in children* (pp. 133–154). Washington, DC: American Psychiatric Press.

Green, W. H. (1995). *Child and adolescent clinical psychopharmacology* (2nd ed.). Baltimore: Williams and Wilkens.

Green, W. H., Padron-Gayol, M., Hardesty, A. S., & Bassiri, M. (1992). Schizophrenia with childhood onset: A phenomenological study of 38 cases. *Journal of the American Academy of Child and Adolescent Psychiatry, 31,* 968–976.

Greenhill, L. L. (2002). Stimulant medication treatment of children with attention deficit hyperactivity disorder. In P. S. Jensen & J. R. Cooper (Eds.), *Attention deficit hyperactivity disorder: State of science—Best practices* (pp. 9-1–9-27). Kingston, NJ: Civic Research Institute.

Greist, J. H., Jefferson, J. W., Kobak, K. A., Katzelnick, D. J., & Serlin, R. C. (1995). Efficacy and tolerability of serotonin transport inhibitors in obsessive-compulsive disorder. *Archives of General Psychiatry, 52,* 53–60.

Grice, D. E., Halmi, K. A., Fichter, M. M., Strober, M., Woodside, D. B., Treasure, J. T. et al. (2002). Evidence for a susceptibility gene for anorexia nervosa on chromosome 1. *American Journal of Human Genetics, 70*(3), 787–792.

Hardan, A., Johnson, K., Johnson, C., & Hrecznyj, B. (1996). Case study: Risperidone treatment of children and adolescents with developmental disorders. *Journal of the American Academy Child and Adolescent Psychiatry, 35,* 1551–1556.

Harris, G. (2009, November 18). Use of antipsychotics in children is criticized. *New York Times.* Retrieved from http://www.nytimes.com/2008/11/19/health/policy/19fda.html

Hazlett, H. C., Poe, M., Gerig, G., Smith, R. G., Provenzale, J., Ross, A., et al. (2005). Magnetic resonance imaging and head circumference study of brain size in autism: Birth through age 2 years. *Archives of General Psychiatry, 62,* 1366–1376.

Hedges, D. W., Reimherr, F. W., Hoopes, S. P., Rosenthal, N. R., Kamin, M., & Capece, J. A. (2003). Treatment of bulimia nervosa with topiramate in a randomized, double-blind, placebo-controlled trial, Part 2: Improvement in psychiatric measures. *Journal of Clinical Psychiatry, 64*(12), 1449–1454.

Kendall, P. C. (1990). *Coping cat workbook*. Ardmore, PA: Workbook.

Keys, A., Brožek, J., Henschel, A., Mickelsen, O., & Taylor, H. L. (1950). *The biology of human starvation*. Minneapolis: University of Minnesota Press.

Lahey, B., Piacentini, J., McBurnett, K., & Stone, P. (1988). Psychopathology in the parents of children with conduct disorder and hyperactivity. *Journal of the American Academy of Child and Adolescent Psychiatry, 27*(3), 163–170.

Leckman, J. F., Walker, D. E., & Cohen, D. J. (1993). Premonitory urges in Tourette's syndrome. *American Journal of Psychiatry, 150*, 98–103.

Lehr, R. (n.d.). *Brain functions and map*. Retrieved from http://www.neuroskills.com/brain.shtml

Leonard, H. L., Swedo, S. E., Allen, A. J., & Rapoport, J. L. (1994). *Obsessive-compulsive disorder*. New York: Plenum.

Lis, A., Zennaro, A., & Mazzeschi, C. (2001). Child and adolescent empirical psychotherapy research: A review focused on cognitive-behavioral and psychodynamic-informed psychotherapy. *European Psychology, 6*, 36–64.

Lock, J., Le Grange, D., Agras, W. S., & Dare, C. (2001). *Treatment manual for anorexia nervosa: A family-based approach*. New York: Guilford.

March, J., Biederman, J., Wolkow, R., Safferman, A., & Group, S. S. (1997). *Sertraline in children and adolescents with obsessive-compulsive disorder: A multicenter double-blind placebo-controlled study*. Paper presented at the annual meeting of the American Psychiatric Association, San Diego, CA.

March, J. S., Frances, A., Carpenter, D., & Kahn, D. A. (Eds.). (1997). The expert consensus guideline series: Treatment of obsessive-compulsive disorder [Supplement]. *Journal of Clinical Psychiatry, 58*(4), 1–72.

Marcus, L. M., Kunce, L. J., & Schopler, E. (1997). Working with families. In D. J. Cohen & F. R. Volkmar (Eds.), *Handbook of autism and pervasive developmental disorders* (2nd ed., pp. 631–649). New York: Wiley.

McGlashan, T. H. (1988). Adolescent versus adult onset of mania. *American Journal of Psychiatry, 145,* 221–223.

McKenna, K., Gordon, C. T., Lenane, M., Kaysen, D., Fahey, K., & Rapoport, J. L. (1994). Looking for childhood-onset schizophrenia: The first 71 cases screened. *Journal of the American Academy of Child and Adolescent Psychiatry, 33,* 636–644.

McLeer, S. V., Deblinger, E., Henry, D., & Orvashal, H. (1992). Sexually abused children at high risk for posttraumatic stress disorder. *Journal of the American Academy of Child and Adolescent Psychiatry, 33,* 313–319.

Mehler, P. S., Gray, M. C., & Schulte, M. (1997). Medical complications of anorexia nervosa. *Journal of Women's Health, 5,* 533–541.

Modzeleski, W., Feucht, T., Rand, M., Hall, J. E., Simon, T. R., Butler, L., et al. (2008). School-Associated Student Homicides: United States, 1992–2006. Posted: March 18, 2008; *Morbidity & Mortality Weekly Report. 57*(2):33–36. © 2008 Centers for Disease Control and Prevention (CDC)

Morrato, E. H., Libby, A. M., Orton, H. D., deGruy, F. V., III, Brent, D., Allen, R., & Valuck, R. (2008). Frequency of provider contact after FDA advisory on risk of pediatric suicidality with SSRIs. *American Journal of Psychiatry, 165,* 42–50.

MTA Cooperative Group. (1999). 14-month randomized clinical trial of treatment strategies for attention deficit hyperactivity disorder. *Archives of General Psychiatry, 56,* 1073–1086.

MTA Cooperative Group. (2001). ADHD comorbidity findings from the MTA study: Comparing comorbid subgroups. *Journal of the American Academy of Child and Adolescent Psychiatry, 40,* 147–158.

National Institute of Mental Health. (n.d.). *National Comorbidity Survey (NCS) and National Comorbidity Survey Replication (NCS-R).* Retrieved from http://www.icpsr.umich.edu/CPES/

Nurnberger, J. I., Jr., & Foroud, T. (2000). Genetics of bipolar affective disorder. *Current Psychiatry Reports, 2,* 147–157.

Pauls, D. L., Alsobrook, J. P., II, Goodman, W., Rasmussen, S., & Leckman, J. F. (1995). A family study of obsessive-compulsive disorder. *American Journal of Psychiatry, 152,* 76–84.

Pliszka, S., Bernet, W., Bukstein, O., Walter, H. J., Arnold, V., & Beitchman, J., et al. (2007). *J. Am. Acad. Child Adolesc. Psychiatry, 46*(7):894–921.

Reichenberg, A., Gross, R., Weiser, M., Bresnahan, M., Silverman, J., Harlap, S. et al. (2006). Advancing paternal age and autism. *Arch. Gen. Psychiatry, 63*(9):1026–1032.

Research Units on Pediatric Psychopharmacology Anxiety Study Group. (2001). Fluvoxamine for the treatment of anxiety disorders in children and adolescents. *New England Journal of Medicine, 344*, 1279–1285.

Reyes, M., Buitelaar, J., Toren, P., Augustyns, I., & Eerdekens, M. (2006). A randomized, double-blind, placebo-controlled study of risperidone maintenance treatment in children and adolescents with disruptive behavior disorders. *American Journal of Psychiatry, 163*, 402–410.

Rogers, S. J. (1996). Brief report: Early intervention in autism. *Journal of Autism and Developmental Disorders, 26*(2), 243–246.

Russell, G., Szmulker, G., Dare, G., & Eisler, I. (1987). An evaluation of family therapy in anorexia nervosa and bulimia nervosa. *Archives of General Psychiatry, 44*, 1047–1056.

Rutter, M., Giller, H., & Hagell, A. (1999). Antisocial behavior by young people. *Journal of the American Academy of Child and Adolescent Psychiatry, 38*, 1320–1321.

Rynn, M. A., Siqueland, L., & Rickels, K. (2001). Placebo-controlled trial of sertraline in the treatment of children with generalized anxiety disorder. *American Journal of Psychiatry, 158*, 2008–2014.

Schatzberg, A., Cole, J., & DeBattista, C. (1997). *Manual of clinical psychopharmacology* (3rd ed.). Washington, DC: American Psychiatric Press.

Scheffer, R. E., & Niskala Apps, J. A. (2004). The diagnosis of preschool bipolar disorder presenting with mania: Open pharmacological treatment. *Journal of Affective Disorders, 82*, S25–S34.

Sedlak, A. J., & Broadhurst, D. D. (1996). *Third National Incidence Study of Child Abuse and Neglect* (contract no. 105–91-1800). Washington, DC: National Center on Child Abuse and Neglect.

Shaffer, D., Gould, M. S., Fisher, P., Trautman, P., Moreau, D., Kleinman, M., et al. 1996. *Arch. Gen. Psychiatry, 53*(4):339–348.

Sikich, L., Frazier, J. A., McClellan, J., Findling, R. L., Benedetto, V., Ritz, L. et al. (2008). Double-blind comparison of first- and second-generation antipsychotics in early onset schizophrenia and schizoaffective disorder: Findings from the treatment of early onset schizophrenia spectrum disorders (TEOSS) study. *American Journal of Psychiatry*, *165*, 1420–1431.

Steiner, H., & Lock, J. (1998). Anorexia nervosa and bulimia nervosa in children and adolescents: A review of the past 10 years. *Journal of the American Academy of Child and Adolescent Psychiatry*, *37*(4), 352–359.

Swedo, S. E., Rapoport, J. L., Leonard, H., Lenane, M., & Cheslow, D. (1989). Obsessive-compulsive disorder in children and adolescents. *Archives of General Psychiatry*, *46*, 335–341.

Tondo, L., Jamison, K. R., & Baldessarini, R. J. (1997). Antisuicide effects of Lithium. *Annals of NY Academy of Science*, 836, 339–351.

Treatment for Adolescents With Depression Study Team. (2004). Fluoxetine, cognitive-behavioral therapy, and their combination for adolescents with depression treatment for adolescents with depression study (TADS) randomized controlled trial. *Journal of the American Medical Association*, *292*, 807–820.

U.S. Food and Drug Administration. (2004, March 22). *FDA public health advisory: Worsening depression and suicidality in patients being treated with antidepressant medications.* Washington, DC: Author. Retrieved from http://www.fda.gov/Drugs/DrugSafety/PostmarketDrugSafetyInformation forPatientsandProviders/DrugSafetyInformationfor HealthcareProfessionals/PublicHealthAdvisories/ ucm161696.htm

U.S. Food and Drug Administration. (2007). *Antidepressant use in children, adolescents, and adults.* Retrieved from http:// www.fda.gov/Drugs/DrugSafety/InformationbyDrugClass/ UCM096273

Volkmar, F. R., & Cohen, D. J. (1991). Comorbid association of autism and schizophrenia. *American Journal of Psychiatry*, *148*, 1705–1707.

Wagner, K. D., Ambrosini, P., Rynn, M., Wohlberg, C., Yang, R., Greenbaum, M. S. et al. (2003). Efficacy of sertraline in the treatment of children and adolescents with major depressive disorder two randomized controlled trials. *Journal of the American Medical Association*, *290*, 1033–1041.

Wagner, K. D., Berard, R., Stein, M. B., Wetherhold, E., Carpenter, D. J., Perera, P. et al. (2004). A multicenter, randomized, double-blind, placebo-controlled trial of paroxetine in children and adolescents with social anxiety disorder. *Archives of General Psychiatry*, *61*, 1153–1162.

Werry, J. S., McClellan, J., & Chard, L. (1991). Early-onset schizo-
    phrenia, bipolar and schizoaffective disorders: A clinical
    follow-up study. *Journal of the American Academy of
    Child and Adolescent Psychiatry, 30*, 457–465.
Wilens, T. E., & Spencer, T. J. (1999). Combining methylpheni-
    date and clonidine: A clinically sound medication option.
    *Journal of the American Academy of Child and Adolescent
    Psychiatry, 38*, 614–616.
Willcutt, E. G., Doyle, A. E., Nigg, J. T., Faraone, S. V., &
    Pennington, B. F. (2005). Validity of the executive function
    theory of attention-deficit/hyperactivity disorder: A meta-
    analytic review. *Biological Psychiatry, 57*, 1336–1346.
Willer, M. G., Thuras, P., & Crow, S. J. (2005). Implications of
    the changing use of hospitalization to treat anorexia ner-
    vosa. *American Journal of Psychiatry, 162*, 2374–2376.
Wing, L. (1980). Childhood autism and social class: A question
    of selection? *British Journal of Psychiatry, 137*, 410–417.

Index

CD Contents